YOU
BE THE JUDGE

Bruce N. Sachar

PublishAmerica
Baltimore

ISBN: 978-1-4489-9186-0
PUBLISHED BY PUBLISHAMERICA, LLLP
www.publishamerica.com
Baltimore

Printed in the United States of America

ACKNOWLEDGMENTS

Given the turbulence and turmoil in my life during the past year this book could never have been written without constant pressures from family members. They were at once editors, critics, readers and possible publishers. They may or may not have realized, that the writing of this saga has served as a personal catharsis for me, and for that I shall always be grateful and indebted.

Special thanks to my sons, Matthew and Michael, and to my daughter, Stephanie Bartram. Great insight was furnished by my sister, Bernice Sommerstein, and by my niece, Dawn Ehrlich. Lastly, I would be remiss if I failed to thank my niece, Andrea Eller, a published author in her own right and a grammarian extraordinaire.

PRELUDE

I can state unequivocally, that Captain Ahab's obsession with the white whale, Moby Dick, pales in comparison with my obsession for gambling. Herman Melville's classic novel, by the way, begins with the famous words: "Call me Ishmael." It occurs to me, that were I to begin this book with "Call me_____," then the readers, with some justification, could fill in the blank with their unpleasant appellations of choice.

It also occurs to me that the famous opening penned by Charles Dickens in *A Tale of Two Cities* is equally applicable to this account. Dickens wrote. "It was the best of times. It was the worst of times." Herein are the results of competing forces acting upon one man's conscious and subconscious, depicted, however, on a far more personal level than those portrayed, or probably even imagined by Dickens.

Readers of this book will be observing first hand a struggle between the forces of good and evil, as they are exposed to the decision-making process of a compulsive gambler, who knew the difference between right and wrong, but nevertheless succumbed to pressures beyond his control. They may be startled by the chronic common threads of thought and conduct found in compulsive gamblers, as revealed during actual meetings of Gamblers Anonymous. They may even be willing to conclude facetiously, that inveterate gamblers have a common marker on their DNA.

In any case, I leave the fate of the author for readers to decide, as they consider this tale of the disbarment and humiliation of a hitherto well-known and respected attorney, of a wife who leaves him, of his ultimate fall from grace, and of a medical prescription from hell.

My earlier book, "From the Chicken House to the Court House," ends with a second degree murder conviction of my client, Bariki "Barry" Seit. This book will provide a conclusion to that saga.

CHAPTER ONE

I toss and turn. I can't sleep. The covers are on the floor. I squint to focus my eyes on the cable box digital clock. The blurry green numbers are the only illumination in the room. It's 2:37 A.M. I think to myself, that my prescriptive sleeping pills never seem to work. I think I'll try the Extra-Strength Tylenol PM. Capsules. They helped before. I'm headed for the bathroom.

Ouch!!! I grab my right big toe. *Jeeeze, I've lived here for five months now, and you'd think that I'd remember where that damn chair was! After all, there are only three rooms!* I'm holding the toe and hobbling around groping for a light switch. "Hey! Dummy! The light switch is on the other wall!" Would you believe it? Now I'm even talking out loud to myself!

I manage to put the lights on and find a chair to sit in. The toe is bleeding and hurts like the devil, but I start laughing. I have to either laugh or cry. I suddenly realize, that not only am I talking out loud to myself, I'm answering out loud.

I'm a basket case! I'm really losing it!

Maybe this whole thing is just a bad dream. Am I going to jail? Absurd! Have I been disbarred as an attorney? Impossible! Did my wife leave me? No way! Did the Masons kick me out? Fat chance! Am I living in subsidized housing? That's ridiculous! It just can't all be true!

I need confirmation that I'm not dreaming. I'm compelled to hobble over to my desk to check today's mail.

"This matter came before the Court, Spina, J., on an Affidavit of Resignation submitted by Bruce N. Sachar, with the Vote and

9

Recommendation of the Board of Bar Overseers filed by the Board on February 17, 2009. Upon consideration thereof, it is ORDERED and ADJUDGED that:

The Affidavit of Resignation be accepted and that BRUCE N. SACHAR is hereby disbarred from the practice of law in the Commonwealth effective immediately upon the entry of this Judgment, and the lawyer's name is forthwith stricken from the Roll of Attorneys…"

I limp to a window and open it wide. The cold air awakens me. It's not a dream. My thoughts and memory are now fully focused. How in God's name could I have done this to my family, my friends, the Bar Associations, and lastly, myself?

What's brought me to this unbelievable state of affairs?

I mull the question over and over before I finally doze on the couch, while the TV plays a Rambo re-run…Not yet fully asleep, I can't help but remember, what I had learned several months ago on TV and internet about Mirapex. I didn't believe it then, and I still find it difficult to comprehend, that a drug manufacturer would actually state, that its product can cause pathological gambling and other forms of obsessive-compulsive behavior.

…The real enigma in my mind, was why would Mirapex blow the whistle on itself? The answer to the question was later revealed to me and all the world…

It never ceases to amaze me, how the mind can travel so far and so fast in mlliseconds. It can carry one from place to place and topic to topic in less than a heartbeat. Because I'm focusing on my lot in life, I am suddenly reminded of a passage from Masonic ritual, which has biblical roots…

"…and just when he thinks his greatness is still aspiring, he falls like autumn leaves, to enrich our mother earth…"

…Suddenly, I'm pulling down the sun visor and heading south…

CHAPTER TWO

...My wife, Diane, is driving south on Route 95 heading towards
Rhode Island. It's a Friday about two thirty in the afternoon, and the sun
is shining brightly into our faces. Her sister, Connie, is a teacher's aide
at one of Lynn's elementary schools, and doesn't get out of work until
2:00 P.M daily; otherwise, we would have been on the road long before
this. The weekend traffic is just starting to build up on the highway, but
it's a comfortable ride in my new and spacious Mercury Grand Marquis.

Connie and my mother-in-law, Rose, are in the back seat, and I'm in
the front right. We're all listening intently to the tape, which Rose insists
that we play. It's a hilarious tape by the Italian comic, Pat Cooper
(Pasquale Caputo, I think). We're all in stitches, although I have to ask
for a translation every now and then. I never realized before just how
much Italian I had learned in my youth, while living in the "Brickyard,"
and working at Singer's Poultry Market.

The ride from Lynn to Lincoln Downs in Rhode Island usually takes
about an hour, more or less. The dog track at Lincoln, like all the other
dog tracks in New England, are taking a financial bath. The State
Lotteries are just killing them. Quality programs airing at prime times on
television don't help either. In order to bail out the dog owners, and, of
course, as a means of increasing revenue to the State, the Rhode Island
Legislature authorized the opening of a casino at the Lincoln Downs Dog
Track.

It's not a true casino in the traditional sense. There is neither a hotel
nor fancy restaurants open 24 hours a day. It's merely a building, that's

part of the dog track. It houses hundreds and hundreds of assorted slot machines. There are no table games at all. My biggest gripe is that the casino closes at 1:00 A.M. on weekends and at midnight during the week.

I would have preferred at all times to spend another hour on the road, and to have made the trip to Foxwoods in Connecticut, even though I realize that the slots are "looser" in Rhode Island. It's new and patrons have to be attracted. What better way, than to increase the odds of winning.

I only agree to go to Lincoln, when prior commitments prevent the longer trip to a real casino. The hours of operation bother me immensely, and I usually have the same thoughts running through my mind, each time we approach the parking lot.

If I'm ahead at closing time and in the midst of a hot streak, I'll want to play some more to make a big score! On the other hand, If I'm losing at closing time, I'm gonna be pissed because they won't give me a chance to get even! I resent it! I don't want anyone to tell me, when I can gamble, and when I cannot!

Diane immediately pulls in to the valet parking section. As soon as she slows down in line, I slip her some gambling money, and literally fly out the door before she's fully stopped for the valet. Even though I may need a trip to the rest room, I usually wait. It's more important for me to get to one of my favorite Keno slot machines. Seconds mean everything! My favorites are located all in a row opposite the Dunkin Donuts booth. There are only six of them. If they're taken, there is no telling how long I'll have to wait for an empty machine.

If the whole row is full I have a real dilemma. Sure, I can play some other kind of machine, and try again later. I often do, of necessity. I can't just stand there and wait, even though I know, that my best proven chance of winning, is at one of those six machines. Time is always running short here. On occasion I get lucky. I'd grab an open seat, and hold any other open ones for Diane, Connie, or Rose.

Keno is only one of the games which one can select on the machines in this row. These machines are also multi-denominational. One can play for quarters, halves or dollars. When I have the money, I play for dollars. Contrary to everyone's advice, I always play the maximum numbers allowed, ten. The Keno game on these machines is called "Power Ball."

If the last number spit out by the machine happens to land on a number, that I've selected, and if it results in a win, the Power Ball multiplies the payoff by four.

I have my own favorite numbers, and various combinations of numbers to play. One could opt to play a "quick pick," and to allow the machine to randomly select the numbers. I rarely used it. Each machine is different. Certain machines have a proclivity for throwing out certain numbers more frequently than others. I've come to know the idiosyncrasies of each of those six machines.

Each machine goes through various periods of being "hot" or "cold." It takes only a few minutes to make the determination. I often bounce back and forth from machine to machine. Sometimes I watch the person playing next to me lose his or her shirt. I'm often writhing in agony when he's losing, and the machine is throwing out my combinations. My thoughts then are always the same. *Why didn't I take that machine when I could have?*

I'm standing and watching the numbers coming out in each of the machines. They're all taken. The triumvirate arrives. Diane is first, followed by Connie. Rose, with her bad legs, brings up the rear. Diane whispers to me, "I recognize most of these players. They're here forever. They'll never quit!"

"In that case, I'll either be near the entrance playing my favorite Joker Poker Machine, or in the new back room playing that Mice Keno game. You guys stay here and wait for a seat, but if the second machine from the left becomes available, hold it and come get me quick! My numbers are coming out on it. I feel lucky today."

"How about getting us some coffee before you leave?"

"Are you crazy? Here's a fin. Let Connie get it! See you later."

The poker machine is taken. I head for the back room. Against the back wall are three of the new Mice Keno machines. I've had some luck with the end machine before.

Just as I'm about to sit down, a very large woman grabs the high stool in front, and attempts to mount it. I watch her struggle for a while. She can't get her behind on the stool. I'm standing behind her about to lose it. I wanna give her a body check to the floor, but they'd probably have to rent a derrick to pick her up. Finally, she throws up her hands, and retrieves her pocketbook from the side of the machine. She turns to face me, and with a disgusted look on her face, says, "This machine is as cold as an iceberg." She leaves. I sit down.

Even though I've won on this machine before, I still don't understand the game fully, insofar as to how the payoffs are determined. I decide to get acquainted. I put in a double sawbuck and start playing for five quarters. I'm playing my favorite combinations, and holding my own for about ten minutes. I see that winning combinations pay more, when three mice appear within the number selections. Some of the mice have numbers on them, multiplying a payoff even more.

I play my favorite vertical combo. The bottom five numbers in the "9" row coupled with the top five numbers in the "10" row. I push the button. My numbers are being hit with mice. Suddenly, the machine starts flashing, and blaring out the song, "You Are My Sunshine." In the center of the screen appears, "Call The Attendant," and in the square at the top, the word "Jackpot" is also flashing. People are gathering around. "Hey, how much did you win?"

"Damned if I know! Can't find it anywhere!"

The guy playing next to me says, "It's in that little block on the bottom left of the screen."

The block reads: " WIN: $4,250.00."

The Rhode Island machines do not pay out in coins, even if the win is only fifty cents. Tickets are printed, then redeemed for cash at one of the windows. But if a hit is $1,200.00 or more, then Uncle Sam comes into the picture. I print out the ticket and stick it in my pocket. I put in another twenty, which I quickly lose. I'm really upset with myself, and while on the way to tell Diane, I have only one thought. *Why in hell wasn't I playing for my usual dollars? It shoulda been $16,500.00! Boy, am I a schmuck!*

Diane and Connie are sitting next to each other. Rose is not around. I know she's probably playing slots on the other side of the room. I stand behind Diane and watch her play. I never say a word. She must sense that someone is standing behind her. She finally turns to look, and says, "Oh, its you! Tried to get that seat you wanted, but some woman jumped in before I had a chance to put my coat on the chair and get you."

I say in a very calm voice, "Well, I'm certainly glad, that you didn't save that seat. I told you that I felt lucky today. I just had a pretty good hit playing the mice."

She answers with no emotion. "Oh yeah? Then how about a couple of bucks? I'm not doin' so hot yet. I make a hit every now and then, but I give it back. Just can't seem to get anything back to back. How much did you win?"

I don't smile or answer. I'm relishing the reaction I anticipate. I merely reach into my pocket, and nonchalantly hand her the ticket. She screams, jumps up and kisses me on the cheek. She tells Connie what I had just won loudly enough for the whole row to hear.

Finally, she says, "Where's my half?"

"Half? We've been through this before. You know I have to pay taxes on it. I'll take care of you, after I cash it."

I instruct the cashier not to take the taxes out of the winnings, and that I'll take care of it myself. I present my license, gave her the ticket, and sign some IRS forms.

Within minutes the cash is in my pocket. I give Diane a grand in crisp new Franklins.

I look around and the seats are still all taken.

I walk around the casino looking for an enticing machine to play. Not once do I entertain the thought of taking the winnings home immediately to pay some outstanding pressing bills. Besides, we just got there! It's only about 5:00 P.M.

The games with "Progressive" jackpots have the toughest odds, and I know enough to stay away from them. But not today! I'm on a roll! I sit down at a Progressive machine, and start playing for dollars. I leave the machine fifteen minutes later, after losing three or four hundred bucks. I walk around, and see from a distance that my favorite Joker Poker machine is vacant. I push people aside, as I run to get the seat before someone else does. I sit down and catch my breath.

This machine has a jackpot of $4,000.00, if one bets the maximum of five bucks per hand.

The big jackpot is paid for a Royal Straight Flush without the Joker. Most Joker Poker machines pay the maximum for five of a kind, rather than for a Royal Straight Flush. I'd had some luck on this machine before. About six months earlier, I'd hit the Royal Straight Flush in hearts. A trip to Rhode Island is never complete unless I play a bit on this machine, even though I've never come close again.

I follow my usual routine. No matter where the ashtray is when I sit down, it has to be in the space on the shelf to the left of the machine. I move it from the top of the machine to where I want it. I put my cigarettes and lighter where they belong on the right side of the machine. I light up a cigarette and am now ready to do battle. I quickly insert an ace. I hit the spot on the screen that allows me to change the setting from quarters to dollars. The machine indicates that I now have a hundred credits at a dollar per.

Kings or better earns a payout. Even though I've had several good hands the ace is soon gone. In goes another. My wad is thinning. I make a couple of good back-to-back hits. The machine now indicates that I have over eleven hundred credits. I sense that the machine is hot, and instead of cashing out and going home with some money in my pocket, I keep playing.

I'm chain smoking as I play. Each time I hit the button for a new game five new cards appear. I have to determine which cards to hold for each hand. I think to myself, what I believe to be fact: *This game is programmed by that little micro chip. I gotta outsmart the sucker and not always hold the obvious cards. It knows exactly what I'm doing. I'll fix the little bastard! In my mind, I'm playing against the little s.o.b., who's inside that machine. It's a real person, who's trying to trip me up! Every now and then, he throw's me a bone. I'll get him yet!*

About an hour later I still have over a thousand credits. I hit the button and a new hand is on the screen. From left to right I get dealt a ten of clubs, a joker, a three of clubs, a queen of hearts, and an ace of clubs. I study the hand. There are so many options staring me in the face, that I can't decide what to keep.

I should go for the flush, but I don't catch it too often. Whatever I do, the Joker will probably give me a winning hand. No question about it. Anyone with this hand would use the Joker, and the little guy in the machine knows it! He's programmed for it and he's just sitting back there waiting patiently.

I look up again at my credits and think to myself: *What the hell, the bet's only five bucks. I'm gonna do something stupid! Why not? I'm here to gamble, right? Of course I am!* I hold the ten of clubs and the ace of clubs. I don't even hold the joker! I hit the button. The lights flash and "California Here I Come" plays simultaneously. I draw a Royal Straight Flush in Clubs. I've just won four grand. I retrieve my ticket for over five thousand bucks, which includes my previous credits. I visit the cashier again. Her machine knows, that it's only the hit for four K, that has to be reported to the IRS.

I go over to Diane to tell her what happened. She's in shock, as I command, "Get everyone together. We're goin' to Foxwoods right now!"

"What about your 6:00 A.M. tee time at Gannon tomorrow?"

"I'll make it, as long as we leave Foxwoods by four in the morning. Hurry up! Get everyone together! I'll meet you at the valet station in about 10 minutes! Gotta visit the little boy's room first!"

CHAPTER THREE

...Loud bursts of machine gun fire coming from the television set awakens me with a start. I don't know where I am until I see Rambo in action. I'm in a pool of sweat. My mouth is dry, and my tongue feels like shoe leather. The clock reads 4:10 A.M. A couple of swallows of bottled water from the refrigerator brings me back to reality. I return to the couch with bottle in hand. I recognize Sylvester Stallone and Richard Crenna. I know they're talking, but I don't hear a thing. My mind is elsewhere...

...It's about a week after Seit's verdict, when I regain somewhat the mental stamina to deal with office matters, the unreturned phone calls, client appointments, and most importantly the preparation of an appeal.

We are in the middle of a prolonged Indian Summer hot spell. The air conditioning doesn't seem to help. By mid morning I've taken my jacket off, and am in shirt sleeves with tie loosened and collar unbuttoned. I go into the library to find my star employee, Joe Machera, and to talk about the appeal. He too is in shirtsleeves and his cuffs are rolled up. An unusual sight for such an impeccable dresser and fashion plate.

"Hey Joe, I think it's high time to discuss the appeal. What've you been doing?"

Joe responds sarcastically. "What the hell do you think I've been doing all week? I'm only a peon here! I can't afford the luxury of a few days off!"

"Never mind, wise guy. Let's go to Mel & Murray's deli. My treat. Easier to talk about it, when my stomach isn't growling."

" Sounds good to me, Boss. Walk or drive?"

"Too damn hot to walk. C'mon, I'll drive."

The brothers, Mel and Murray Cohen, run a smooth operation. The food is great and the surroundings are new and pleasant. Murray, behind the take-out counter nods as we enter. The stools at the counter are all taken. We look around and spot a couple leaving a table. We hurry over and sit down, even before it is cleared by a waitress.

Eventually, Trudy D'otolo arrives to pick up her tip, clean the table and hand us menus. Her long flaming red hair is in sharp contrast with her white uniform. She always has a smile and a story, or some gossip to tell. She has a nice figure for a woman in her 40's, and the custodial parent of two teenagers.

"Do you guys need time to study the menus?"

Joe quickly responds. "Not unless they've changed for the first time in this decade!"

"Okay, what'll you have?"

With a straight face Joe says with his best Italian accent: " 'Scusa me senora, but how come, I'ma no see ravioli, or lasagna, or antipasti on disa menu?" Not batting an eyelash, Trudy responds. " You no lika to mangia da corna beefa, den you cumma to mia casa tonight, whena the bambinos goa to sleepa, and I'ma makea you pollo cacciatori anda pasta. I gotta nicea surprise for da desserta, and itsa no spumoni!"

We order. Trudy turns and leaves. She swings her hips in a suggestive manner. Joe watches her leave, and comments, "She's a looker!"

"She always was, Joe. We lived in the same house at 56 Estes Street, when I was living with Phyllis. She and Phyllis are both still there."

"Okay, enough of this small talk. Tell me what your thoughts are for the appeal, and what you've been doing."

"I've spent a lot of time reviewing and reading the various statutes relating to appeals of criminal cases. Not many choices. We can write to the clerk's office, and claim an appeal. Then it's the clerk's responsibility to assemble the record, and of course, we'll have to order the transcript of the entire trial. We can also file a Motion for a New Trial."

"I've given it some thought too. Unfortunately, I've been down this road before. The way I see it, is that one option would be to do just as you say, and claim an appeal. We also have a couple of other choices, which may give us a couple of more bites at the apple.

I want you to look up the statute for a Motion To Revoke and Revise the Sentence. There are time constraints, as to when it may be filed. Like you say, we can file a Motion For A New Trial, but it also may have filing-time constraints. If we file them quickly enough, we might get lucky, and avoid a full appeal to the appellate court. Too bad both Motions are required to be heard by the same judge, who presided over the trial."

Joe is now visibly upset. He raises his voice, and says, "For cryin' out loud, Bruce, you know what he did to us at the trial. What makes you think he'll be any different with the Motions? He denied every request you made. He didn't even let you put on your expert witnesses. He smiled at the jury, and spoke pleasantly to them, whenever he made a ruling, which favored the prosecution! He was sarcastic and demeaning, whenever it came from our side. What makes you think he'll change with the proposed Motions?"

"During the trial he had a jury to control. He wanted a guilty verdict and had to convince the jury to make the finding. That's why nearly every objection made by the Commonwealth was sustained, and ours over-ruled. The old geezer was dumb like a fox. He knew exactly what he was doing. That's the reasoning behind his attitude and demeanor, when addressing the jury. His voice inflections and smiles to the jury were nothing more than blatant attempts to gild the lily for the prosecution.

I don't envision any change in his attitude, when he hears our Motions. There will be no jury to influence, so he'll probably be very polite and pretend to be interested before his rulings stick it to us once again. The short answer to your question is, that I anticipate nothing new from him with regard to our Motions. It's a mere formality, which we must undergo in order to preserve our appellate rights."

Customers at nearby tables begin looking our way. I whisper, "You're probably right, and that's precisely why we have to do the research, as though it's a full appeal. We can use the same cases and arguments in the Motions, and get two more shots at His Nibs. We'll use the Motion To Revoke And Revise, to convince the s.o.b., that the verdict was against the weight of the credible evidence, and that it would be more consonant with justice to set aside the verdict, and enter a conviction of manslaughter instead."

My mouth is so dry, that I polish off a glass of water without stopping to catch my breath.

"Boy, did I need that! Now I want you to listen to my rationale. The Motion For A New Trial will make the same argument and point out all of flaws in the Judge's rulings on the admissibility of evidence, as well as, his refusal to allow our experts to testify. I have to admit that it'll be a tough sell trying to convince him, that his rulings prevented Seit from getting a fair trial.

The Motion will also give us another chance to try and convince him, that he should have allowed at least some of my Requests For Instructions to the jury, and shouldn't have kept our experts from testifying. The jury never got a true picture, and Seit never had a fair trial!"

"Let's face it, Saitch, what are the odds of Sullivan reversing himself? If the rulings were good enough and proper for him at trial, how can you expect him to reverse himself and admit that he was wrong?"

"You're right, Joe. That's why I don't waste my time filing Motions To Reconsider, whenever a Judge rules against me in a civil case. It's usually an exercise in futility."

"If they're usually futile, why bother? What makes this case so special?"

"The difference here is, that he'll know for certain, that we're contemplating a full appeal to the appellate courts. If he thinks one of our arguments has some merit, or that one of his rulings might be considered a reversible error, then he might cut some slack, and give Barry a break.

We both know that no judge likes to be chastised by the appellate courts and reversed. We also know, that most attorneys and judges in the Commonwealth read the published opinions of the appellate courts. Who would want to be remembered, as The Judge, Who Got Reversed by Denying a Defendant a Fair Trial?"

The pastrami sandwiches arrive, and with a twinkle in her shining green eyes, Trudy looks at Joe and says, "Well, lover boy, you a gonna cumma to my housea tonight, whena da suna goesa down?"

" Gracias, signorina, but I'ma gonna takea raina checka! You keepa da chianti ina da icea boxa. Onea day, I'ma gonna knock ona da door, and I'ma gonna geta da dessert!"

"I'ma holda my breath. I'ma no sleepa, 'til I heara da rapa ona da door!"

She winks at us, places a bill on an adjoining table, and is gone.

"Oh, by the way Joe. You better order the transcript from the court stenographer. My best guess is, that there'll be anywhere from six to ten volumes. The cost will probably be about two grand. No sense billing the Seits."

"Scusa me, Boss, gotta go to the little boys' room. I'ma cumma right back."

My mind dwells on the financial aspect of the case. I recall what has transpired to date and then draw some realistic conclusions. Barry's in the hoosegow, his wife is working two shifts to feed the kids, and Barry had never even paid for the full trial. I've taken a financial bath on this one. I even sent most of the small retainer to another lawyer, as a referral fee. Even so, I just don't have the heart to bill him for the enormous amount of time I'm about to spend on his appeal. At this point I just want to see it through. I won't send another bill for the time spent on trial and research. Likewise, I don't have the heart to send him a bill for the appeal, Motions and research to come.

Joe returns and states, "I'm all set. You about ready to leave?"

"Yeah. Let's vamoose. By the way, Joe, when the bill comes for the transcript, I'll take care of it, as well as the bills for printing our brief, and the entry fee for the appellate court."

Joe's response is a simple nod of the head.

We return to the office, and Joe walks directly into the library, reaching to one of the shelves for the volume containing relevant chapters and sections of the Massachusetts General Laws. There are about six shelves of those green books, but watching him, I know he's taken a volume dealing with appellate procedure.

CHAPTER FOUR

...The sound of the water bottle hitting the floor shakes me out of my reverie. I run to the kitchen for the roll of paper towels. I'm now fully awake. I put some coffee in the coffee maker and never move; I just stand in that spot until I hear the final hissing. One Sweet & Low, and I'm sitting behind my desk, enjoying both the caffeine and the aroma of the coffee.

I'm glad, that the kids convinced me to take my office desk with me, when I closed up shop. The memories attached to the desk help get me over the reality of the situation, but most of all, it makes me feel somewhat comfortable during these trying times. I reach for my book of New York Sunday Times crosswords, and turn to an unfinished one. I go to a numbered clue, but the whole page is a blur. I stare off into space, as I dwell on my predicament and become absorbed in self-pity.

I don't have the chutzpah to think that the heights and abysses in my life compare to The Rise and Fall of the Third Reich; or The Rise and Fall of the Roman Empire, but it sure as hell is a story of "Riches To Rags." I guess it all really started at 60 Lewis Street...

...The law firm of Gordon, Sachar, Pearlmutter, Tobin & Shactman, is located on the third floor of Sam Levine's Commerce Building at 113 Broad Street at the corner of Silsbee. It was in 1964, that Tessler, Gordon & Sachar became the original tenant in those quarters. Then in June and July of 1969 we are enticed and induced by real estate entrepreneur, Saul Gilberg, to enter into a ten year lease for a first floor and basement suite at 60 Lewis Street. Pearlmutter and I design the offices for the new building. We are its first tenants, and Gilberg builds and furnishes according to our specifications.

In 1971, Lynn's Mayor, Patsy Caggiano, appoints me, from a long list of contestants, as the first lawyer-prosecutor for the Lynn District Court. I've always had a sneaking suspicion, that the fine hand of the inimitable Freddie Goodman, is instrumental in the selection process.

(I had known Freddie and his brothers since grammar school days. He was one of my first clients. I was a witness to his involvement in the oil delivery business, which followed a stint as a delivery boy for Singer's Poultry, which was then followed by a tour of duty as a dog trainer for my brother, Solly.

In the early 60's I incorporated the Goodman Oil Company. His first customers were drawn from the delivery list of Singers poultry. He later became a real estate entrepreneur and his own best customer for oil. I drew so many real estate trusts for him, that the names just seem to run together. A testament to his vision in the real estate area are the several apartment buildings, which he built, and which are all named for members of his family.

He became involved in politics. Although he once ran for mayor, his real forte in the political arena, was the uncanny ability to schmooze the local politicians. He became a go-between for those seeking political help or connections. It was this role which contributed to his downfall and subsequent incarceration.

Apparently, shame and bad press in local newspapers, were never a deterrent to Freddie's skullduggery. He was certainly one of a kind. In fact, the title to my first book was originally "Freddie and I.")

I'm soon appointed, as a Special Assistant Attorney General for the Commonwealth, and as an Assistant District Attorney for Essex County. Thus begins my prosecutorial career. It proves to be in sharp contrast with my former court appearances, as a criminal defense attorney.

Before accepting the job, all the partners meet. Morris Gordon calls the meeting to order. He's the first to speak. Morris has seniority, having passed the Bar first, and being the oldest of the conglomerate. As usual, he wears a dark-colored conservative Brooks Brothers suit with a color-coordinated bow tie. A gold chain is visible dangling from a vest pocket. He takes off his glasses, and holds them in one hand. When he is assured, that he has everyone's attention, he clears his throat and begins.

"We all know why we're here. Bruce, we'd like to know how you can justify taking on the new job? Who will pick up the shortfall, when you're out of the office? Who'll try our office cases in your absence? How much time will it take? What happens to our criminal cases? You certainly can't defend and prosecute at the same time. I foresee a huge conflict of interest here, especially in Lynn. We're all concerned. Can you enlighten us ?"

"I'll try. I didn't take the job without first addressing each of the issues you raise. I've spoken to Lieutenant Fred Stinson several times. He's taking over as the Lynn Police prosecutor from Lt. Fran Brodbine, who I'm sure, most of you know. I've been helping Stinson on my own time at night. We've been studying the "Blue Book" together in order to help prepare him for the Captain's exam. It started as a gesture of friendship with my new associate to be. I guess the word spread. I'm now being inundated with calls for help from officers who are aspiring for promotions.

He and Brodbine have both assured me, that it will be a rare day, when I won't be back in the office by noon. Don't forget, that Marblehead still has Lt. Dick Fullerton to prosecute, Swampscott has Lt. Jim Hanley, Saugus, Sgt. Jimmy Monico, Nahant, Chief Melanson, the Registry of Motor Vehicles has Bo Granger, and the M.D.C. has Sgt. John Galvin.

Stinson and I will divide the Lynn trial cases and I'll only try the tough cases from the other cities and towns. I'm supposed to be primarily an advisor in the law and the rules of evidence for the police prosecutors, who, by the way, have been doing just fine without me for decades.

Let's look at the facts. Fred Pearlmutter has been doing the Workmen's Compensation cases for us, and has been helping me with the tort files. He can certainly cover for me for a few hours in the morning, if I'm not here. Morris Tobin and you are sharing real estate and probate cases, and you also are handling domestic matters. David Shactman is involved with insurance company work.

It's only when one of your cases gets into suit, and has to be tried, that I come into the picture. I've been juggling court appearances since I started practicing. I've often scheduled trials in the afternoons. The local Clerks of Court are all accommodating. I don't foresee any problems here."

Good or bad, I know I have their attention. Gordon is a tough read. He's absolutely poker-faced, but every now and then, I catch Tobin and

Pearlmutter nodding in assent to my comments. My mouth is dry. I take a sip of water before continuing.

"Gentlemen, I fully understand Morris's conflict of interest concerns. One certainly should not be a prosecutor and a defense lawyer in the same court at the same time. It's the appearance of impropriety, which must be avoided. In this regard, I point out that Essex County District Attorney, John P.S. Burke, who'll be my boss, has already given me guidelines. The only court where I won't be able to represent any criminal defendant is in the Lynn District Court. The good news is, that I can still try civil cases in Lynn.

Lastly, the position now pays either $7,500.00 or $10,000.00 a year, depending upon to whom one speaks. In either case, I plan to deposit all of it into the firm's account. I think this should allay your fears, and answer all your questions. Anything else, gentlemen?"

There are none. After a salient pause, Gordon says: "By a show of hands, are there any objections to allowing Bruce to take the job, and remain with the firm?" Not a hand is raised. But it's first time I realized, that my position in the firm has been in jeopardy.

Ever since I could remember, The Lynn Item's Court Reporter, had been Earl Stern. He had received a promotion, and his replacement was, Bill Kettinger from Saugus. However short Bill was in stature, he was tall in his command of the English language. He had an inquisitive mind, and was never bashful, when it came to asking questions. We had become friends. His accolades, which have appeared in the press, are often embarrassing to me and make me blush. I had no idea at the time, that he would eventually become a client of mine in a very difficult product liability case against a well-known manufacturer.

The new prosecutorial team of Fullerton, Hanley, Monico, Melanson. Galvin, Granger, Stinson and Sachar, has its debut in the basement of a church near the Salvation Army Building on Franklin Street. It is here, following a lengthy and complicated trial involving members of the Norsemen (later the Hell's Angels) receive sentences calling for incarceration. Of course, their lawyers all appeal to the Superior Court for a new trial.

One of the lawyers is the well-known and talented, Harvey Brower, who approaches me after the trial, and whispers goodnaturedly, "Hey, Saitch, how's it feel now that you've traded in a black hat for a white one?"

The old court building has been demolished, and a new modern edifice stands on the site. I have the honor of trying the very first case in the First Session of the new court. Henry Mayo, its First Justice, presides. He's about six feet tall and doesn't appear to have an ounce of fat. His thinning black hair is streaked with strands of gray.

He's a former Assistant District Attorney for Essex County, and is death on drunken drivers. I'd had several real estate closings with him before he became a judge, and I felt comfortable trying before him. Hannon & Mayo was located diagonally across from the Lynn Daily Evening Item Building on Exchange Street, and they often did mortgages for the Essex County Bank & Trust Company.

Judge Mayo rarely sits in his chair. He generally stands behind it, and paces back and forth. He has an ulcer condition, and continuously pops Gelusil or Maalox tablets, as he walks to and fro. Instead of a belt for his pants, he always has a necktie running through the loops, which he ties loosely in the front.

Public drunkenness is still a crime in Massachusetts, when the new court opens.

It's common knowledge, that certain habitual inebriates throw rocks through glass windows of businesses right in front of police officers. The rationale is obvious. Usually, it's during the winter, and incarceration means warmth, a bed, and three meals a day. Oh, but it's different in the spring and summer. They fight tooth and nail to convince the judge to enter a not guilty finding, or anything else, that would keep them out of jail.

So here we are on opening day in the new court. After Judge Mayo assumes his position behind his chair, the Court Officer calls the Session to order, and tells everyone to be seated.

The Judge looks to the audience in the crowded room, and welcomes everyone to the plush and modern surroundings. He then turns to his left, faces all the drunks in the dock, and politely says, "Gentlemen, in honor of this great and auspicious occasion, I hereby dismiss the Complaints for all defendants charged with Public Drunkenness, and will enter findings of 'Not Guilty'. You are all free to go."

There is a roar of approval from the dock. Stinson and I look at each other and laugh. Just then, a defendant in the front row of the dock cries out, "Wait just one damned minute!" He's a seedy looking character wearing a dirty and wrinkled green army field jacket. He's in dire need of a shave, and obviously has a hangover. He places both hands outside the railing, and with his palms facing each other, he begins to move them back and forth clapping his hands. He resembles a seal, as he barks, "Great f......Judge!"

What follows is a most unusual sight: A courtroom where everyone, including the Judge, is actually laughing.

And that's the highlight of opening day.

Little did I know then, that defendants, some of whom were Hell's Angels, I would prosecute, and often sent to jail, would become clients, when I retuned to full private practice.

To my dismay, the partnership on Lewis Street is short-lived. Shactman and Pearlmutter leave. We are now, Gordon, Sachar & Tobin. Pressure from my remaining partners mandate, I give up a role, I had truly come to love, having served the Commonwealth for almost two years.

CHAPTER FIVE

...The phone startles me, as I'm concentrating on number 7 Across. I'm trying to think of a 6 letter word for "Fund-raiser's target." I have an "f" for the first letter, and a 't' for the last. It's a few minutes past eight in the morning, and I know who's on the other end of the line without looking at the screen on the phone. My daughter, Stephanie, is making her first daily check to see if I'm ok. "Hi, hon. How ya doin?"

"I'm Ok, Papa, how do you feel? You all right?"

"Yup. I'm just drinking coffee and doing a crossword."

"The kids are both sick and throwing up. Jennifer has a fever again. Paul just got home, and is gonna watch the kids, while I get a few things at the supermarket. You need anything? I'll drop it off at your place."

"No thanks, I'm all set. The only thing I need is a wheelbarrow full of 50's"

"Yeah, yeah, yeah, I know." She says, "That's all you ever say! Love you!"

"Love you too. We'll talk later."

I chuckle. It's not my son, the doctor. It's my daughter, the lawyer! I look at her picture next to my desk. I'm not out of line, and I'm not biased, and the whole world is right, she's just absolutely gorgeous. It's no wonder that the male Judges are so good to her!

I start looking at other pictures in the room. She resembles my sister June. I start thinking about June's big case. I wish it were yesterday, so that Steph could have been there with me for the experience and the exposure....

31

You win some and you lose some. Long ago I had decided that any lawyer who claimed to have won all of his or her cases was immediately suspect. Either the lawyer never actually tried cases, or chose only absolute-no-brainer cases. I'd learned the hard way that there are very few perfect liability cases. There is always a wrinkle even in the best of them.

In 1954 my sister, June, and her husband, Shep Salinsky, moved from the first floor of the three decker at 125 Lawton Avenue in Lynn. They'd bought a large Cape Cod style home at 18 Thompson Road in quaint, historic Marblehead. June's pride and joy were her flower gardens, located strategically around the house and in the spacious back yard. Almost from the day they bought the house, they were besieged by brokers and neighbors wanting to buy the back yard for a house lot, but using the yard for cookouts, touch football and badminton for the kids and their friends was more important to June and Shep.

It's the winter of 1971. The intercom rings in my office. One of our most proficient and talented secretaries, Margie Lane, is on the other end. She tells me June is on the line.

I ask, "And to what do I owe this unexpected pleasure, Madame?"

"Shep and I need a bit of legal advice. How about coming over for supper tonight?"

"Is it serious? Anything going on between you two?"

"No, no, no, nothing like that. How about six o'clock?"

"O.K. see you later."

The house is located on the left, half way down the small block. It's white with red brick stairs in the front and tall evergreen trees on either side. In keeping with the old seafaring tradition of the town, there is even a so-called, "widow's watch," high above the second floor.

I know the house well. I lived there for about a year after Phyllis and I had separated.

No need to knock. June opens the door and greets me with a hug and a kiss. Even before I'm seated in my usual chair in the kitchen I come out with it, "Now what's this all about?" Shep responds with, "Let's eat first!" June quickly serves me a steak and salad, and of course from their bakery there's a basket of hot rolls in the center of the table.

Shep is totally predictable. I know exactly what he's going to say next. He doesn't disappoint me.

"It's *sangua, sangua, sangua* (blood, blood, blood). She always gives you the steak and I get the chicken!"

We go into the dining room to talk while having dessert and coffee. I finally ask, "Who's going to break the ice?" Shep responds, "June remembers the details better than I. Let her tell you."

She begins. "Well, it happened so long ago, that I don't remember all of the details; it was sometime in 1958. Shep and I were watching TV when we saw a commercial we'd heard many times. We watched and listened as Walter Cronkite extolled the virtues of Alcoa Aluminum Siding. I can hear him now. He said something like...

'...*It will last a lifetime. Just cover your house with it. It'll keep you warm in the winter and cool in the summer. It's virtually maintenance-free. Just hose it down every now and then. This product is fully guaranteed for as long as you own your house. It will not bend, crack or become subject to pitting, as with other inferior products. Just call this number or look in your local Yellow Pages to contact an Alcoa dealer...*'

Well, the house paint was peeling and cracking; we'd either repaint or use Alcoa. Sheppie made the ultimate decision. He thought that a paint job would last at best for a few years because we're so close to the ocean with all the salt in the air. The siding cost considerably more, but it's a one-time shot. I agreed."

I learn piecemeal as they tell the story that June called Perma-Home Corporation, which the Yellow Pages listed as an Alcoa dealer and installer. They were located on Broad Street in Lynn. A representative appeared and gave them a choice of Alcoa or a less expensive product. They opted for Alcoa. They took out a bank loan to pay for the project. It took nearly six weeks for the installation. As the work progressed, the workers stored cartons containing materials for the job on the premises and in the driveway.

June tells me that whenever she waters her flower beds, she hoses down all of the exposed siding. She says she has to reach behind the tall trees flanking the house to spray the siding behind them. This routine lasted from the installation of the siding in 1958 to the summer of 1971.

By that time, the well-watered and manicured trees had grown so tall, they covered the widow's watch and blocked sunlight from entering the windows on the second floor. June and Shep decided to cut the trees, greatly reducing their height. It was after the trees were cut when she discovered that the siding, which had been hidden from view behind the trees, was pitted and significantly discolored.

Out came the ladder. All attempts to clean the siding with Mr. Clean, Barcolene, and other highly touted cleaning agents were unsuccessful. Remembering Cronkite's spiel about a guarantee for as long as one owned the house, June made a call to Alcoa's home office in Virginia or Georgia or one of the Carolinas.

Wonder of wonders! An Alcoa representative actually showed up! From the ground, he observed the defective siding. He told June that this was a first for him. He'd never seen such a condition in all the years that he worked for Alcoa. With a screwdriver and hammer in hand he scaled the ladder and pried off a piece of siding. He climbed back down, siding in hand.

He announced somewhat self-righteously, "Mrs. Salinsky, this is just as I had suspected. This is not an Alcoa product. We have a special patented chemical treatment to prevent pitting and discoloring such as this. No other company has it. Here, look at the inside of this piece of siding. It's stamped 'Alcan' and not 'Alcoa'. I'm sorry to say, but you've been had!" He replaced the siding and left.

I asked, "Anything else I need to know?"

Shep shrugged his shoulders, but June said, "Oh, I forgot to tell you. We don't have the contract anymore, but I did get a copy from the bank that lent us the money. It's barely legible—a carbon copy—and it's hard to tell if it says 'Alcoa' or 'Alcan'. I never read the damn thing. I just signed it. Oh. We have an estimate of seven thousand to take off the Alcan and replace it with Alcoa. I think that's about it. What do you think? A case or not?"

"Holy smoke! There are so many problems, that I don't know where to begin. Bear in mind, that what I say now is off the cuff and without the benefit of any research. The first hurdle, is to find out whether or not,

Perma-Home Corporation is still in existence after all these years. I know that they sure as hell are not on Broad Street in Lynn.

Let's assume for the sake of argument we can find a viable Perma-Home Corporation, or its successor to sue. The bigger problem is the Statute of Limitations. In a breach of contract case you have to bring suit within six years. Hell, we're talking about 13 years, as we sit here! If we bring suit and claim fraud or deceit that's a tort, and such cases ordinarily carry with it a three year Statute of Limitations. A tort, by the way, is a civil wrong as opposed to a crime. So in this case, you would have until 1974 to sue in tort and until 1977 to sue for breach of contract. Remember, you discovered the fraud perpetrated upon you, when the Alcoa representative arrived and made the discovery in 1971.

Massachusetts clings to its own interpretation of when its statutes of limitation begin to run. Most other states follow the Federal rules. A recent ruling by the Massachusetts Supreme Judicial Court in a medical malpractice case might later prove to be relevant in your case in the event of an appeal. The Court endorsed a sensible rule stating that the statute begins to run, when you learn of the defect, or when you reasonably should have known about it. Maybe it's time to convince the Court, that its malpractice stance should also apply to cases involving fraud, deceit or fraudulent concealment.

The rule in the Federal Courts, incidentally, where we cannot bring your case, is that if there is deceit, concealment or fraud, the limitations statute is suspended until the fraud is discovered."

Shep asks: "What do you think this will run?"

"I'll make you a deal. If there is a case and I think it's worth a shot, you pay all out-of-pocket expenses as we go along. I'll eat the fee. Literally. It'll cost you a steak once in a while, so that I can enjoy watching you eat your chicken! *Sangua*, pal, *sangua!*"

The Yellow Pages reveal that there's a Perma-Home Corporation in Wakefield. A trip to the Secretary of State's office in Boston confirms that even though there are now different officers and directors, it is in fact the same entity.

We brought suit in the Essex County Superior Court on January 30, 1973, claiming fraudulent misrepresentations upon which the Plaintiffs had relied, and that Perma-Home negligently installed an inferior product, which was other than as ordered. I threw in the negligence language hoping that I'd hear from their insurance company, which might enhance the possibility of a settlement without a trial. (Massachusetts didn't have a consumer protection law at the time.)

Attorney Santo J. Ruma (who would later become presiding Justice of the Peabody District Court) filed an Answer to the Complaint denying "each and every allegation." He also filed an Affirmative Defense claiming that our action was barred by the applicable Statutes of Limitation.

Now, eight years before this, Gail, June and Shep's 15 year old daughter, contracted aplastic anemia. The doctors looked for family members with her blood type and characteristic; both Red Sommerstein (my brother-in-law) and I underwent bone marrow transplants. They proved to be of no avail and she soon passed away. (I believe she would have survived today given the medical advances in the field.)

Quite understandably, June and Shep were shattered. As a means of therapy, June began working for Tessler, Gordon & Sachar; it's how she got to know Santo Ruma. In those early years Ruma had worked for a collection firm, and when he had a scheduling conflict he'd called June to see if someone from our office would cover for his office. We usually accommodated and in turn weren't bashful in asking him for coverage in Suffolk County.

It's always makes life a lot easier to know an attorney on the other side. He had no authority to settle, and the case had to go to trial, but we agreed upon many things in order to save time at trial, and to make both of our jobs a little easier. Since almost all of Perma-Home's key players were either of parts unknown or deceased, we agreed to allow hearsay statements of deceased persons to be admitted so that we could avoid cumbersome legal technicalities. Some of the defendant's workers were still alive and remembered the work in question. They would be able to relate relevant conversations of deceased PH employees with the Salinskys, if they happened to hear them.

Criminal trials are given precedence over civil cases by law. The Superior Court in Salem, where we would have been otherwise was busy making a dent in it's criminal case backlog, so civil cases were being shipped out to Peabody, Newburyport and Lawrence. We ended up trying the case for two days in the District Court of Peabody with Judge John Forte presiding.

Judge Forte was actually the Presiding Justice of the Concord District Court, but was able to sit in the Superior Court by special dispensation, when some committee came up with the idea that because in reality we had only one Trial Court in the Commonwealth, any judge could be assigned to any court. Those responsible for this brilliant innovation apparently lost sight of the fact that not all District Court Judges are suited for the complexity of the cases in the Superior Court. Nor do all judges have the background, experience or training to sit in the Probate Court dealing with the myriad of domestic issues.

As far as I was concerned, and without casting any aspersions upon the able and competent Judge Forte, it created a legal abortion in the Courts of the Commonwealth long before the United States Supreme Court spoke on the subject in the famous case of *Roe vs. Wade*.

It doesn't happen very often, but the case was tried in virtually text-book fashion. There were no unnecessary delays, displays of histrionics, unwarranted objections or other wasteful and dilatory tactics. June was our key witness and needed little preparation. She recited the facts in believable terms just as she had that evening at her dining room table. Our siding expert testified about his observations, and the cost of doing the remedial work.

Ruma presented a Motion for a Directed verdict at the close of the evidence based upon the Statutes of Limitation. He was asking the Judge to enter a verdict for his client based upon the law. If allowed, the case would not go to the jury for a decision. The Judge denied his Motion; now I thought that we had a real shot. Closing arguments followed. The Judge gave his instructions to the jury on the laws pertaining to the case. The jury went to private quarters to deliberate.

The jury came back with a verdict right after the free lunch provided by the Commonwealth.

We were looking for seven thousand, and that's what the jury awarded us—by a unanimous vote. The hugs, kisses, and handshakes were short-lived, however. Attorney Santo Ruma was now on his feet: "Your Honor, may we approach the bench?" With a nod of the head the Judge responded with: "You may."

We approached. Joining us were the Clerk of the Session and the Court stenographer. In barely audible tones Ruma addressed the Court on a side of the Judge's bench out of the hearing of the jury. "May it please the Court, and without trying its patience, I have here a Motion For Judgment For The Defendant Notwithstanding The Verdict. It's based solely upon the applicable Statutes of Limitation. In plain and simple terms, this case was just brought years too late. I will rely upon the brief which I previously filed with the Court in support of my earlier Motion To Dismiss for the same reasons."

In equally hushed tones the Judge responds: "Yes, I'm aware that this case was not entered in accordance with our existing Statutes of Limitation. The Supreme Judicial Court has ruled that in situations such as this, it's better to let the case go to the jury. If they find for the Defendant, the question then becomes moot. If they find for the Plaintiff, the preferred action is to allow a Motion For Judgment Notwithstanding The Verdict. And I do so now. Mr. Clerk, will you kindly announce my decision and adjourn the Court. I will speak to the jurors in about twenty minutes. Thank you gentlemen for a well-tried case. It's always a pleasure to preside, when competent attorneys do battle."

Needless to say, we were all very disappointed. June still managed a smile and a kiss on the cheek. June is truly amazing. Years earlier, when the medical bills relating to Gail finally arrived, they put everyone into a state of shock. No one was prepared for the astronomical amounts due the doctors and the hospital. June and Shep both refused my initial advice to file for Bankruptcy. With head held high, and right in the face of this new adversity, she proclaimed: " I don't care how long it takes. We'll pay them every penny! I'm grateful for all of their efforts on Gail's behalf." I'd like a nickel for every letter I sent to the medical providers, collection agencies and lawyers. I also knew that just about every penny she earned working in my office went for those damned bills.

A light bulb flashed in my head as I realized how important the verdict really was. They were still making monthly payments—nine years after Gail had died.

I felt very humble and feeble when all I could muster was: "Let's see if we can convince the Appeals Court that Ruma and Forte are both wrong. If I can't, there's also an outside chance I can convince the Court that it's time for Massachusetts to join the rest of the Union."

Rumors regarding Ruma were rampant in the legal community, and shortly before oral arguments were scheduled at the Massachusetts Court of Appeals, his picture was in the papers. He was counsel to Speaker of the House, Thomas McGee and was awaiting appointment as a District Court Judge in Roxbury or West Roxbury. Doomed. No matter what I'd say in the Appeals Court it would fall on deaf ears. They ain't gonna change the law on *this* case! Who ever said that I was paranoid? Ruma is about to be one of them! Who the hell am I?

Ruma and I appear for oral argument dressed in our most conservative attire. The Court listens attentively to both of us and ask cogent questions. I talk about fraudulent concealment, which would have delayed the running of the statute of limitations until the defects could reasonably have been found. I mention the Federal rule, which delays the running of the Statute in cases where fraud or deceit were involved. I further point out that this is also the rule in the vast majority of our sister states. I remind the Court of its recent decision in malpractice cases when it had ruled that the statute of limitations did not begin to run until the negligent act was discovered.

In closing I say, "With all due respect, I would urge the Court to keep step with the rest of the country and allow Massachusetts to come out of the dark ages and enjoy a breath of fresh air. There must be many good reasons for other states to follow the Federal Rules, and I am confident that this Court will consider them in making its decision in this case. Thank you for your indulgence."

Months later the opinion of the Court on our case mentions the Federal rule, but the Court doesn't adopt it. The decision also says that the facts of the case don't support any fraudulent concealment. It acknowledges the malpractice standard, but says that this case does not involve conduct by any professionals. The Court comments upon the fact that the carbon copy of the contract leaves a doubt as to whether it says 'Alcan' or 'Alcoa'.

Lastly, the Court hints that maybe the Plaintiffs should have paid more attention to the markings on the boxes of materials stored on their property during the six week installation period.

The law is often unfair. If there is justice it must be in heaven; it's not often found in the courtroom. It never ceases to amaze me that very often injured people with meritorious claims and with whom it is easy to empathize, end up with a big zero. On the other hand, far too often the malingerers and other nefarious characters end up with undeserved windfalls.

We have to resign ourselves to the fact that the jury giveth and the Court taketh.

*****

It was a different story altogether with Bill Kettinger, Court reporter for the city's newspaper, *The Lynn Daily Evening Item.* Kettinger came to my office one day in late July of 1974, his right hand heavily wrapped in bandages.

He said that about two years ago he'd bought a Black & Decker electric hand saw that came directly from a window display in a hardware store on Munroe Street in Lynn. There was no box, operating manual or instruction booklet of any kind, nor were there printed warnings on the saw. The salesman said that it was the only one in stock.

Bill was very articulate. He said calmly, with a slight nasal twang, "I was in my garage cutting some boards on July 16th, when the saw suddenly bucked back and struck me in the stomach. I instinctively tried to push it away with my hand. The blade was still turning. My fingers got cut. They started to bleed profusely and they were dangling in the air. I nearly passed out, but my screams brought help. I was rushed to the hospital. My fingers were sewn back together and splints were used for the severed bones. I lost the entire middle finger of my right hand. I'm a reporter, and I'm afraid I won't be able to use my right hand for typing. Do you think that I have any redress?"

Red ("give you ice in the winter") Mahoney was the adjuster for Liberty Mutual. He had the reputation in the legal community for being the stingiest adjuster around. He undervalued nearly every case he had. As far as he was concerned every case had a flaw. If liability was not in issue then the injuries were minor. He hated to part with a buck. He treated Liberty's coffers as though they were his own. I coined the phrase and teased him about it often.

Black & Decker had an insurance policy with Liberty, which provided that no claim could be settled without B&D approval. In order to discourage suits, they rarely assented to any out of court settlement. They apparently had the law on their side because there were very few plaintiff's victories throughout the country.

Liberty Mutual was often represented by the very able Attorney John Ronan. When he was elevated to the bench, Liberty stayed with his brother, Jim Ronan, who became counsel for Black & Decker in this case. Red Mahoney acted in this case, as he had never done before in any of our previous dealings.

We both wanted to settle, but B&D didn't. The closer it came to trial the more I asked for in settlement, and Red was keeping pace with my demands. His settlement offers increased with each new figure from me. But B&D wanted no part of any settlement.

The case was tried to a jury in the same courtroom as the Salinsky case. Judge Samuel Adams presided. In essence, our mechanical expert opined that there should have been some warnings given at the time of purchase, or in the very least a warning on the handle or other convenient spot, that one should not operate the saw without first reading instructions.

The crux of his opinion was that the bucking of the saw was caused by the upper and lower guards rubbing against each other. He explained that the circular saw blade is covered by an upper and lower guard. Together they housed the blade to protect the operator. When the saw is used to cut a piece of wood, the guards separate and allow the blade to move forward into a piece of wood. The deeper the blade goes into a piece of wood, the more the guards separate and the more the blade is exposed. The failure of the guards to fully separate as Kettinger was cutting caused the entire saw to buck, or retreat from cutting, and instead to snap back towards the operator. It was as though the blade had come into contact with a hidden piece of metal, or had run into a wall, that made it buck backwards.

Our expert reasoned that sawdust had accumulated inside the guards and prevented their free movement and separation as cutting progressed. The guards were rubbing against each other and sticking, which ultimately caused the whole saw to snap out of the wood and head in reverse towards Kettinger.

Our expert in mechanical engineering told the jury that the saw in this regard was negligently designed by B&D. For about two or three cents it could have installed a thinner washer at the bearing site between the housing and the guards. This would have prevented sawdust from accumulating. Simply put, he reasoned logically, a thinner washer would have created more space between the guards.

The jury found for Kettinger in the amount of $74,500.00. It also said that Kettinger was 35% contributarily negligent. The net result was about $48,425.00 for Kettinger, plus interest at the statutory rate of 12% per year from the date of entry of the case.

The B&D representative who had not permitted a settlement was one of their vice-presidents. He took the stand and appeared as an expert on behalf of the company. He ended up being my best witness.

It was his opinion that Kettinger must have dropped the saw on some hard surface. He held the saw up for the jurors to see a slight dent in the upper guard which housed the lower guard. He claimed that it was this dent, rather than an accumulation of sawdust, that caused the rubbing and sticking of the guards. His ultimate conclusion was that Kettinger was negligent in using a damaged saw.

During cross-examination he conceded that it was quite possible that the slight dent was caused when the saw hit the cement floor in Kettinger's garage, after it bucked and cut his fingers. He flushed when I confronted him with an assortment of B&D advertisements, which claimed that its circular power saw was built to withstand rough handling including accidental drops to the floor during use.

His embarrassment would be complete, when I further confronted him with some test results performed by Underwriting Laboratories. He had just agreed that testing by U.L. was mandatory and design changes are often made as a result of its testing. U.L. sets the standards in the industry. So I began.

" Mr. X, how can B&D advertise to the world that its saw was built to withstand drops to the floor, when this U.L. test result which I now show you indicates substantial disabling damage to the guards from drops of only five feet?"

"I don't know."

"Mr. X, would you agree with me that a thinner washer between the guards and the saw housing would create more space for sawdust to flow freely and prevent sticking?"

"I believe so."

"Thank you, sir, I have no further questions."

Jim Ronan said that he'd been ordered to appeal. I told him that if B&D paid the judgment, I would waive the interest and costs. B&D again refused to settle and the case went to the Court of Appeals. About six weeks following oral argument, the Court wrote a short opinion upholding the jury verdict. I then sent a letter to Jim Ronan requesting a check to satisfy the judgment, including costs, and every penny of interest. It also contained a per diem rate to account for any mail delay. It came.

Hooray for the good guys! You may lose some, but then again, you win some!

CHAPTER SIX

...I'm still looking at the pictures on the wall, when I realize that it's almost nine and I'm famished! I can visualize and actually smell a well-done omelet at Brother's Deli on Market Street. Damn! I can't go there ever again! I know too many people, and besides, it's too close to the Court House. It'll be too embarrassing, if I run into someone I know.

I decide to stay faithful to the Atkins Diet. I've lost 35 pounds in the last two months and my blood-sugar level has dropped significantly. Maybe I can get to the point
where I can dump all the diabetic meds.

I grab a frying pan and throw in half a stick of butter. I grab a bowl and beat a couple of eggs. I nuke a cup of coffee and a few minutes later I'm sitting alone at the kitchen table eating a cheddar cheese omelet with sautéed peppers and onions.

My living room reminds me of my old office. My old desk sits against the wall and faces the center of the room and a black leather couch from the waiting room also faces center. Two green and two blue leather wing chairs, formerly used by clients, are on opposite sides of the room. A television set, three small bookcases, and a couple of equally small two-drawer wooden file cabinets line the perimeter walls. A lamp table, a coffee table, and two black oriental cabinets complete the décor. I feel very comfortable in my living room/office/den, and find myself spending most of my time at the computer behind the desk.

In accordance with the suggestions of two of my children, Matthew and Stephanie, (the third, my eldest, is Michael, and he's in Maine), the entire ten-foot-long wall behind the desk displays many of my diplomas, citations, and awards. The majority of the diplomas are laminated in clear plastic with wide green and gold borders, color-coordinated with the green paneling in my former office. On another wall hangs the John Jennings Advocacy Award, the highest honor the Greater Lynn Bar Association can bestow upon an attorney. The engraved silver bowl sitting on top of a bookcase is the Ronan Family Jurisprudence Award, the highest award the Essex County Bar Association presents. It's an award which is not often presented. I'm proud to have the distinction of being the only person ever to have been presented with both awards.

I've programmed the computer with some of my favorite oldies, and in the background I can hear the unmistakable voice of Bobby Darin singing, "Mack The Knife." My eyes glance around the living room from the kitchen table where I'm seated. They scan the wall with all the diplomas, and then focus on the only one with a large prominent red seal.

Once again, I'm eating, but don't taste anything. I no longer hear the music in the background. I keep staring at the red seal, as though hypnotized. And as if by magic, I'm in another place at a time long ago...

...It is almost ten years to the day following my honorable discharge from the army (I had served in Germany as a First Lieutenant with the 7th Tank Battalion of the Third Armored Division) when I receive a large, unsolicited certified-mail envelope from the office of the United States Attorney General.

I have no clue as to what the letter is about, and can hardly wait to open it. As I look for a letter opener, I start thinking to myself, and almost say out loud, Damn! What did I do wrong now?

There's a cover letter signed by The U.S. Attorney General, Nicholas Katzenbach. The signature is not a facsimile. It's actually signed personally by the man himself! The only other document in the envelope is an enormous diploma from the office of the Attorney General Of The United States. Directly under its title is an American Eagle with wings fully extended. I can't imagine what it's for as I begin to read the Old English lettering:

"TO ALL WHO SHALL SEE THESE PRESENTS, GREETING:

Know Ye, that reposing special trust and confidence in the patriotism, fidelity and abilities of BRUCE N. SACHAR of Massachusetts, I do hereby appoint him a Special Hearing Officer for the Department of Justice to...."

I've been appointed to conduct interviews, investigate, and hold hearings in Conscientious-Objector cases during the Viet Nam conflict. Soon thereafter I receive a booklet containing instructions and the standards used to determine whether a person is qualified to claim Conscientious Objector status and to receive a deferment from active duty in the service.

Packages soon arrive from all over New England containing the files of claimants. I conduct the hearings in my office. It becomes clear that in a small minority of the cases there is absolutely no basis for obtaining CO status. The attempt is obviously to avoid the draft, and I quickly dispose of those cases by rejecting the claim.

But the validity of the vast majority of claims is more difficult to determine since the definition of a CO is cloudy at best. It leaves too much room for speculation; a decision has to be made mainly by assessing the candor and credibility of the claimant. My role is no different than the role of a Judge in a jury-waived case.

There are very few whom I find to be true CO's. In the remaining number of cases where there is room for reasonable doubt, I cover both my behind and my conscience. I write opinions finding that the claimant should not be exempt from active duty, but that he should be assigned to non-combatant duties, such as service in the Medical Corps.

The decade of the 70's has more ups and downs than I can remember. I do know that the highs and lows would resemble a Wall Street broker's chart or the printed result of an electrocardiogram.

I date often following my fourth and final voluntary separation from Phyllis in 1966. She continues to live in Lynn, and our son, Michael, is with me every weekend from Friday after school until bedtime on Sunday night. We also spend an evening or two together in the middle of the week as well as every holiday. Although he's a very bright student, I truly regret and feel guilty that I'm not there for him every night to help with or check his homework. A visiting father has only so many things to do and places to go. Consequently, Michael becomes a great bowler. We also both become avid and devoted fishermen.

It proved to be a long and grueling series of difficult elimination matches, but at the age of 15, Michael is awarded a huge trophy in honor of his being crowned as the "World Candlepin Bowling Champion." I take great parental delight, whenever I sit in the audience watching him compete in live television bowling matches.

I begin dating Fred Pearlmutter's secretary, Christine Ingalls Jackson. She's both extremely bright and attractive. Her shoulder-length auburn hair interspersed with streaks of blond, is worn in a variety of the then-popular styles. On any given day it would just fall loosely to her shoulders. On another, she would sport a ponytail or an updo.

Her mother's maiden name was Ingalls. She was a former Marbleheader. Pictures of her forebears bearing the family name were prominently displayed on the walls at Town Hall. Many of them were former politicians or dignitaries. Her Ingalls ancestors were among the first settlers in Lynn and Saugus.

In order to make ends meet, Chris takes a second job at night as a cocktail waitress at the Harbor Lounge in Lynn. In my mind, the mandatory short skirts and silk stockings accentuate her sexy figure and long shapely legs. As is the custom, she has a variety of wigs to match her mood or attire. Her vivacious smile reveals a perfect set of shiny white teeth. The end result is lots of generous tips.

I'm in love and smitten. On March 16, 1974, after eight years of separation, I divorce Phyllis. On May 3, 1975 Chris and I are married at the Hawthorne Hotel in Salem. We spend our honeymoon in Las Vegas with her best friend and her husband, Angela and John Barnes. We're married by "Marrying Sam." He's a traveling Rabbi from New Hampshire who performs mixed marriages.

The Hawthorne Hotel is now owned by none other than my erstwhile client, Freddie Goodman. He furnished the hall for the ceremony, meal and dancing. He also provided overnight accommodations for John and Angela and the newlyweds. He had asked me to pay him in cash. After the ceremony, when the guests are dining, I enter his office. Behind the desk sits the perfect clone of the movie actor, Peter Ustinov. I hand him a stack of one hundred dollar bills, which he immediately puts in his pocket without even counting. We shake hands. With a big grin on his face, he says, "I really wish you guys all the luck in the world. Be sure to have a good time on your 'funnymoon' and I'll see ya when ya get back."

Attorneys Jim Valerie from Lynn and Morris Gordon had represented me in the earlier court proceedings involving Phyllis. Morris was my attorney years before when the original support order was entered. It was $150.00 per week. I later learn that at the time it's one of the highest support orders entered in the Probate Court in Salem.

I make the payments faithfully, albeit at times with great difficulty. The support payments often curtail what I'm able to do for Michael during my visitations; this adds to my feelings of guilt.

The ever popular and affable Salem attorney, Phil Strome (a dear friend and sometimes mentor) becomes my new attorney in the never-ending saga with Phyllis. Phil's specialty is Bankruptcy, a unique and totally foreign subject to most other lawyers. He also represents a Salem bank and does all of its title work and mortgages. He is well-liked and respected by everyone including most of the local judges.

A trip up the long flight of well-worn wooden stairs gets me to the second floor in the hallway outside the door to his office. The glass on the door has his name emblazoned in the usual manner with black and gold painted lettering. The old building itself is attached to the bank he represents. It's on Washington Street and diagonally across the street from both the Superior and Probate Courts on Federal Street.

I enter nervously even though I had been there many times. It reminds me of my good friend Attorney Irving Estrich's office. Files are scattered everywhere. They're on desks, chairs, and cover every inch of space on the floors. His inner office door is just off the waiting room. The door is open. He's seated behind his desk when he spots me and beckons with his hand to come in and sit down. He's laughing and talking on the telephone.

I feel a little uncomfortable listening to his phone conversation, having to pretend not to hear the advice he's giving to a local well-known restaurant eer on what has to be done to remain open for business. Eventually he hangs up. Without even taking a break or greeting me, he begins to tell me a joke in Yiddish. I've heard it before, but laugh dutifully. Suddenly he becomes serious and says in Yiddish : *"So, boychick, vie gehst deine tzimmes? Vas machst du eppis? Shpicht tzu mir!"* ("So, kid, how are your problems working out? How are you doing? Speak to me!") I have at that moment no idea that the decisions about to be made will have a profound effect on the rest of my life.

Before I can respond to his questions he quickly says, "Listen, *boychick*, I already spoke to your wife's lawyer, Alan Chapman. If you want this divorce to end quickly and smoothly, you'll have to forget about a decrease in your child support payments. There's no way in hell that they will agree to reduce them."

"Christ, Phil, they're already outrageously high and you know it!"

"Right, Kiddo! But do you want to postpone your wedding and have a full-blown trial in about a year? I suppose in that case, you could get lucky and get a reduction. I read all of the detective reports about Phyllis, and obviously some judge from another county will be assigned to hear the case. You'll probably prevail on either adultery or cruel and abusive grounds. The downside is that you're a lawyer. The judge may feel compelled to even increase the support."

"I can't wait another year. It's already been much too long, and I don't relish the thought of publicly airing the dirty laundry during a trial. Besides, my bride-to-be, has already made all sorts of arrangements. She's given deposits to the band, the printers, and the florists."

"OK, that's what I wanted to hear from your lips. I have some thoughts with regard to the child support payments."

"Shoot!"

"The way the child support order stands today, you don't get any kind of a tax break. If I can somehow get the order to read 'unallocated alimony and child support', you'll get to write off and get a tax deduction for the full amount. The fact that she'll have to declare the whole sum as income shouldn't bother Chapman. After all, she only works part-time as a hairdresser, so it shouldn't affect her tax return at all.

In any case, you'll have to pay alimony until she either remarries or dies. Judging from the detective reports, she won't stay single for long,

50

and you might as well take advantage of the tax deduction in the interim. What do you think, Kiddo?"

"Sounds like a plan. See if you can pull it off."

"I'll call Chapman and give it my best shot. I'll call you with the results, but no matter what happens, we still have the court date set for March 16th, which is right around the corner. I'll see you there about 8:30 in the main ballroom."

"OK, Phil, thanks a lot. I'll see you there."

Chapman rejects our proposal.

Judge Henry Mayo is on the bench. He had recently been elevated from the Lynn District Court. I feel right at home as I watch him dispose of other cases, while he paces back and forth popping his antacid tablets. Whenever he puts his hands in his pockets he spreads his robes apart, and the ever-present necktie supporting his pants is exposed.

Eventually, the clerk calls our case. I think he wants to save me from embarrassment because except for us the courtroom is now empty. He then proclaims. "All witnesses who are to testify in this matter please stand and raise your right hands."

Phyllis and I stand, as does my corroborating witness, Attorney Ben Tessler.

"Do you swear that the evidence you are about to give in this matter, will be the truth, the whole truth, and nothing but the truth, so help you God." In unison the three of us say, "I do."

The judge asks the parties to approach the bench. "Good morning Mr. Strome, Mr. Chapman, Mr. Sachar, and I presume, Mrs. Sachar."

We all respond with, "Good morning Your Honor."

"I see from reading the file that Mr. Sachar is the Libellant. I'll hear from you first Mr. Strome."

"Well, Your Honor, as you can see, this is to be a trial on the merits in which my client alleges that a divorce should be granted on the grounds of cruel and abusive treatment. We will waive the other grounds alleged in the Libel. We have a disinterested witness present to corroborate Mr. Sachar's claims. It should be noted, Your Honor, that we are basically in agreement with respect to obtaining a divorce, but we have reached an impasse with respect to alimony and child support."

Strome lets this sink in, clears his throat and continues: "Your Honor, as you can see from the file, my client has been paying child support in the amount of $150.00 per week. We made a proposal to Mr. Chapman that the order be revised to an unallocated payment of alimony and child support. As the Court knows, this would allow my client a significant tax reduction which would lessen the burden of such a significant payment. There really does not appear to be any downside to this proposal since Mrs. Sachar works only part time. We submit that her reporting of the payments as income will not affect her in any significant way or manner. Thank you, Judge."

"I'll hear from you now, Mr. Chapman."

"Thank you, Your Honor. I respectfully submit that the addition of $7,800.00 a year to my client's taxable income is not insignificant, but in fact will place her in a different tax bracket when added to her part-time wages. I believe that Mr. Strome's proposal will lead to an unjust result, and that the existing order for child support only should stand. Thank you for your indulgence, Your Honor."

The Judge scribbles some figures on a piece of paper and looks in the file. He stands up. He begins pacing and stares at the ceiling, and then at the windows, and then at the floor. He appears to be in deep thought for what seems to me to be an eternity.

Finally, he speaks. "I feel that this is a classic situation calling for compromise. I suggest that the order of $150.00 per week continue, but that a fair solution to the problem would be to specifically allocate $75.00 per week to alimony and $75.00 per week to child support. In my mind this would be an equitable solution. It would also eliminate the need for a trial in the future in the event of the remarriage of Mrs. Sachar. There would not be a need to have the Court attempt to divine what portion of the $150.00 was really meant to be alimony. Gentlemen, I'm about to take a mid-morning recess. I suggest that you talk to your respective clients, and we will reconvene in about 15 minutes."

We go outside for a breath of fresh air. I light up a Camel. Strome and Tessler each bum one from me. Our concensus is that it's still a good deal. Tessler speaks with a straight face as he observes: "The ball is now in Chapman's Court."

Strome responds with: "True words of wisdom from our newest legal scholar!"

Chapman soon finds us, and as he lights up a cigarette he announces that we have a deal.

As we enter the courtroom, I hear Chapman tell Phylis to remain in the hall until he comes for her. The clerk advises the lawyers to approach the bench and they report the agreement to the Judge, who almost instantaneously directs me to take the witness stand. He reminds me that I'm still under oath.

Strome asks me a few questions directly from the Libel. He asks when and where I was married, and when Phylis and I had last lived together. He then asks for Michael's date of birth.

"Mr. Sachar, is it true that you have brought this Libel for divorce alleging cruel and abusive conduct as grounds therefor?"

"Yes, Mr. Strome."

"Will you please tell the Court in your own words the facts upon which you rely in support of your claim of cruel and abusive treatment."

I then relate three separate incidents together with dates and witnesses. When Strome finishes, the Judge asks Chapman if he has any questions. He responds that he has none.

Strome then turns and beckons for Ben Tessler to take the stand. The Judge holds up his hand and halts Tessler in his tracks. He then faces Strome, and asks if that's my corroborating witness. When Strome answers in the affirmative, the Judge says very sincerely, "Look, gentlemen, let's dispense with this great fiction of ours. I don't want to hear from any such witness."

He continues sarcasticly. "Someday, in its infinite wisdom, the legislature will allow Massachusetts to recognize no-fault divorces, and this great charade can end once and for all. It will stop a lot of deliberate lying on the stand while under oath."

Chapman goes into the hall and brings Phyllis back with him and the Judge asks everyone to approach the bench. Chapman obviously hadn't wanted her to hear my testimony about the cruel and abusive incidents. Had she heard, she might not have agreed, and could have transformed the case into a fully contested matter.

The Judge compliments Phyllis and I for having chosen such excellent attorneys.

He then declares us divorced and says that it would be final in ninety days. He recites the alimony and support breakdown. He also makes an order that I am to be responsible for medical insurance, as well as any uninsured medical, dental, and pharmaceutical costs. He then wishes us both good luck. We leave.

*****

Angela (Chris's friend) makes a call home to check on the kids the morning after our arrival in Vegas. Once off the phone, she can't wait to tell us the news. The Hawthorne Hotel has been destroyed by fire. I had noticed during our stay that none of the valuable paintings and other artwork I'd seen before were displayed on the walls. When I had asked Freddie about it, he simply said that he had put them in storage during remodeling.

In those days the Barneses and the Sachar's are inseparable. I point out and convince the group that we should try and get into the real estate business. If it worked for the likes of Freddie Goodman, George Clayman, Saul Gilberg, the Backman Family, and many more, then it should work for us.

"I see how my clients and others do it. I think we should give it a shot. It's all very simple. Generally, you make a small down payment, assume the seller's first mortgage, and the seller will usually take back a second mortgage to cover the small down payment. In lots of cases you don't even need any front money. The second mortgage will take care of it. Then all you have to do is collect the rents and pay the bills."

I also tell them that over the course of time real estate values always increase. After owning the property for a few years, all we'd have to do is "refinance the first mortgage based upon the increase in the value of the property, pay off the second and walk away with a few bucks in your pocket. It's foolproof."

They agree. We start to buy multi-family dwellings throughout the city. Each building goes into in a separate Trust. In case one goes bad the others will still be protected. Thus are born the Shore Line Realty Trust, Egg Rock Realty Trust, Red Rock Realty Trust, and others. On paper each venture looks like a sure winner and a sound investment.

Every Saturday Chris and Angela go rent collecting. We soon learn that not all tenants pay rent on the due date. Some don't pay rent on any date. Tenants complain about every miniscule problem and they withhold their rent. It becomes common for tenants to move out in the middle of the night without notice, and of course, owing us rent.

Almost everything in life is based upon timing. Unfortunately, the climate for real estate ventures could not have been worse than in the early seventies. We have several so-called Section-8 tenants, whose rent is paid by the State. The concept is great because it's guaranteed every month. The problem is that the Section-8 office makes outrageous demands of us which we can't afford. If we don't put in a new separate staircase, or cover the house with aluminum siding, for instance, all rent is withheld. Without the rent we can't pay our obligations. Foreclosure letters begin to make us nervous.

Section-8 alone is bad enough, but we now see rent control rear its ugly head in Lynn. It becomes impossible to evict a tenant for any reason without the Rent Control Board's approval. An owner can't even get a rental increase without the Board's permission. The RCB arbitrarily denies all requests. We have insufficient personal assets of our own to continue; we then have no choice but to liquidate as soon as possible.

The sales give us enough to buy adjacent empty lots on Priscilla Road in Swampscott from the Gallo family. The Barnes's build first. John is an electrician and acts as his own contractor. He finally has a beautiful home with an in-ground pool in the back yard. He then helps with our house next door. We obtain a construction loan from the Winthrop Savings bank and build a Tudor-style house at 10 Priscilla Road. The total cost in 1975 to build the house according to our specifications and to acquire the land is about $43,000.00.

Chris moves into my three-room attic apartment at 8 Michigan Avenue in Lynn when we return from our honeymoon. Soon the foundation for our new house is completed and the actual construction begins. The apartment is about ten houses from the office and Priscilla road is about a half mile away in the other direction. We visit the site at every opportunity which is usually several times a day, and we are able to watch the contractors at work. We often have them accommodate us as we deviate from the original plans.

Towards the end of the summer Chris goes to the site less frequently. She claims that the new construction smells make her nauseous. We soon learn that her due date is in April. We move into the house just before Christmas in 1975.

CHAPTER SEVEN

...the phone rings. I jump. At first I don't know where I am .By the time it rings for the fourth time I'm standing behind the desk looking down at the phone. Shit, another bill collector! I don't answer. The unfinished omelet ends up in the disposal and the cold coffee goes down the drain.

The stove clock reads 9:48 A.M. I can't believe that I was out of it for nearly an hour. A fresh cup of coffee is what I need. I love the Keurig one-cup coffee maker which the kids gave me when I moved here. I insert a small container labeled Columbian Breakfast Blend, put a cup under the spout, pull down the lever, and in less than a minute, the aroma of fresh coffee permeates the room.

I'm back at the desk savoring the taste of the hot coffee. I'm surprised that I can remember what I had just been thinking about. Usually, when I wake up my mind draws a blank even though I know that I had been dreaming. My thoughts are disjointed. There's no particular chronology to them nor can I understand why certain apparently unrelated matters became intertwined.

This time I deliberately and intentionally zero in on Seit's appeal. It works!...

...It's a Friday a few days after Machera and I had first talked about the Seit appeal. It's about 11:00 o'clock in the morning. The Indian Summer hot spell had disappeared as quickly as it had arrived. I open my brief case, remove a file, and put it in a filing cabinet with the other tort cases in its proper numerical spot. I grab my messages from the spindle on Margie's desk and go into my office. I return a couple of calls, put the rest in the middle of the blotter, and head right for the office library.

I startle Machera with my entrance. He says, "Hey, what the hell are you doin' here this early? Weren't you supposed to start trial in Lynn on that dog shit intersection case? You know, the one where the lawyer kept calling the office for extensions in answering Interrogatories? You always assented, but when you had a conflict on a Motion date, he wouldn't continue it for you."

"Good memory. That's the case. We settled it in chambers ."

Joe is now practically shouting, "Hey, the guy was adamant. He wouldn't offer a plugged nickel. How'd ya do it?"

"I did nothing. I was ready and expected a full trial. I even answered 'ready' at the first call of the list. As luck would have it I caught an old friend for a judge. Former Town Counsel for Saugus, Gus Gannon, hit the bench. I knew then that my case and probably every other one on the list would settle today.

He's the greatest thing since sliced bread for plaintiffs in tort cases. He once told me at a Bar Association Dinner that he hates to listen to the same garbage in virtually every tort case. They're usually all the same. Just change the names and dates."

"Well, you know I'm here to learn. How'd he do it?'

Joe gets up and closes the library door. He shoves his books and notes aside and waits impatiently for my response.

"He merely did what he always does. As soon as we entered his chambers and exchanged greetings he spoke. It just happened, Joe, so my memory is still fresh. I'll try to give it to you exactly as though you were in the room with me and privy to the following scenario: Some lawyers become intimidated just being in a judge's chambers. I'm not. After all, this is Lynn and I know the judge well."

He begins. "I see that you are counsel for the Plaintiff in this case, Mr. Sachar. Tell me what it's all about."

I respond with, "Well Judge, my client was on Western Avenue in Lynn heading north towards Salem. He had stopped for several seconds in a line of traffic at the lights at the intersection of Chestnut Street. Suddenly he heard the sound of screeching brakes behind him followed by a loud bang. Before he was able to brace himself or even look in the rear view mirror he was belted by the car behind him. It had previously been stopped in traffic with him. The impact was so severe that it pushed my client at least six feet forward into the car in front of him. That car in turn impacted the front car in line.

My client was thrown backwards and forwards in the car. His knees were bruised from hitting the underside of the dashboard. His chest and head bent the steering wheel upward. His left arm and hand hit the door on his left.

He was taken by ambulance to the Lynn Hospital where numerous x-rays were taken. He was given some medication for pain. He had five stitches in his forehead. My client is not a malingerer. The last treatment for injuries related to this case was about six months following the accident."

I then add. "Here are some pictures, Judge, showing the damage to my client's car, the rear of the car he hit, the car which hit him and the car which caused it all from the rear. You can readily see that my client's car was totaled and that he was a very fortunate man not to have been injured more severely than he was.

The only defendant in this case is the operator of the car with the screeching brakes. He was 18 years of age at the time. He was driving a souped-up 1969 red Ford Mustang. He left skid marks in excess of 50 yards on a main thoroughfare where the traffic was anything but light. He was cited by the Lynn Police for speeding and driving to endanger.

Based upon the liability, the medical bills, my client's loss of earnings for two weeks, and the six month period of disability, I have made a demand for settlement in the amount of $9,000.00. There has been no offer. By the way, Your Honor, here are copies of his lost wage statement from the General Electric Company and his medical bills."

I continue. "Then 'Good Ole Gus' made a neat pile of all the papers, put them on top of the court file, pushed the whole stack to a corner of the desk, pulled an ashtray towards him, leaned back in his tall swivel chair, lit up a cigar, filled the room with cigar smoke, looked at the other lawyer, and finally spoke quite calmly.

'Well, counsel, if what Mr. Sachar has said is true how come there's been no offer in this case? I'd really appreciate an answer to that!' The other lawyer responded with an absolute straight face."

Joe starts to laugh and leans forward to hear me better. "What happened next, Bruce?"

"He said. 'Firstly, Your Honor, you should be made aware that I have no authority to settle this case. It's all in the hands of the claims adjuster. He has taken the position that the Plaintiff's minor injuries either were not caused by my client, or if they were, then the Plaintiff still cannot recover from him because the Plaintiff's contributory negligence in this case is a complete bar to his recovery.' At first Gannon just stares at him and says nothing."

I take a sip of coffee and continue. "Then Gannon says sarcastically, 'That's a very interesting theory. I'm only a District Court Judge. You'll have to enlighten me further as to your rationale.'

Again with an air of sincerity I hear, 'It's our contention that the Plaintiff's injuries were caused as a result of the impacts from the parked cars behind and in front of him. It is our further position that the car behind him was stopped too close to the rear of the Plaintiff's car. If the operator of that car had maintained a proper distance from the rear of the Plaintiff's car, it never would have struck the Plaintiff's car, after it was hit by my client. The Plaintiff should have sued that operator. Not my client.

We further submit, Your Honor, that the Plaintiff was also stopped too close to the rear of the car in front of him. We claim that most of his injuries were caused by that impact. He was, therefore, guilty of contributory negligence and cannot recover. The bottom line, Judge, is that he sued the wrong party and was also contributorily negligent. That's why the Company has decided not to make an offer of settlement. We believe that following a trial there will be a finding for the Defendant.'

I couldn't believe my ears, Joe, and neither could Gannon." I knew Joe was a captive audience and I enjoyed the suspense created in my little story. I continue. "Turning red and practically hollering the Judge blurted out, 'That's all very nice Counsel, but I think it's the biggest crock of shit that I've ever heard! I'm gonna take a fifteen minute recess. I strongly suggest that you call the adjuster handling this case. You be sure to tell him, that I'm the Judge who's going to hear this case today and that I think Mr. Sachar's demand is far too conservative. You got that?'

The now completely flushed and trembling lawyer responds meekly. 'Yes, Judge, it couldn't be more clear.' Well Joe, what do you think of those egg rolls?"

"I just can't believe the whole scenario."

"If you were there, Joe, you would have seen that lawyer run down the stairs to the first floor and head right for the pay phone. Ten minutes later we settled for $7,500.00, which is just about what I thought the case was worth. It's the figure I had in mind all the time. If I told you how many times I've heard Gannon say those words to an insurance company lawyer, you'd never believe me. He's an old school Judge. Unfortunately, they're a dying breed and in the minority."

"Did you tell the Judge?"

"Yeah. With Casey's permission I knocked on the door to his lobby. He was just coming out and opened it. I said, 'Thank you, Judge. It's settled'."

He smiled as he said, "I thought it would. What'd you get?"

I said, "$7,500.00."

He winked at me and said, "Good job, son!"

Joe keeps shaking his head from side to side in disbelief as he opens the library door. Before he even has a chance to get comfortable I tell him that, "The real reason I came in here was talk about Barry's appeal. I've given it a lot of thought and I think that we should keep it as simple as possible. Let's forget about the Motion to Revoke and Revise the sentence. I'm not sure that he even has the power. The statute is somewhat gray in my mind on that score.

We should, however, definitely file a Motion For A New Trial using virtually the same arguments we plan to use in the formal appeal. Our major point is that the Judge should have allowed our expert ballistician, Joe Caproni, to testify about the phenomenon known as an 'involuntary firing reaction'. Seit, you recall, fired four shots, but could remember only the first one. Caproni's testimony would have contradicted the Commonwealth's theory that Barry shot the decedent from the back.

Caproni would also have testified, that there was enough muzzle velocity from the 357 Magnum bullet leaving the chamber of the 38 Special to have caused the victim to spin around when a glancing bullet hit him in the forehead. It was a subsequent shot which hit him in the back of the neck severing his carotid artery causing death.

Remember, Joe, that on cross-examination of the state's coroner I got him to change the opinion which he gave in direct testimony. He reluctantly admitted that the glancing subcutaneous wound to the victim's forehead was from a frontal shot, and that it was not the fatal blow. Pagoni was found by the police lying on his stomach with the carotid artery shot appearing to have entered from the rear. It was that wound which was the actual cause of death. Never lose sight of the fact, that this was a self-defense case. Every witness for the government tried to prove otherwise claiming that it was a first degree murder.

Just as a sidelight, Joe, Attorney Bob Stanziani, (later to become a District Court Judge) who has the distinction of having defended more first degree murder cases than any other lawyer in the Commonwealth, had a case called, *Commonwealth vs. Carita*, which I recently came across.

Guess what! He, too, had the misfortune of having the same trial Judge as we did. A part of his appeal was based upon the negative tone of voice and inflections used by the Judge when making comments or rulings involving the defendant. Sound familiar? Unfortunately, all the Appeals Court Judges will see are the written transcripts of the testimony. One cannot hear the words spoken. Maybe I can somehow comment upon it during oral argument. Read the case and see if there's any way we can use it."

"OK, Bruce, I'll get right on it. Got time for lunch?"

"Yeah. How about a pizza at Monte's?"

"Sounds good. I'll not only drive, but I'll treat!"

"You'll treat? Incredible! Let's hurry before you change your mind!"

CHAPTER EIGHT

...I'm still drinking the Keurig coffee and am no longer concentrating on a particular date or event...but here I am again in the 70's...

...It's a Friday in 1975 just after Christmas and before New Year's Eve. The weather is mild but it's raining steadily. It's about 10:30 in the morning when I enter the office. I instinctively reach for my messages on Margie's desk, when I hear Morris Gordon through his open door behind Margie's desk and slightly to the right of it.

There's a sense of emergency in his voice as he hollers, "Hey, Bruce, will you come in here for a minute!"

It seems more like an order than a request. I answer. "Sure, just gimme a second to hang up my raincoat. It's all wet."

As I enter his office I see that Morris Tobin is also there. He's seated near the wall on the left. The open door had obstructed my view of him. I sit down in a vacant chair in front of the desk and as I'm seating myself Tobin rises to close the office door.

I'm suddenly asking myself, what the hell is this all about? Why the emergency? Why is there a need to close the door?

My fears are temporarily allayed, when Gordon calmly and politely asks, "How come you're back so early from Court? I know you've been preparing all week for a trial today. I saw the stack of witness subpoenas you had served by the constable."

" Some things just never change, Morris. Billy Casey was the Clerk assigned to the Third Session. He called the Trial List at 10:00 o'clock sharp. There were about twenty cases on the list. As I'm sure you can imagine, the room was packed with lawyers, litigants, and witnesses. Every seat in the house was taken and people were several rows deep along the walls.

The end result was that there were about six or seven cases where the lawyers had answered ready for trial. Casey then announced that there would be about a five or ten minute recess. I went outside for a quick smoke with the lawyer on the other side of my case. Still couldn't settle.

When the Session reconvened, Clerk of Courts Charlie Flynn, entered the room and went to the upper level. He actually stood next to where a Judge should have been seated. He announced that there was a shortage of Judges and that those who were there were all hearing criminal cases. He told us to arrange for new trial dates with Billy Casey and he left.

There were the expected bitches from all sides about the wasted time in preparation for trial, as well as for the costs expended for summonses. The major gripe, however, was that there had only been about five or six civil cases actually heard the whole year. And that, my friends, is why I'm back here so early."

The mood in the room quickly changes. In a somber voice Gordon speaks to me but all the while his eyes are focused on Tobin. "Bruce, we've come to the conclusion that this partnership of Gordon, Sachar & Tobin is over. I've already given Joe Machera his notice."

I'm in a state of total shock as I try to gather my wits and respond. Finally, I feebly utter incredulously, "What do you mean, 'over'? You can't be serious! You gotta be joking!"

"No. It's true. We came to this conclusion for several reasons. As far as criminal cases are concerned the Public Defender's Office is handling the bulk of them. Neighborhood Legal Services, as you know, entered the domestic area and is giving free legal representation to allegedly indigent litigants. Motor vehicle tort work is drying up with the advent of the No-Fault legislation.

Trial work is phasing out. Pretty soon there won't be a need for any trial lawyers. Tobin and I primarily concentrate in the non-litigation aspects of law practice. We intend to form a new partnership of Gordon & Tobin. We have also decided to keep young Jeff Musman in our employ. As you know, he's been doing a significant amount of real estate work for those guys downtown in the Security Trust Company building. Musman has indicated that he will remain with us."

And then at least for me comes the *coup de gras*. The words which have stuck in my craw ever since Gordon uttered them on that memorable and fateful day. At first I don't know what he means. It takes a few moments to solve the riddle.

"Bruce, you're like a blacksmith in Detroit!"

I don't have a clue as to the meaning of his analogy. I sit there like a dummy. I just can't put it together. Finally I regain the ability to speak.

"What the hell are you talking about? What do mean by that?"

He again looks at Tobin. So do I for the first time. Tobin is slouched into his chair as though he wants to disappear. His neck and cheeks are flushed and there are some beads of sweat on his forehead. I turn again to face Gordon as he starts to speak. He begins to lecture me as though I'm his student in a classroom.

"Detroit just happens to be the number one automobile manufacturing center in the world. I really hate to disillusion you, Bruce, but horse and buggy days are gone forever. Detroit no longer has a need for a blacksmith nor does any place else!"

I sit there in disbelief. I just can't believe what I'm hearing. I wonder just how long these two partners of mine have been planning this meeting. I then and there decide that I've been on the defensive long enough. It's time to become a little bit aggressive.

In a loud and unmistakably sarcastic tone of voice I inquire. "And may I ask you two gentlemen just when this dissolution is supposed to take place?"

Gordon quickly responds. "Now! Immediately! Forthwith!"

An unexpected calmness comes over me. Nevertheless I'm still loud and sarcastic as I reply. "Hey, even a tenant gets a thirty-day notice! There's lot of paper work and many other things to be done here. As far as I'm concerned, February 1st is a great day to call it quits."

They look at one another and nod their heads in assent.

I could not have been more sarcastic as I continue to speak. "I certainly want to thank you both for the timing of this announcement. You both know that I just built a new house and that I moved in only about a week ago. You are certainly aware that my wife is pregnant and is due in about three months. You can hardly be oblivious to the fact that I now have a mortgage to pay in addition to my other financial obligations. Did you give any thought to the fact that your decision will put an end to my weekly draw? Did it ever enter your minds, that I may have relied upon that draw in order to stay afloat with the new baby or to keep current with my new mortgage? Obviously, gentlemen, you just didn't give a shit!"

The only response was dead silence. I leave the room without another word. I'm deeply hurt.

I come to realization that come February 1st I will have to begin the practice of law all over again for the fifth time. Once, when I had initially passed the Bar; once, when it became, Tessler, Gordon & Sachar; once again, with, Gordon, Sachar, Pearlmutter, Tobin & Shactman; then again with, Gordon, Sachar & Tobin; and now full circle to where I started, just plain: Bruce N. Sachar, Attorney At Law.

This divorce is destined to create many problems. Foremost is trying to determine which files belonged to which person. My own words are now coming back to haunt me. It now seems to be eons ago when my first partnership was in its preliminary stages and the subject of compensation arose. Was one to be paid based upon the volume of new cases generated by that person? Was salary to be dependent upon how much new money a partner generated? Was any consideration going to be given to the hours one spent doing work for the partnership?

I suggested at that time to my partners-to-be that none of their proposals would promote harmony in the new venture. Their choices for determining compensation would only lead to jealousy and could ultimately foster contempt for one another. I reminded them that we were about to enter into a new venture based upon trust in each other. Our partnership was to be based upon a division of labor. Each of us would have a particular function and specialty. As long as we each do our job we should divide the profits equally.

I remind them that I generate a lot of tort cases. Would they think it fair if I settled one for megabucks and then demanded a bigger piece of the pie? Compared to the tort cases neither of my future partners could compete with the fees to be generated in their respective specialties. Lastly, I said that we shouldn't create a situation whereby a partner could think to himself, *Gee, I brought in the case that just settled. Boy, if I were alone I could have kept the whole thing!* They agreed with my reasoning and plan for compensation, as did each of the successor partnerships.

Due to my faith in the integrity of my partners and my philosophical approach to compensation there are absolutely no records as to the origin of a particular case. Whenever I received a phone call from a prospective client about a divorce, I merely told the person that I would refer him or her to my partner Morris Gordon, who was a specialist in such matters. A call regarding a trust, real estate, or corporate problem, was likewise referred to Morris Tobin.

Now to myself. *Jeeeze, Sachar, what do I do now? I can't possibly remember the names of all those people who called me. Maybe we should have kept records regarding the source of cases.*

Nevertheless I try to remember. I have no other options. I go through every open file in the office and made a list. I then write a note to each Morris listing those cases which I feel really belonged to me. I give them a choice of giving me the files now or a referral fee later when they receive compensation. I receive only the files which relate to my relatives. I've already taken virtually every tort case in the office. I brought them all in anyway.

Deep down, I think that they were influenced in their decision to split because of the large volume of cases which each of them was handling and the potential for future fees. I personally thought that they may have been lulled into a false sense of security. My rough calculations lead me to believe that between eighty and eighty-five per cent of the pending cases in the office had been generated by me.

February the First arrives and I have some reason to inwardly gloat a little, when Morris Tobin announces that he would prefer to be a solo practitioner rather than enter into a partnership.

I had been entertaining a sneaky suspicion all along that Tobin had never really intended to enter into a new partnership with Gordon in the first place. His ultimate decision convinced me that he had actually conned Morris Gordon. I thought that it was really a stroke of genius on

Tobin's part. The partnership had to be dissolved first before he could opt to be a sole practitioner; otherwise, there could have been prolonged and nasty litigation involving each partner's equity interest, the monetary figures appearing in each partner's capital account, and a real battle over the ownership of every file in the office.

Since we are all signatories to the original lease which is still in effect, we all remain in the suite at 60 Lewis Street and enjoy each other's company. For the same reason Fred Pearlmutter is still in the suite.

A short time later Gordon & Musman move to the Security Trust Building. A short time after that Musman takes his files and joins the prestigious Boston law firm of Goldstein and Minello.

How does that old saying go? "...the best laid plans of mice and men..."

.

CHAPTER NINE

...with all these memories flooding my mind I forgot to take my morning pills. I enter the bathroom and open the medicine chest. The top two shelves contain my morning and evening medications. Automatically the pills are in one hand and a half cup of water in the other as I close the door with my elbow and look at myself in the mirror...

...My legs had been virtually killing me for years. I had already experimented with every over-the-counter medication which I thought might remedy my problem. Nothing worked. I dreaded the nights. My legs prevented me from sleeping or lying down. I couldn't sit down to read, or study, or prepare for a trial at night. They ached. They wouldn't stop moving and twitching. I was experiencing involuntary spasms and movements. They would force me to jump up from a reclining position. I tried walking, hot packs, cold packs, and body creams to calm them down, so that I could get a little rest. I even took suggested vitamins and organic herbs and salves. Nothing worked.

I had seen several doctors in my quest for relief. No one could put a name to my condition. I was generally given some form of sleeping pill or tranquilizer. They were all a waste of money and never helped. My mother had the same affliction. The doctors told her that it was arthritis which caused her problem. Whatever she was advised to take never helped. She suffered until the day she died. I believed that my affliction was genetic and that I had inherited it from her.

I ultimately came to the conclusion that I too would take my condition to the grave. I had been suffering for at least a decade. One would think that by 1994 medical science and technology would have recognized my condition and found a cure or at least a treatment.

I don't remember whether it was an acquaintance or a primary care physician who suggested that I see a neurologist. I soon found myself sitting in a waiting room where the majority of patients were wearing a wide variety of collars and braces. Some were using canes. A feeling of embarrassment came over me. *Hey, Sachar, what the hell are you doing here with all these really sick people? You should be ashamed of yourself by taking up the time of a neurologist.* I was contemplating leaving at once and destroying my intake sheet, when a nurse called my name and told me to follow her.

I'm now in a small room with the doctor. "Your intake sheet is quite detailed. You have certainly set forth your complaints. Let me take your blood pressure." \

I roll up my shirt and soon feel the pressure of the sleeve. The doctor stands beside my chair, loosens the sleeve, and is looking at his watch. He's of slight build and not very tall. Judging by the absence of gray or white in his closely cropped hair I surmise that he's a lot younger than I, but no means is he a kid fresh out of med school.

"Would you remove your shoes and socks please and hop up on the examination table. Just sit on the edge and dangle your legs."

He uses a small rubber percussion hammer as he tests the joints in my arms and legs for reflex activity. When he finishes he slips the x-rays which I had sent to him previously under the clips of his well-lighted x-ray reader.

"First things first, Mr. Sachar. Based upon your medical records which came with the x-rays and my examination today I believe that you have hypertension. I'm going to prescribe the mildest medication available. It's really a diuretic called Lisinopril. Take one each morning. That should bring the blood pressure down significantly. If you lose some weight you might even be able to dispense with the medication. You can check your own pressure daily at a Stop & Shop or CVS store."

There's a significant pause as he flips through the papers in his file. At long last he speaks. "Can I call you 'Bruce'?"

"Absolutely."

"Well, Bruce, you have a classic case of R.L.S."

"What the hell is R.L.S.?"

"It's Restless Leg Syndrome."

"Holy smoke! You're the first doctor to put a name to what I have! I was beginning to think that I'm a psycho and that I really needed to see a shrink!"

Jokingly he says, "That's really not my field but one never knows."

"Now that you labeled my symptoms can you tell me something about what I have and what's the cure?"

"There's no cure. RLS is like an incipient or mild form of Parkinson's Disease. Let's just say that they're both in the same family. The same area of the brain is involved for both. The treatment lies with the use of drugs which will have an effect upon the chemical or enzyme imbalance in your brain. Research has discovered, that wonders can be accomplished in Parkinson cases by the use of drugs, which are in the so-called El-Dopa family."

"That's just what I need! A drug to make me dopier than I am, if that's possible!"

"Just give me a few minutes while I try and glean some info from this little gadget of mine."

"OK."

He has in his hands a little computer. It resembles a cell phone of today. He keeps pushing the buttons with a pencil. He tells me that he's logging into the latest edition of the Physicians Desk Reference book and is looking up some drugs. Finally he takes his eyes off of that little black box, puts it down, and looks towards me as he speaks in a scholarly manner. "I'm going to start you off with a prescription for Depakote. You start taking it tonight. Give me a call in about a week and give me a report."

"Sounds like a plan. I'll pick some up at CVS on my way home."

"Don't bother yet. I'll have my nurse give you some samples which should last for about a week. Be sure and call here and insist that you speak directly with me."

"Will do."

I make the call and report that the medicine has no effect upon me whatsoever. He then tells me to stop by the office for a new script calling for double the original dosage and to call again in a week.

"Doc, I think it's starting to work. Finally getting some sleep. Actually watched a whole movie on television. Only trouble is I'm exhausted all the time."

"The Exhaustion should pass once your system adapts to the new medicine. Drop by the office. I'll leave a script with the receptionist. Call me if there are any problems. I'll see you in three months at your next appointment."

"OK. See you then. Thanks Doc."

Eventually, the drug helps no more. It is then followed by a series of other drugs. None really work. I begin to feel like a lab rat. Quite by accident I come across a television ad. It's about RLS. I'm shocked to see it on TV but I soon become a dues paying member of the RLS Foundation and receive its newsletters. Until then I had no idea as to how large a segment of the population was affected and afflicted with RLS. The pamphlet is replete with articles by doctors and letters to the Editor.

Each drug I had taken is mentioned in the various articles. They work for some and not for others. There appears to be a consensus among the Foundation authors that RLS is found in those individuals who are lacking certain minerals in their system. Many report relief from the ingestion of magnesium. In my desperation I make a trip to a pharmacy and discover that magnesium is available in several strengths. It doesn't help one iota.

Finally, I receive a prescription for Klonipin. It's widely used by individuals who are prone to epileptic seizures. The drug works. I remain on it for about a year. The side effects are horrendous. I have vivid dreams almost nightly; I'm constantly being attacked; I'm always fighting for my life; I thrash and thrash in my sleep; the bedcovers are usually found on the floor intermingled with torn sheets; I kick my wife with my feet; I belt her with my hands and elbows; I wake the neighbors with my ungodly screaming and moaning when the windows are open in the summer. Needless to say, I'm totally exhausted every morning.

I'm unable to concentrate at work. I just can't stay awake and think. Everywhere I go I sleep. I have neither the energy to go out at night nor to participate in family functions. I may have physically occupied a particular spot but as sure as God made little green apples I'm never there mentally. I've become merely a mass of flesh and bones. A jelly fish or a sponge has a more active life.

"Doc, we've been experimenting for about two years now. You gotta get me off of this shit! That damned Klonopin has stolen a year of my life. You gotta help me, and fast!"

"I too get lots of literature related to RLS. I also read about it from time to time in various medical articles and journals. Wait a sec while I write out this new script. Take two at night before you go to bed and one in the morning when you wake up. Call me if you have any problems. Give it about a week or so to get into your system and kick in."

"OK, Doc, thanks again."

The new drug "kicks in" within a couple of days. I slowly come back to earth from outer space. The sheets are still on the bed in the morning. I start to live a normal life once again. I swear by my doctor and recommend him to anyone who will listen.

Little do I know that the prescription which was handed to me on that fateful day in 1996 will have such a profound impact upon my family, my clients, my friends, and myself. Unanticipated and unrecognizable side effects gradually take control of my mind, my body, and my soul.

CHAPTER TEN

...I should have taken the pills much earlier. It's not even noon and I'm getting drowsy. I begin to argue with myself..."Go take a nap!"

"How can I at this hour?"

" You've got nothing better to do with your time. Don't forget you're retired."

"You're right! My social calendar is clear! Good night!"

The shades are still down. The bed is still unmade. I crawl under the covers and wait for blissful sleep to take me away from bad memories. Does it? Of course not. I'm exhausted but can't sleep. I toss and turn but just can't get comfortable. I'm wide awake with my eyes closed as I again visualize the graph of the 70's. There's no question. The lowest point is 1976...

...Times are tough. Bills remained unpaid. Phyllis is hollering for her weekly checks. There's no steady income. It's truly, *deja vu.* The only difference between now and 1960 is that I have a small backlog of pending cases, am well-known in the community, and have developed a following of faithful clients. When the word spreads of the dissolution of Gordon, Sachar & Tobin, many of the clients whom I had previously referred to Gordon and Tobin take back their files and give them to me.

Fred Pearlmutter hires Florence Jacobs as his secretary. Chris now works for Morris Tobin. I have no secretary following the schism. Just cannot afford the luxury. I do most of the typing and other secretarial work by myself. Chris, although pregnant, pitches in and helps the cause in no small degree. It's her salary in those early weeks which puts food on the table. In a pinch or other emergency I hire either Florence or

Margie on a per diem basis. It's mainly the tort case settlements which kept us afloat and allow us to play "catch up" with financial obligations.

A few years before, Irving Estrich, was on the board of directors of the Lynn Credit Union, which is now located across the street next door to Saul Gilberg's office. Irving used his influence and saw to it that I was given the Credit Union's delinquent accounts for collection. The diminutive Joe Freedman, who lived on the second floor of our office building, was then and still is the chief cook and bottle washer for the LCU. He manages its every day operations. Joe has snowy white hair strategically located just above his ears and just below his shiny bald head. He's a perfectionist in all that he does and has a reputation for being difficult to deal with. He guards the coffers of the LCU as though each penny is his own. We get along famously after I start sending him money from the collections on a regular basis.

Little by little he starts sending me mortgages to do for the credit union. Deep down I think he knows that I'm having financial problems and is taking pity on me. It was probably even more obvious to him when I refinanced my automobile in order to obtain some money for living expenses. In those days mortgage work is easy. The Federal Government has not yet fully plagued us with its plethora of mandatory and often repetitious documents. In order to cut costs I try to do the title work myself, but if there is a problem I give it to Morris Tobin.

My father somehow managed to get a ride before sunrise every day to Ahabat Sholom the orthodox synagogue on Ocean Street in Lynn. Every day following the morning prayers he and his cronies would have a belt of *schnapps*. Usually it was Four Roses or some other cheap rotgut. In honor of a special occasion, however, they would consider themselves fortunate if someone made a donation of Canadian Club. In addition to his daily shot of booze he smoked Tiparillo Cigars. Apparently he had discovered the formula for longevity. But on April 4, 1976 while being driven home by Florence Jacobs' father he succumbed in the car. I often wondered, whether it was the daily dose of whiskey or the cigars, that did him in at the tender age of 84.

It's now April 11, 1976, a week later to the day, that our son Matthew Eric Sachar is born at the Salem Hospital. I pass out Tiparillos to everyone including the ladies. I hang around long enough to make sure they smoke them.

One of Lynn Police Officer John Main's sons is Glenn "Hoppy" Main. He had polio as a youngster and thus the nickname "Hoppy." He's a member of the Norsemen and destined to become a Hell's Angel. I had prosecuted him during my stint as an Assistant District Attorney a few years before.

In the blink of an eye he becomes my brother-in-law. He marries Chris's younger sister, June. Glenn is instrumental in referring his buddies to me when they have problems with the law. I soon find myself doing even more criminal defense work than I had previously done. I become a regular visitor in the Lynn, Salem and Peabody District Courts.

I'm out of the office and in some court almost every day. I no longer have the time to do essential secretarial work. Needless to say, Chris is busy at home with Matthew. I need help and inquire of Florence and Margie as to whether or not they know of any legal secretaries looking for a job. Margie indicates that when she worked for Jaffe & Tauro, she met a woman who might now be looking for a change in scenery.

It's less than six months following the break-up when I hire, Melinda Hatfield, a tall attractive woman with short and somewhat curly blond hair, as my full time secretary. She lives in Nahant with her husband and two teenaged sons. Her maiden name was Sears. The Sears family went back for generations in Nahant. In fact her mother, Samantha, was and is the Town Historian.

Melinda has a pleasant personality and is a pleasure to work with. She's a super fast typist, has a fantastic handwriting, and is a great organizer. She makes friends quickly with clients. She's becomes at once a talented legal secretary and receptionist.

The LCU can no longer compete with the Brotherhood Credit Union, which is the largest and most financially secure credit union in the area. It's stronger and sounder than some of the local banks. Ultimately the LCU closes its doors and transfers its assets to the BCU. Sam Sherman was its founder and is now its well-liked and respected President. Arthur Levine is its in-house attorney who does all of the mortgage transactions. I'm disappointed in losing the LCU as a client.

I begin sending the proceeds from the LCU collections to the BCU, which is located in cramped quarters on Mount Vernon Street underneath the Boston & Maine Railroad tracks directly across the street from the Registry of Motor Vehicles. To my surprise I receive legal work from the BCU, whenever it involves former customers of the LCU . If a problem arises regarding a LCU mortgage it usually also comes to me. Arthur Levine even sends me an occasional mortgage to do for the BCU, which is unrelated to the former LCU.

We're still digging out and feeling the after-effects of the February blizzard of '78, when Chris gives birth at the Salem Hospital to Stephanie Ingalls Sachar on March 11, 1978…

…The Mount Sinai Lodge of Masons meets at least once a month for its regularly scheduled meeting. Another night is used for rehearsals. When the list of candidates for membership gets to be exceptionally large an additional monthly meeting is held. The Lodge was first located above Kennedy's Men's Store on the corner of Market and Summer Street. The destruction of the building forced the Lodge to hold its meetings at the Saugus Masonic building. Eventually, the Lodge settles in with all of the other local Lodges in the Masonic Building on Market Street.

Mount Sinai has so many lawyers in it that the meeting hall resembles a courtroom. I followed my brother Abbott's lead and served as Master of the Lodge a few years before. I'm truly flattered and honored when asked to become its Master again for another two years. With Chris's assent I accept…

…Some families may have lived in Swampscott for thirty years or more but the "Townies" still considered them to be newcomers. Our status in town is no different. Nevertheless, I become involved in town politics. I knew many people just by having been a delivery boy for Singer's Poultry and some of the Summer street butchers. One thing is for certain. I feel that I know the location of every street in town.

It isn't long before I decide that some day I'm going to run for a seat on the Board of Selectman. When Town Meeting votes to increase the number of Selectmen from three to five, I throw my hat in the ring and get elected.

The exposure in Masonic circles and weekly appearances on the locally televised broadcasts of the Selectman meetings serve to enhance my law practice. Things are certainly looking up more quickly than I had ever anticipated.

I'm absolutely astonished and crushed when the love of my life, Chris, announces that she wants a divorce. She had apparently fallen in love with someone else. They eventually marry.

CHAPTER ELEVEN

...The Seit case is on my mind the entire weekend. I'm thinking about it on Saturday night at a restaurant. People are talking and I'm lost in thought. I'm on a different planet.

Someone says, "Hey, Saitch, we keepin' you up?"

"Naw, I'm sorry. Just thinking about a case. Keeps nagging me to death." My face turns red and I feel guilty. I spot the waiter and motion him to set up another round of drinks for the table. It's difficult, but I force myself to concentrate and pay strict attention to the idle chatter going on. The drinks arrive and the guilt feeling goes away.

Sunday is no better. I'm in left field playing softball at Phillips Park in Swampscott. I'm pounding the pocket of my glove, as the next batter comes to the plate. He's a dead centerfield hitter when he makes contact. I instinctively move several steps to my left and deliberately turn my body in that direction. I don't dare leave the left field line any more open than it is. The fastest guy playing on either side is Attorney Joel Mazer. He's our centerfielder today and I know that he can cover lots of ground. We've been playing on teams together for over 20 years so I'm perfectly content to stay where I am.

It's the last of the ninth and the score is tied. There are two outs. We're playing our first game of the morning. The winning team has a guarantee to play the second game. The losing team joins those on the bench who either came late or weren't picked. They all go into a pool and hope to play when they buck up after this game is over.

All of a sudden the only thing on my mind is Seit. I picture him behind bars at Walpole. The Motion for a New Trial has to be filed this week. Mazer's an attorney. I oughta ask him if he's familiar with Section 33E. The batter keeps fouling off balls.

I cup my glove and bare hand on either side of mouth. At the top of my lungs I holler in his direction. "Hey, Joel, ever have any dealings with Chapter 278, Section 33E? He turns in my direction, puts his gloved hand to his ear, and hollers, "What did you say?"

Somewhere between the words "what" and "say" the batter hits a screaming line drive to right centerfield. The ball bounces about twenty feet in front of Joel, but behind his back because he's facing me. Everyone is hollering, but by then the ball is well on its way beyond the distant tennis courts.

No sense chasing after it. The batter is already rounding second. I don't hang around to see if I get picked for the next game. 33E keeps bugging me....

...The next morning I'm in the office Library at 6:30. The first thing I do is scan the backs of the books. I reach for and pull out the green volume containing Chapter 278. I'm thumbing through the pages looking for Chapter 278, section 33E. I find it and put the book on the table next to my yellow pad and pen. I sit down and begin to read.

I'm disappointed in the wording. It's not entirely as I had hoped it would be. I turn the pages until I come to the last sentence of the statute. I drop my eyes to the annotations which follow. I know that the annotations will contain the name and citation of every case decided by the appellate courts in which this statute was mentioned.

There are not many decisions involving this particular Section. Nevertheless, I write down the names of the cases cited together with the references indicating in which volume of the appellate courts cases the decision may be found. I turn around and face the left library wall. It's about fifteen feet long and about ten feet high. The shelves on this wall contain every decision which had previously been made by the Supreme Judicial Court and the Massachusetts Court of Appeals.

I quickly find the five volumes which will contain the five cases cited in the annotations. I place them on the library table. With pen in hand and yellow legal pad in front of me I open the volume containing the oldest case cited. As soon as the right page is found I begin to read the case and

YOU BE THE JUDGE

take notes. A cold shiver comes over me…*Holy shit, it's 1960 and I'm in Izzy Bloch's tiny library doing his stupid research. It can't be!…*The feeling passes quickly. I'm back to reality.

I have mixed emotions as I read the cases interpreting the language in the statute. Once again an appellate court is attempting to divine the intent of the Legislature, when the statute had been enacted several years before. I'm in the middle of reading the last case when Joe Machera enters the library with a cheerful, "Good morning, boss." The clock on the shelf in front of the window indicates that it's nine o'clock on the nose.

Pretending to be upset I don't even look up at him. My head is down and my eyes are on the page in front of me, as I say, "I thought you were a lawyer and not a banker. It's now after nine o'clock!"

"My watch says that it's not yet nine o'clock. I've got two minutes to go! Besides, with the slave wages you guys are payin' me I really shouldn't come in until noon!"

"OK, wise ass. Have a seat. Let's talk."

He takes a seat at the far end of the table where all of his Seit papers are located.

"OK Bruce. I'm ready when you are."

"I read your drafts of the Motion for a New Trial and the Memorandum of Law in support of it. It's a good job. You hit every point and discussed every issue which we were considering. Normally, I'd say just call the Criminal Clerk in Middlesex, find out when the Judge is due there, and mark up the Motion for hearing on that date.

But this case has been tearing me apart. It's on my mind constantly. I remember that in the past few years the SJC in a couple of rare instances reduced the jury verdict to a lesser crime, and then remanded the case back to the Superior Court for re-sentencing."

"Under what circumstances do they remand? Is there a common thread in those cases? What do the cases say?"

"It usually occurs when the defendant has no record, was a good family man, and was a hard worker. Although the Court doesn't actually say it, I think it looks at the whole picture to see if he got a fair trial or if the verdict is against the weight of the evidence."

"OK. I get it. You want me to include it in the Motion."

"You're such a geniass, Einstein!"

"I gather that the cases are in the books in front of you?"

"Brilliant, Sherlock!"

"It's elementary, my Dear Watson, elementary!" Almost as an afterthought I add, "By the way Holmes, the statute is in Chapter 278, Section 33E."

"I know it Watson. Your book is open to that page! Any other clues for me to follow?"

"Just one important fact. The statute says that the SJC has the power to reduce the crime at anytime after a case is entered in that Court. The statute is silent as to whether or not a Superior Court Judge has the same authority. Our job is to try and convince the Judge that he does have the authority because the case has not yet been entered in the SJC."

"Got it. I'll let you know when you have to appear for argument."

It's a great feeling and an absolute relief to finally get that off my chest. The tension has disappeared. An unusual calmness comes over me as I retrieve my messages from Margie's desk and enter my office.

CHAPTER TWELVE

"…Where in hell is that can of Epsom Salts? I know it was in one of the boxes that Stephanie had unpacked. It should be on this closet shelf with the bandaids and all those cold remedies. I'm getting more upset by the second as I push things aside looking for that tin can while my toe keeps throbbing. I step back a few feet to survey the closet at a distance. Aha! There it is on the shelf above with all of the furniture polish and cans of spray paint. I grab the can and laugh to myself, as I ponder what relationship my daughter had perceived to exist between Epsom Salts and the other items on that shelf.

"The tea kettle water is almost at a boil when I pour a few inches into a bowl, add some Epsom Salts, and stir until it dissolves. I sit down at the kitchen table and attempt to put my foot into the bowl on the floor. The water is too hot. I notice for the first time that my toe is turning blue. In the background I hear "…Swanee, Swanee, how I love ya, how I love ya, my dear ole Swanee…" According to my watch it's just after two. Never thought I'd ever see the day when I'd be home at this hour on a Friday afternoon. My toe is now fully submerged and I'm humming to myself, "Foxwoods, Foxwoods, how I love ya, how I love ya, my dear ole Foxwoods…"

…"I just love the speed pass on the windshield. Don't you, Bruce? It saves so much time…Bruce, did you hear me?" She glances to her right, sees my eyes closed, and gives me a poke in the ribs to wake me up. I had fallen asleep as soon as we hit Route 128 South. I look at the clock. It's only about quarter to three. I quickly calculate that we've only been on the road about a half hour. The toll booth behind our parked car confirms it.

" Diane, what the hell are we doin' stopped over here? It's dangerous. We could get killed by one of those trailer trucks coming onto the Pike."

"The roads are slippery. The snow is right in our face and getting worse by the minute. I think we're heading right into a blizzard. You'll have to drive."

"OK, I'll go around while you crawl over here." I open the door and am greeted with a blast of cold air which forces me to walk backwards to the driver's door. I finally get seated comfortably behind the wheel and adjust the seat and put on the seat belt. "You're absolutely right. We're heading directly into the bad weather." I think it significant that no one says, "Let's just turn around and go home." Besides, I'm already prepared to say "no." Under perfect conditions Exit 10 is only a half hour away. The wheels spin for a few seconds before the car moves forward.

The driving is treacherous. The traffic is just crawling. The snow blowing directly into our faces keeps the wipers busy but snow still accumulates underneath them. I'm following the red tail lights of a car in front. All traffic is confined to the center of the road. I hear the blast of a loud horn behind me. A peek into the rear view mirror reveals a large flashing orange light coming up behind me in the lane to my left. The horn doesn't stop. It sounds like a fog horn. I know it's a State vehicle.

From the left rear seat I hear my sister-in-law Connie shouting, "Hey, Bruce, there's a bunch of trucks that wanna pass us!"

"Yeah, I know it. Just where in hell do they think I can go? There's no lane open on the right! Oh, shit, here goes nothin'! Hold on!" I cut sharply to the right and go all the way over to the breakdown lane. Luckily it's not too bad because cars are using it as they enter the exit ramps.

I spot snowplows passing on my left. I count five of them as they pass one behind the other in the far left lane. When the last of them passes a new tandem of plows follow each other in the center lane temporarily clearing a path to the west.

"OK, guys, hold onto your socks!" I gun the engine and take an angular path to my front left. I make it through the unplowed portions of the highway and find safety following the trucks in the middle lane of a plowed surface.

We come to Exit 10. I'm in the process of exiting the Pike from the break-down lane when Diane nonchalantly comments, "That wasn't bad at all. Instead of a half hour it only took us three quarters of an hour to get here." My hands ache from gripping the steering wheel. My eyes feel like they're glued open. I've got a pain in my lower back that just won't quit. I say nothing, except, "Only an hour to go and we'll be back home in Dizzyworld!"

"Bruce, there's no sense in tryin' to come home tomorrow. The roads are still gonna be tough. I should call Donna or Bud at the casino and hold the room for two nights."

My mother-in-law, Rose, has been sitting quietly in the back seat all along. If it weren't for the rear view mirror I wouldn't even have known that she was in the car.

The first words spoken by her indicate that she agrees with Diane.

"No need to call the casino for rooms anymore or to wait in line to register. The last time we were here I was told to go directly to the VIP registration room in the corridor next to the gift shop. All I gotta do is hand 'em my Hampton Club Wampum Card. I now get preferences for rooms and they're always free. I only took a change of clothes for one day but I'll make do. What promotions do we get today? I saw that you wrote them on the calendar next to the computer but I forgot."

She rummages through her pocketbook, puts on her reading glasses, and pulls out a stack of cards and letters from Foxwoods. After looking them over she says, "I get a $25.00 cash bonus ticket today and another $25.00 available on Sunday morning after five o'clock. I can also pick up a $25.00 free gas card in the Grand Ballroom any time after 6:00 P.M. tonight. Connie told me that she got a couple of vouchers for the Buffet and $10.00 cash today and Sunday. Don't know what Ma gets. She's too secretive!"

"What do I get?"

"I told you before but you just don't listen!"

"My mind is usually elsewhere. Tell me again, please."

"OK. You get a $100.00 free gas card at the Grand Ballroom after 6:00 tonight; a set of serial-numbered gold-plated commemorative quarters from the Franklin Mint on Sunday after 3:00 at the Fox Theater reservation booth; and to top it all off you get a ticket for $1,500.00 today and $500.00 on Sunday after 5:00 A.M."

"Great! I can use the cash. I'm not holdin' much but I got a couple of checks just in case."

In disbelief Rose exclaims, "$1,500.00? I can't believe it! How much do you bet anyway? I play as long as you do and sometimes right through the night."

Diane picks right up on it and asks me, "Seriously, just how much are you betting?"

I never directly answer the question. Instead I invent an answer as I go along. Some parts may be true and others not. I'm not really sure. But I tell them, "It's not necessarily the amount of the bet you place, although I'm certain that dollar players are placed in a different category than quarter or nickel players. Somehow, when you put your Wampum Card into the machine the House knows all. It can tell what you're playin' and for how much. I understand that coin turnover is a big factor. I guess the combination of the amount bet and coin turnover determines one's status and the rewards you get."

Luckily I'm at the entrance before I get any more questions. I take a right turn towards the casino as I simultaneously reach into my back pocket for my wallet. I manage somehow to get my Hampton Card and not lose control of the car. We're in a small tunnel leading to the garage. At the end I take a left. I spot the Hampton Club Sign and take another left. I stop and open my window. I swipe my Hampton Card in the box on my left. A yellow bar which prevents entry into the Hampton parking area suddenly rises vertically into the air. I drive by it and pull into an open space right in front of me. The elevator to the hotel and casinos is about twenty feet away.

I pop open the trunk and throw my gym bag's strap over my shoulder. The others grab their luggage. In less than a minute we're in the casino. Fuddrucker's is directly in front of us as we exit the elevator. We take a right and head for the down escalator. I walk so fast that I leave them all in the dust. My heart is racing. I want to get started. I dislike the delay caused by getting the room. I'm going down the escalator to the hotel lobby. I start walking down the moving escalator rather than waiting for it to get to the bottom.

I take a left and walk down the corridor to the right of the gift shop. I see the VIP sign above a door on my right and enter. There are three desks in the room. Two are occupied. I literally run to the open desk and in one motion I put my Hampton Card in front of the host and sit down.

"Welcome to Foxwoods, Mr. Sacker."

"It's pronounced "Saychar.""

"I apologize, Mr. Saychar."

"Don't worry about it. Been called a lot worse in my lifetime."

After swiping my card he asks, "And how long will you be staying?"

"Two nights."

"I see from your prior visits that you want two double beds. Smoking or non-smoking?"

"Doesn't matter. Whatever's available is ok. By the way, how close to a room number ending in '14' can you get me?"

"Lucky number?"

"No. My mother-in-law is 93 years old and has bad legs. All rooms ending in '14' are right across from an elevator."

He searches in his desktop and asks, "How's Room 1014?"

"Great! You're a good man!"

"How many key cards?"

"Three, please."

He turns around facing the credenza behind his chair and inserts something into a little machine on top.

"As you are aware your room is comped. There's no charge. Here are your key cards."

"Thank you very much. Good service deserves a reward."

I attempt to give him a tip and he says, "Thank you, Mr. Saychar. I appreciate the gesture but it's not allowed. I could get fired. Enjoy your stay and good luck."

"OK, and thanks again."

My gambling companions are in the hall next to the gift shop waiting for me. I buy a carton of Marlboros using my wampum points. I give a few packs to Diane and Connie and put two packs in my pocket. I place my gym bag and the rest of the cigarettes on top of Diane's suitcase with the wheels.

"Here are the keys. It's Room 1014. I'm gonna get my bonus at a wampum booth first and then I'll start playing upstairs at the circle of the 'Quick Hit' machines. If they're taken I'll be next to them at the '12's slots. If the machines are cold I could be anywhere. Let's meet for supper in the VIP Lounge in the Pequot Casino."

I dutifully hand Diane $200.00 or $300.00 to start depending upon what's in my pocket. They head for the elevator to go to the room to drop off the luggage. Before they ever reach the elevator I'm running up the stairs on the moving escalator. I gotta play! I can't wait! I've already wasted too much time!

CHAPTER THIRTEEN

...During my reverie I'm not exactly sure when it is that my attention is directed to the relationship between the state of the economy and my law practice...

...I'm in a long line of traffic during the days of the "gas crunch" in the 70's. I'm just praying that the station doesn't run out of gas before I get to the pump. Cars which try to cut into line are greeted with horns and vulgar epithets. I can still hear the cheering as a cop ensures that the interlopers are relegated to the end of the line.

The economy is suffering. It's a time of "double digit" inflation. Legitimate mortgage rates at the banks are not uncommon at around 12%. Second mortgage lenders are having a "field day" with interest rates over 20%. Money is tight. People are not paying their bills. The small claims lists in the local courts are indicative of the times. They are twice the usual size.

I'm seated at my desk in the office and am talking to myself again. How come I can't think of something original? I guess the old adage that "timing in life is everything" will have to suffice. Business sucks. It's just one helluva time to begin my practice all over again...

...It has to be a trip on a fabled flying carpet from the *Arabian Nights*. In what seems to be a millisecond there's a soft rap on my office door.

"Come in." Melinda enters and is standing there with her short-hand note book.

. "Got a minute?"

"Yeah, of course, sit down. What's on your mind?"

" Bruce you know we're busy as hell. Were in the 80's now. It's totally different from the 70's. The Brotherhood is flooding us with mortgages. I'm having problems trying to stay current. The rest of my work isn't getting done. It's as though the Credit Union is your only client. We've gotta do something and it has to be quick."

"I thought I did. I thought we had a pretty smooth running operation. I hired my sister Bernice. She gives you a break by answering the phone. When the title searches come back she calls all the prior mortgagees and gets the payoff figures with per diem rates. That's a big help and time-saver. I also hired Florence Jacobs on a part-time basis. Her only function, as far the mortgages are concerned, is to send the original mortgages back to the Credit Union after the Registry of Deeds returns them to us. She also makes sure that mortgage discharges come from the prior lenders so that she can close the file. In addition to all that she does all the correspondence in the PIP portion of the tort cases. Remember when you did all of those chores? What else can I do? Just what do you want?"

"I think we're operating in the Dark Ages. The trend today in offices is the use of computers. The work gets done quicker. A computer remembers what it does. We can even throw away all the carbon paper."

"Computers! I don't know the first thing about them! This isn't the General Electric!"

"Look, Bruce, it will save you a lot of time dictating. Once a form or document is in the computer it stays there. If you have a need in the future for a similar document I can call up the old one on the screen, and all we have to do is change the names and the date. Everything is stored on discs."

"I suppose that little book in your hand has all the details including cost?"

Sarcastically but good naturedly she says, "You just know everything! You're sooooo smart! Of course my book has the details!"

" OK, Let's hear them."

"I took a course at night in Boston. There were reps from all the leading manufacturers and each one gave a lecture complete with graphs and charts. I studied their pamphlets and made comparisons as to what each computer could do."

"And the results please, Doctor Hatfield!"

"It really was a no-brainer. Head and shoulders above them all and the best for our needs is the CPT. The downside is that it costs about $9,000.00 but they're all in that price range. They will also make arrangements for financing if necessary."

"Whew! Nine grand! Are you shittin' me? I just don't happen to have that kind of bread hanging around here with nothin' else to do!"

"Yeah, I'm aware of that, but what about financing?"

"Lemme give it some thought."

"OK. Gotta get back to work."

She leaves and closes the door softly behind her.

It's not uncommon for my Trustee's Account to have over $500,000.00 in it at any one time, especially if I had deposited several mortgage checks. My bank accounts were all at the Century Bank in its new building on Market Street. At lunchtime I visit the bank and obtain a personal loan for $10,000.00.

"Melinda, I don't want to deposit this because I'll probably spend it. Here you hold it until I need it. You can call CPT and order the damn thing right now." I hand the check to my beaming secretary and go about my business.

The 80's are good to me. I'm current with my child support payments to Phyllis and to Chris. Phyllis has not remarried so my full payments continue. Chris did not seek alimony.

For what now seems to be one brief moment I had life insurance policies for each of the kids; term and straight life coverage on my life for about four million dollars naming my trust as beneficiary for the benefit of the kids; a pension-retirement plan; some Israeli Bonds; a new Lincoln; and a stack of credit cards with zero balances.

...It was late 1961. I had been practicing less than two years when Saul Gilberg urged me to leave the Grossman Building and to become his tenant in the Professional Building at 156 Broad Street. When I moved back to Lynn with Phyllis at about the same time, he also became my landlord at 56 Estes Street. A year after Phyllis and I separated he became my landlord again, when I rented a third floor attic apartment from him at 8 Michigan Avenue. In 1969 he was my landlord once more at 60 Lewis Street.

In the early 1980's I'm still on the Swampscott Board of Selectmen. When Chris and I split she remains at 10 Priscilla Road with the kids. I need to find a place to live in town. There's only one person to see. He's usually at his real estate office at 89 Lewis Street diagonally across the street from my office.

I enter the newly renovated suite at 89 Lewis Street. The walls are covered with state of the art expensive paneling. A tall man wearing a brown business suit is standing behind the counter. He smiles and says, "Hey, what're you doin' here? To what do I owe this unexpected pleasure? Your rent isn't due yet!"

In less than ten minutes we're both standing in the long sun room of a second floor apartment located opposite the middle of King's Beach watching the waves coming to shore. Behind us is a kitchen a bathroom and one bedroom. "Saul, it'll be very cramped but I need something right now. I'll take it."

"That's good Mr. Selectman. I'll take $50.00 off the rent I quoted. I'll drop off a lease at the office."

"Great Saul. Thanks again."

We shake hands, as he says, "Oh by the way, my son Bobby Lives upstairs, so don't make too much noise!"

"Now you tell me!"

I head to Portland Street in Boston and buy some furniture wholesale from a former client. Michael leaves Phyllis immediately and moves in. He's finishing up his college career at Salem State. He sleeps and studies on a couch in the sun room/den. Matthew and Stephanie are about six and four respectively and sleep in bed with me on week-ends. Michael and I are both besieged almost immediately with phone calls. We both entertain frequently in those cramped quarters.

In July 1985 I buy 15 Donnelly Drive in Lynn while it's still under construction. It's a two-story house located in a new development on a hill behind the Union Hospital. There are three bedrooms, a kitchen, a living room, a den, a dining room and two full baths. Eventually I have the basement finished into an office complete with built-in shelving. The shelving in an adjoining room serves to display Michael's bowling trophies. The floor space is occupied with an exercise bicycle and a full set of weights and bench. The walls in both rooms have individually hand-crafted raised panels stained in mahogany.

Michael has his own room which I furnish with a large brass bed and a soft white rug. The kids' room has two sets of bunk beds and wooden furniture. All the pieces are of dark oak. The deck in the rear holds a large outdoor grille. A huge flagstone patio in the backyard serves as a sun deck complete with chaise lounges and a table with chairs and an umbrella. The deck and patio are connected by a flagstone walkway.

The house is never empty. I buy a round card table surfaced in green felt, which can accommodate eight players. It surfaces in the trophy room once a week for Michael's card-playing buddies. My sister-in-law. June, divorced "Hoppy." She now lives across the street with her new husband and two children from the former marriage. Her son Scott is with us daily. The weekends are hectic. Matt and Steph usually arrive with various contingents of friends for sleepovers. In the morning it's not unusual to see the bunk beds full and bodies in sleeping bags on the stairs and on the floors. The pullout couch in the living room is used often. It can accommodate two youngsters. I become quite proficient in flipping pancakes while still in the pan.

One year in the month of April I receive a phone call from my grandnephew Louis Ehrlich. "Uncle Bruce, I need a place to stay for a couple of days. My mother and I are constantly arguing and are in each other's hair. I gotta get the hell outa here for a while. Can I stay with you and Michael?"

"Yeah, no problem." He sleeps in one of the bunk beds.

The same year about a month later I get a phone call from my sister Bernice's son Fitzy, who's about to enter law school. "Uncle Bruce, I need a place to stay for a couple of days. My mother and I are constantly arguing and are in each other's hair. I gotta get the hell outa here for a while. Can I stay with you and Michael?"

"Yeah, no problem." He sleeps in one of the bunk beds.

Michael, Louis and Fitzy were all about the same age and had hung around with each other before. Now they become even closer. When Matt and Steph arrive I feel as though I'm back in the dormitory at UMASS. The weather is getting warmer and most of the meals are cooked on the grille and eaten outside. The delivery people from Domino's and Fauci's Pizza are ringing my door bell almost nightly.

I toy with the idea of putting up a "No Vacancy" sign on the front lawn. When Michael's card players arrive I feel that I should charge admission to this zoo. There are never any leftovers. If there were, the card players would devour them all. Michael always prepares a light repast for his card cronies to eat during the nightly break. I envision a new refrigerator being delivered with a chain and a lock and key.

The words "for a couple of days" in April and May lasted a little bit longer. The house felt like a morgue when my house guests left in September just in time for opening day in school.

CHAPTER FOURTEEN

Sometime in the late 70's or early 80's I'm appointed to sit as a conciliator of civil cases in the Essex County Superior Court. I'm flattered to be following in the shoes of some of Essex County's finest trial lawyers. The names of Max Nicholson, Vinnie Curcio, and George Ankeles, are the first which come to mind. It's a challenge to listen to the positions of the lawyers from each side and attempt to bring about a resolution of their differences. The aim is to reduce the staggering number of pending cases on the trial docket.

Each time I sit I have a list of cases starting at 9:00 in the morning. The cases are usually spaced about thirty minutes apart with the last case scheduled for 4:30 in the afternoon. I am given a State Identification Number and am actually paid by the hour for doing what I love. When the State stops paying conciliators I nevertheless stay and serve for years thereafter.

During the same time frame I'm again honored when asked to accept an appointment to the Executive Committee of the Essex County Bar Association. Of course I enthusiastically accept. I have long felt that the Association needs some input and a voice from the Lynn area. I attend the monthly meetings faithfully. It's never a chore. It's a great night out at some local restaurant where lawyers can get together and swap war stories. The free exchange of information often proves helpful with my own cases.

One night when Matt and Steph are with me for the weekend we're watching television together. The name of the movie is "War Games."

It's a fantasy about a high school student who's using his computer at home one night and somehow logs into the United States Air Force's military defense system. It's called "NORAD." It's a system which can tell if Russia is launching missiles, and if so, where they're heading. The system is also capable of launching a retaliatory response by the United States. It's a movie for kids but I enjoy it thoroughly.

The movie is on my mind for the rest of the weekend. I know nothing of computers at the time. I'm a total computer illiterate. The one thing that amazes me the most is the ability to have a computer at home and somehow log into a computer at a different location. This is the only thing that I can think about. The concept is absolutely astonishing to me.

It's Monday morning and I'm in the car driving directly from home to the Salem Registry of Deeds. I have to record a mortgage before I go to the office. I'm just now becoming familiar with the computers recently installed at the Registry. I have to do a short title rundown from the date when the title search ended to the present. I have to make sure before recording the mortgage that no attachments have been put on the property in the interim.

I'm drinking my Dunkin Donuts cup of coffee and trying to visualize the computer at the Registry. I'm thinking of the sequence of buttons that I have to push on the keyboard in order to do the rundown. It suddenly comes to me in a flash! I can hardly contain myself!

Holy shit, if that kid could log onto the NORAD computer from his house, then a lawyer from his or her office, should be able to log into the Registry computer!

I find a spot to park and literally run up the stairs to the Registry of Deeds. I hasten to the back without stopping at the rows of computers available to title examiners, lawyers, and the general public. I take a right at the end and find the door to John O'Brien's office. He's the Register of Deeds for the County. I enter and am greeted by Mike Miles the Assistant Register.

"Hi Mike. How're you doin'?"

"Can't complain. What can I do for you so bright and early on a Monday morning?"

"Is John around?"

"No. He's home with the flu?"

"Anything I can help you with?"

"I have a couple of questions about the computers."

"Well, you're talking to the right guy. I designed and installed our whole program. What're the questions?"

"I think I can sum it up with two simple questions."

"Fire away!"

"Is it possible for a lawyer in his or her office to tap into the Registry computers and have access to its data?"

"Absolutely."

"How? What has to be done?"

"All a lawyer needs is a computer, a modem and a dedicated line."

"Forgive me for being stupid but what's a modem and what's a dedicated line?"

He gives me an explanation and I don't know what the hell he's talking about. I don't understand a word. He's talking in a foreign language!

"Look Mike, I'm gonna leave all you said to the experts. Suppose I want members of the ECBA to have the ability to tap into your computers. Would there be any cost other than having the right equipment in the office?"

"Someday I envision no problems. Anyone in the world will be able to log on without cost. Unfortunately, we're not yet at that advanced stage of technology. In order to do what you propose I'd have to rehire the technicians, who did the original programming for our system and to redo the whole thing. Right now this is strictly an in-house operation. We have no ability to transmit outside this building. We have no arrangements with the telephone companies to use their wires. This my friend would be a costly proposition."

"I'm Just thinking out loud Mike. What if we make it available only to members of the ECBA and charge them a yearly stipend for the privilege. It may be a windfall for us. I can envision every title examiner and real estate attorney in the State becoming members of the ECBA. Why make a trip here in traffic when you can do it from the office?"

Mike seems to be pondering the topic. With some hesitation apparent in his voice he finally says, "Maybe we can make a deal that will benefit us both. The State and not the County now controls our budget, and the powers that be are a bunch of stingy bastards. Come out front with me for a minute."

I follow. He points to an aisle containing hundreds of old books on the shelves of metal bookcases.

"You see those old books. There are hundreds more in the basement. They're all in line to be rebound before we lose the old deeds. The State won't give us the funds to complete the job. We have to steal from Peter to pay Paul. What do you think the reaction would be if we ask for more money for the computers?"

"Well, what's the deal that will benefit us both?"

"If you think that the ECBA can generate some serious money by way of dues and user fees, then some of that money could be paid to us to help defray the costs for binding and reprogramming."

"What if we were able to send you monthly, quarterly, or yearly checks?"

"Ah, me bucko, therein lies the rub! If the State Auditors pick up the added income on our books they'll recommend an offsetting budget cut. The only way to handle it is that you keep all the money and whenever we think it appropriate we'll send you a bill. We might even ask that you send the checks directly to the party rendering the service. How's that grab ya?"

"Sounds good to me but I'm only one person. I have to bring the whole thing before the Executive Committee and get its reaction. It could easily be rejected because I don't think there are many real estate lawyers on the Committee. I'll get back to you when I get an answer."

"OK, and don't forget I gotta run it by my boss too."

We shake hands, I do my search, record the mortgage and leave.

At the next meeting of the Executive Committee, when the President asks for "new business," I give a long dissertation beginning with "War Games." A committee consisting of computer literates and real estate conveyancers is appointed. I'm named chairperson. We subsequently meet often with Mike Miles and the program eventually begins. Anyone wanting access has to be a dues paying member of the ECBA. There is an additional user fee of $100.00 per year.

Thus it comes to pass, that many prestigious Boston law firms including the likes of Hale & Dorr and Ropes & Gray become members of the ECBA whose coffers begin to rise.

Sometime later I'm nominated and elected to the office of Secretary of the ECBA. The term is for two years. It's eventually followed by Treasurer, Vice-President, and then President. During those eight years while awaiting my ascendancy to the throne, I slowly see to it that Lynn and Saugus lawyers become members of the Executive Committee.

I'm the first to have the honor and distinction of having served as President of both the Greater Lynn Bar Association and the Essex County Bar Association. Lynn Attorney, Anne Gugino Carrigan, becomes the second. It was several years earlier, while serving one of my terms as President of the GLBA, that I arranged to have her appointed to the office of Secretary, so that she would eventually become the first woman President of the GLBA. Likewise, as President of the ECBA, I arrange to have her nominated and elected as its Secretary, so that she would eventually become an ECBA president. After all, there's no need to spoil a good thing! Besides, I have now fulfilled my goal of ensuring that Lynn would have a strong voice and representation in the ECBA.

I would be remiss, if I failed to mention that Lynn Attorney Donald Bumiller is the President of the ECBA, as this is being written. I wonder how?

CHAPTER FIFTEEN

...Sure, I enjoyed going to the dog track with my father and brothers when I was a kid in high school. I loved to sit in my brother Solly's exclusive box at the finish line. He and his partner Aaron Kulchinsky owned greyhounds. In 1951 they had the World Champion "On The Line." The box was a perk provided by Wonderland Dog Track in Revere. It was only on rare occasions that I even had the two bucks to make a wager. I was content to listen to Solly as he was handicapping a race about to be run. I felt a sense of pride when gamblers came to the box and asked for Solly's selections. I enjoyed the excitement of the race itself and the fans rooting and shouting for their selections.

Sure, after I became a lawyer, I enjoyed playing cards once a week with my brothers and their cronies. I was the "baby." They were all about twenty years my senior. Sure, I bought an occasional scratch card and sometimes prayed or begged for a hit. Sure, as a kid working for my brothers at Singers Poultry I bet a nickel or a quarter for a week's play of the daily number. Scullio the bookie came to the store every Saturday and everybody played.

I never thought twice about my gambling. I only did what everyone else around me was doing. It was never a matter of life or death. I never felt compelled to go to the track, play cards, or place a bet with a bookie. My gambling was not an all-consuming thing. I could take it or leave it. It really didn't matter one way or the other...

...I'm on line logged onto a site suggested by the Boston Globe in a gambling article. I read: "...It is not only the speed of the games that makes so addictive the playing of new-style electronic gaming machines...The machines produce a highly intense and continuous experience for players…there is no waiting for the horses to run or the wheel to stop spinning…brain studies have shown that gambling causes the release of dopamine, a feeling good chemical that spurs the desire to repeat a pleasurable behavior…that is involved in drug addiction…The pleasure comes from not just winning, but from the process of playing and anticipating a possible win…"

…It's still Friday. It's about five in the afternoon and I'm not moving from the computer. I find it difficult to believe that the television ad by Mirapex admits that its use can cause gambling. Why in hell would Mirapex blow the whistle on itself?

Ahhh, here it is. I'm on the home page for Mirapex. I move the mouse around and scroll up and down and side to side until I spot the words "side effects." I hurriedly hit the spot. In seconds I'm reading a very long article. Will you look at that! I've got most of those damn symptoms! I keep reading. Near the end it says that the use of Mirapex can cause over-indulgence in eating, as well as other forms of compulsive behavior including pathological gambling.

Well, at least they haven't changed this part of the information. It's the same as I first read several months ago. Just think, I've only been takin' this shit for twelve years! I then pose a question to myself. Do I have a predisposition for gambling which made it easier for Mirapex to have had such a profound effect upon me? I glance again at my watch. It's only a few minutes after five. I'd normally be at Foxwoods at this hour. I can actually see and feel myself playing Joker Poker. The sad thing is that in spite of all that's happened I wish that I were there this very moment!…

…I've been practicing law for about two years, and am still working in the chicken store, delivering meat for nearby butchers, and managing the Lynnway Recreation Center's bowling operation on weekends. It's a Sunday afternoon and I'm behind the counter at the alleys. Diane Lussiano and her high school girl friends are there every week. I do my best to accommodate by assigning them an alley as close to the guys they're obviously chasing.

I never seem to be able to take my eyes off of the tiny blondish-brunette little girl who's wearing a Classical High School cheerleader's sweater. That's exactly how I visualize the pretty Diane Lussiano today and its forty six years later!

She's always the spokesperson for her group. I observe that she makes friends easily with her winning smile and a quite obvious "gift of gab." My secretaries to date have all been relatives working part-time. There was my cousin Judy Katzoff and my nieces Anne Sachar and Dawn Ehrlich. One Sunday, following a brief spelling test, I hire Diane on the spot. She becomes my first full-time secretary and remains loyal to me throughout my various partnership ventures.

Despite the ten year difference in our ages and my marriage to Phyllis I manage to hide my secret "crush" on her. I'm terribly upset when she marries Russ Caswell who has just been discharged from the navy. It's 1964 and she's only twenty years old. I know even then that my marriage to Phyllis just isn't going to last. Secretly I want Diane for myself…

…My mind is racing everywhere in time. Now it's somewhere around 1990. The combination golf outing and annual meeting of the ECBA has just concluded at General George S. Patton's former Country Club in Hamilton. It's a humid night in June. My nostrils fill with the unmistakable scent of horses as I pass the polo field. I'm about to pull out of the driveway of the Myopia Hunt Club. I'm waiting for traffic to pass so that I can take a left onto Route 1A. I may have had a little too much to drink at dinner but my head is suddenly clear enough to remember that Diane lives in Hamilton.

I represented Diane and Russ when they bought 222 Linden Street. I made sure that she got to keep the house when I represented her in their divorce. I had been there before and I know it's only a short distance ahead. I spot a convenience store on my right with an outside phone booth. I immediately grab the phone book and look up the number. The phone rings a few times before it's picked up.

"Hello."

I immediately recognize the raspy high-pitched voice. It's her mother, Rose. I'm not prepared for someone else to answer the phone. I'm not sure how the call is going to be received at about 9:30 at night. Eventually I manage to speak.

"Hello. Is this Mrs. Lussiano?"

"Yes. Who's this?"

She doesn't recognize my voice and I'm convinced by the tone of hers that she's upset. I guess that it's probably because of the hour.

"This is Bruce Sachar. How are you?"

"Who?"

I respond a little louder. "This is Bruce Sachar. How are you?"

"Oh, I'm fine. Can I help you?"

"Is Diane at home? I'd like to talk to her."

"Is something the matter?"

"No. This is a social call." I feel stupid. Did I really say that?

"Hold on a minute, I'll get her."

After what seems to be an eternity I finally hear her voice.

"Hi Bruce. Anything wrong?"

"No. Nothing's wrong. Just got through with a Bar meeting at Myopia. I'm in Hamilton and naturally thought of you. Any chance you'd like to go for a cup of coffee and catch up a bit with each other's lives?"

I can tell she's surprised. After a short pause she says, "It's kinda late, my hair's a mess, and I'm all dressed for bed. It's really short notice. Maybe some other time."

"OK. Take care. Be good. I'll catch you another time. Good night."

"Good night."

All the way to the entrance to Route 128 South I keep wondering how I could have made such a jackass of myself.

Just before Christmas about a year later I'm in Brother's Deli in Lynn with a very attractive and very young woman. She's from some southern State and is visiting her mother whom I represent. We had just left her mother's house. I do not fight her suggestions to take her to lunch and to go out on a date later that night.

She's already told me what she wants for lunch. I escort her to a booth and head for the line of customers waiting to give their orders. As I reach for a tray and silverware I hear a voice from the line in front of me.

"Hey, Sachar, what a surprise! How're you doin'?"

I look up and see Diane, her sister Connie, and their mother, Rose.

"Fine, Connie. Long time no see. How're you doin'?"

"Great!"

Diane gives up her place in line and comes over to stand next to me. We're face to face a few inches apart.

"Diane you get better and better looking with age. How do you keep your figure?"

She blushes a bit but never answers my question. My ears don't believe the first words out of her mouth.

"I work at Cardinal Health in Peabody. Tonight's their annual Christmas party. I don't want to go alone again. I hate to sit around while everyone else is dancing. How about taking me?"

"You gotta be pullin' my leg."

"No. I'm dead serious. I need a date for tonight. How about it?"

"I'd love to but I can't. Not tonight."

"Why not?"

I point to the booth near the window and whisper, "I've already got a date tonight with her."

"You robbin' the cradle? Kinda young isn't she?"

With a smile on my face I tell her, "That's what keeps *me* young!"

"You sure you can't take me tonight? How about breaking your date and make it another night?"

"I normally would but she's goin' home somewhere down south in the morning."

"OK, it's your loss!"

"I'll take a rain check. I'll give you a call."

"OK. Give me a call."

The Lussiano clan go to their table and I to mine. I'm sitting with this lovely creature but keep looking across the room at Diane. I eventually make the call and soon thereafter we began dating each other exclusively.

...Didn't know it then, but it was the beginning of my eventual gambling addiction followed by my disbarment and eventual fall from grace...

CHAPTER SIXTEEN

...It's a little after seven. My stomach is beginning to make strange gurgling sounds. I can't believe that my crazy and disjointed recollections can appear to be so vivid and real. I'm now overcome with a craving for a pizza from Monte's across the street. I can smell it and taste it from here. I can even see myself placing a call to make an order. Gotta fight this! It'll take about three days to get the carbs out of my system so Atkins can kick in again. It's not worth it. I head for the kitchen and quickly fry up some scrambled eggs and corned beef.

I'm eating at the kitchen table and wishing it were pizza. I console myself by thinking of all the weight I've lost. Just think I only started at Christmas... Christmas?...

...It's Christmas Eve 1981 at 10 Priscilla Road in Swampscott. Matt is five and Steph is three. It's about nine o'clock at night and they're both asleep upstairs. Chris is also upstairs in the kitchen making her famous ice cream pumpkin pie for tomorrow's dessert. She had just finished decorating the wrought iron railing on the side of the stairs leading to the floor above. I'm the den in the mahogany paneled basement sitting on a couch and not paying attention to the television against the wall facing me. The entire wall to my far left is made of red brick. A fireplace in the center of the wall is surrounded by built-in brick shelves, which contain selected books and scattered knickknacks. I can feel the warmth, smell the smoke, and hear wood crackling, as the fire blazes in the fireplace.

The assembly directions for Matt's "Big Wheel" is nothing more than a large diagram which is spread out on the floor in front of the couch. A huge box showing a picture of the completed plastic car is on the floor to the left of where I'm sitting. In large print the box advises that assembly requires only a hammer, a screwdriver, and a block of wood. All three items have been in and out of my hands for over an hour as I attempt to follow the diagram in front of me. I'm swearing to myself in utter frustration when I realize that I had installed the seat backwards. The phone rings just as I'm about about to take it apart and put it back properly.

Chris hollers from the top of the stairs. "Bruce, there's a Jim Monico on the line for you."

"OK. Thanks, I'll take it down here."

"Hi, Sarge, Merry Christmas!"

"Doesn't look like it's gonna be one."

I can tell from his voice that he's obviously distraught.

"Why? What's the matter?"

"I sure as hell hate to bother you on Christmas Eve, but I'm down here at the Lynn Police Station and don't know what to do. They've got my son, young Jimmy, under arrest and they're in a room questioning him. Please Bruce, I need your help and I need it now. Can you come down here?"

"OK. Just calm down Jim. What's the charge?"

"Two Counts of Murder One."

"What'd you say?"

"Two Counts of Murder One."

"You gotta be shittin' me! Where and when?"

"Tonight. He supposedly plugged two guys comin' outa the White Eagle Café in West Lynn."

"Look Jim, I'm in dungarees. I'm not even gonna change my clothes. Be down in a few minutes. Stick your head in the door. Tell him I'm on the way and to keep his damn mouth shut!"

"Gotcha, pal, thanks."

On the way to the station I can clearly see the short, dark complected, and unmistakably Italian figure of Jim Monico. He's been the Police Prosecutor for Saugus at the Lynn Court ever since I was there prosecuting nearly a decade ago. I haven't seen him in Court for at least two or three days. Sure, his black hair is thinning out a little, and he's not

110

quite the skinny guy that he was, but he's never lost his sense of humor. Jimmy's personality made everyone like him. I betcha, that he's done more favors for people than anyone else around.

I'm still on a first name basis with almost every cop in Lynn. I enter the old building on Sutton Street and climb a couple of stairs. From there I can be seen through the chicken wire, which separates the entranceway from the officers in the combination booking room and signal station. Great. A familiar face. Before I can put a name to the face I hear, "Merry Christtmas, Mr. Sachar. They're waitin' for you upstairs." I hear the door in front of me being buzzed open. I'm pushing as I'm saying, "Thanks a lot. Merry Christmas to you too!"

Jim stops me as I approach. He's shaking all over. He can't stop the coffee from spilling from the cup in his hand. He's so excited that he's having trouble getting the words out of his mouth. His eyes are red and watery. He's on the verge of crying. He looks around to make sure that no one can hear us. He finally speaks to me in a whisper.

"Those dirty bastards threw me out of the room, when I said that you were on the way and for Jimmy to stop talking. I was in there earlier for about ten or fifteen minutes and listened to the questions and Jimmy's answers. He's absolutely off the friggin' wall. He's totally incoherent and keeps changing his story. In one breath he says that only one guy is involved not two. In another breath he says that he was attacked by a black guy. A second later he says that *they* were Hell's Angels. Can you believe it? They threw *me* outta the room! Me! Me of all people! I'm supposed to be one of them! When I think of all the favors I've done over the years for those Lynn cops and their families..."

"Who's in there with him now?"

"Lynn detectives, a State Trooper from the DA's office, and I guess a couple of the officers who were at the scene."

"No point in hurrying to tell him to keep his mouth shut. According to you he's already spilled his guts."

"I asked those ungrateful sonsobitches with the short memories for a simple favor. I asked them to cut my kid a little slack. After listenin' to Jimmy's rantin' and ravin' a moron could tell that it was clearly two on one. They attacked him first. It's an open and shut case of self-defense.

All I asked for was for them to charge him with manslaughter instead of Murder One. They practically laughed at me!"

"Ok. Settle down, Jim. Follow me."

I open the door to the interrogation room without knocking. Without raising my voice I merely say, "Gentlemen, this interrogation is now over. Would you all please leave so that I can be alone with my client." There are several nods of acknowledgement as they pass by me and exit the room.

Jimmy is covered with blood. It's all over his face and clothes. He has a cut lip and a gash on the back of his head. I observe the gash as I tenderly move to the side the bloody dried matted hair covering it. Before I utter a word I make a quick search of the room looking for a tape recorder. A favorite place once shown to me by Captain Stinson was a desk drawer. They were all empty.

Even though I'm very anxious to talk with my client I simply tell him that we'll talk later when we're alone. I take him by the arm into the hall where all the police are standing. No one is near Jimmy's father who's standing alone near the stairway to the floor below. I turn Jimmy to face the Lynn Police contingent. Pointing to his head I sarcastically but politely ask, "Did anyone think to make arrangements for him to be taken to the hospital?" There's no response.

Would someone please call the Clerk of Court who's assigned to bail duties tonight and have him come right down. An unfamiliar voice coming from behind an open door to one of rooms booms out for all to hear. " Are you shitin'? Bail on a charge of Murder? What the hell are you smokin'?"

It doesn't matter to me which clerk will appear. He'll be a sympathetic friend of both Jim and myself. He'll be a clerk who has worked with us both for years and who still sees and works with Monico every day. He appears, reads a police report of the incident, announces that Jimmy is in dire need of medical treatment, has no prior record, has strong family ties to the community, and does not pose a threat to flee. He sets a modest bail. Jim's wife, Boots, arrives from Saugus and pledges a bank book as security for bail.

"Hey, before you guys leave for the hospital, I wanna make sure that all of you are in my office tomorrow night at about six o'clock. I don't care if it's Christmas or not. I'm gonna go back upstairs now and see if I've still got enough influence around here to get some of the police reports. See ya tomorrow!"

Jim sticks his head out of the open driver's side window. He points a finger at me and calmly utters what is definitely a promise on his part. "Every dog has his day and mine's still comin'. Brucie baby, it's a long road with no turns. Someday, I'll get every one of those forgetful bastards even if I have to live forever. So help me god!"

They show up just before six. The story and the defense begin their embryonic journey...

CHAPTER SEVENTEEN

...The eight o'clock western movie playing on Encore stars James Garner in one of my favorite Maverick reruns. The movie opens with Bret Maverick playing poker on a Mississippi river boat. As usual, he's wearing his trademarked ruffled shirt. The camera pans the players sitting around the table. It stops abruptly and quite predictably when it reaches the beautiful and buxom Samantha. Obviously, no one is looking at her hand. They're all gawking elsewhere as an Ace is deftly slipped into her hand from a loosely fitted blouse with wide sleeves...

...Is it pre-ordained or just plain coincidence that at that very moment I hear the voice of Hank Williams coming from my computer. It's a favorite oldie..."Yore cheatin' haaart will tell on you...the tears come down, like fallin' rain..."

...It's really impossible to point to a particular date and state with certainty, "That's the day when I became an addictive gambler!" The truth of the matter is that it's a slow and gradual process. The victim hasn't even got a clue that it's happening. It's just like old age. One often doesn't feel it coming and then one day it's just there.

November 15, 1995 is the big day. Diane and I are married in the second floor function room of the Continental Restaurant on Route One in Saugus. It's a small affair attended only by our immediate families. My good friend and sometimes confidant, Judge Joe Dever, performs the ceremony. We also sing "Happy Birthday" to my mother-in-law, Rose.

My mother has apparently done her job well. She has raised me in the true tradition of a Jewish mother. Hardly a day passes when I don't feel guilty about something. Real or imagined guilt consumes my soul. When Diane moves into 15 Donnelly Drive she insists that her cat, Priscilla

Mullins, live with us. The fact that Michael is allergic to cats doesn't seem to phase her at all. The overwhelming guilt that I felt then is still with me. Michael is forced to move from the house which I had promised would someday be his. I've sold out my son and traded him for a cat!

...The Lussiano Girls, Rose, Connie and Diane, were bingo regulars long before I came into their lives. The routine continues after we're married. One night it could be St. Mary's near City Hall Square in Lynn and another at the Knights of Columbus Hall on Lynnfield Street. On other nights they could find themselves in Stoneham or at St. Anthony's Church in Revere. Trips for bingo to Salem or Portsmouth, New Hampshire were also not uncommon. One of the spots was at the Rockingham Race Track. I can still hear them talking about the bus junkets, which they took to Foxwoods long before there was a casino on the site. It was reportedly the largest bingo hall in the country. I often joined them at the various locations before we were married. I had never played bingo in my life prior to those trips.

It all started something like this..."Bruce, we're goin' to Salem, New Hampshire tonight for bingo. Wanna come?"

"Bingo! Are you kiddin' me or what?"

"No. I'm serious. It's a night out. It'll do you good to relax and forget about the office."

"Do you think for one instant that I'm gonna sit there and listen for numbers being called, so I can cover them with those foolish colored daubers you guys use? Besides, I'm hard of hearing. I'd probably miss the call anyway."

"Got a call today from your old flame, Millie Sandler. Bumped into her recently in the super market. Wanted to know if our relationship was purely Platonic. She couldn't believe it when I told her we were getting married. To make a long story short, she and her husband Alan go to bingo together often in Salem, New Hampshire. Said she'd give me a call someday to see if we wanted to join them. That was her call this afternoon. Told her I'd get back later."

"You mean to tell me that Alan actually plays that old lady's game!"

"As much as you don't wanna believe it he obviously does."

YOU BE THE JUDGE

Condescendingly I finally agree to go. "OK. Call her and make the arrangements. Take an extra dauber for me so I can try out this sissy's game."

To my astonishment the parking lot is jam-packed. How can it be? Bingo doesn't start for another hour. I drop Rose and everyone else at the door while I look for parking spot. I finally find one. Jeeez, I'm so far away that I'll probably need a passport to get in. I suddenly find myself in a huge room which appears to be larger that a football field. There are wooden tables lined up side by side the entire length of the hall. Every now and then there's a space between them for an aisle. The folding chairs at the tables look uncomfortable and I see some people putting soft cushions on them. People are literally running to find a strategic spot. Many of the chairs are empty but have a coat or a bag on them. Some tables have makeshift cards on them saying "reserved."

There's a long line at the far end of the hall. I quickly determine that they're buying their bingo cards. I can't believe that there are so many men in the hall. In the front center of the hall where all the chairs are facing there's an even longer line. It's the refreshment stand. I see pizza, fries, onion rings, subs of all kinds, nachos covered with melted cheese, hot dogs, hamburgers, fried dough, chili, and god knows what else.

I'm looking around for my newly-found bingo buddies. I spot Diane in the line waiting to pay for the privilege of playing. At the same time I see Connie with her hands in the air waiving to get my attention. I find a seat with them at a table near the back of the hall. We're with the Sandlers at the same table. Diane joins us carrying not cards but large blocks of paper sheets. She distributes several blocks to Rose and Connie and then places a large pile in front of her chair. She hands me two blocks and a dauber. I look around the hall to survey the situation. Some tables are occupied by only one or two people but the entire table is covered with blocks of paper.

"Connie, how come that woman over there is all alone and has the table covered with these bingo sheets? Why doesn't she just make a stack and use a page from the top as each game is played?"

She laughs and says, "She's playin' ten or twelve games at a time."

"Oh. OK." Not until the games actually start do I realize what a feat it is.

Diane comes over to explain the procedure. "I got you two sets of sheets. You'll be playin' two games at once. You see those TV's all around the room just below the ceiling?"

"Yeah."

"Well it doesn't matter that you can't hear the caller over the microphone announcing the numbers. Just look at one of those monitors and the ball with its number will appear."

"How much can you win here anyway?"

"The payoffs in the first few games, known as the 'early bird specials', pay anywhere from $50.00 to $150.00. It all depends upon the design called for in that big screen above the canteen."

"What design?"

"Here, look at this sheet I gave you with your package. It tells you what you have to get to win. One game is just for five numbers in a row anywhere. Another pays for a diagonal and another pays for a win without using the free number in the center. After the 'early birds' the payoffs get higher. The big ones come after intermission. The last game of the night is the 'coverall.' You gotta fill the card in forty-eight calls."

She looks at the board in front and proudly proclaims, "Look up there. No one has hit it in forty-eight calls for weeks. The grand prize is then carried over to the following week. That's the reason for the big crowd tonight. The payoff is $9,000.00!"

Bewitching time arrives. The room is suddenly quiet. I feel like I'm at a funeral or in a church. I focus on the stage in the front of the hall and actually see the balls popping up in the air in a wind machine. A random ball lands in a cup and is picked up by the caller. He looks at it and I can actually hear the words, "B-1." I look up at the monitor in front and see the ball itself. I look everywhere on my sheet for the spot to daub. I have no idea where the letters and numbers are. I don't realize that the letter "B" stands for the first letter in the word "Bingo" and that it is always the first vertical row. By the time I find it and daub he's calling another number and I haven't even daubed my second game sheet.

I'm up tight and frustrated. I can't keep up. I'm hunting while everyone around is holding a dauber in the air waiting for the next call, and that includes the woman who's playing all those sheets at once. This is no fun. Whoever said that it was a relaxing night out is full of shit! Suddenly, several people simultaneously holler, "BINGO" and raise their hands. Attendants go to each of them. I surmise the sheets are being checked for accuracy. Eventually the caller announces whether it's a win or not. There are five winners in the first game. They each are paid the whopping sum of $10.00, which arrives and is paid by an attendant during a later game.

By the time intermission arrives I'm wound up like a drum, even though I'm beginning to remember where the letters and numbers are. I really don't want to reveal my ignorance again without being asked, so I don't ask anyone why I keep hearing, "I've got a wait!"

Genius that I am, I finally figure it out. When someone has only one number left for bingo, it's a "wait." I never get to socialize with the Sandlers, or anyone else, for that matter.

At first I went with them infrequently. I could play a few hands at once but never the amount played by my traveling companions. One day I come home early from the office and am about to sit down and watch television. Before I can get comfortable Diane comes into the room holding a flier. "Bruce, remember that place we went to with the Sandlers?"

"Sure."

"Well, according to this flier they've just installed computers. For an extra couple of bucks you can rent one. No need to hunt and daub. You can play up to fifteen games at once. Wanna give it a shot? There's a new coverall worth five grand."

"Sure. Why not? When?"

"Tonight. OK?"

"Let's go early so I can find a parking spot in this country."

"I'll call Connie and Ma and we can leave as soon as they get here."

The computers are terrific! I love 'em! I play the maximum cards often. I can even do crosswords in-between games. One button allows me to look at the best fifteen cards at once. Another lets me see the top five cards from the fifteen that I'm playing. When I have one number to go the machine flashes and tells me that I have a "wait." If I catch a winning hand the machines tells me to holler "Bingo."

I'm luckier than the bunch of them put together. I win often. The machines come to Portsmouth. I like that place better than all the others because there are poker slot machines in the back room. They don't payoff in money but credits are issued for an assortment of prizes. I'd forego the bingo and stay there for the night if they didn't close the room when bingo started. I've also become a regular New Hampshire scratch card player. The tickets are available in the Portsmouth hall.

There's no question about it. My lucky season is usually from the middle of October to the middle of November. Diane knows it as well as I. It's sometime in the late 90's. It's November 7th . It's my birthday. We're playing somewhere in New Hampshire. At this point in time it's all a blur. I can't recall if we're in Salem or Portsmouth. I win a game for a couple of hundred bucks and don't have to share it with anyone else. I'm the only winner. We're now playing the coverall in the last game of the night.

My numbers just keep coming and coming. The computer tells me that forty-two numbers have been called. I push the appropriate button and my best five cards are displayed. One card indicates that I only need two numbers to get the coverall within forty-eight calls. I nudge Diane and point to my machine. As I'm pointing I catch one of them. The machine flashes and tells me that I have a "wait." Diane tells Connie and Ma. Within seconds everyone in the surrounding tables is aware of what's happening. I need a 33. It's the year of my birth and has always been a lucky number for me.

Forty-six numbers have been called. Two chances left. My heart is throbbing. The palms of my hands are sweaty. We all look up at the monitor where the next number will appear seconds before the caller makes the announcement. When 33 shows on the screen there are loud screams from Diane and Connie. Everyone in the hall is looking at us. The announcer calls 33 as the computer tells me to holler "Bingo." I holler. I then look around the room to see if anyone has hit it. Silence. An attendant is now at my side to check the serial numbers on the winning card in the computer. He relays the information to the caller.

The hall is emptying rapidly when the caller finally announces, "We have one winner tonight. The coverall pays $5,000.00. The attendant asks if I want cash or a check. Naturally I opt for the cash. By the time the money is counted out into my open palms the room is just about empty.

"All right guys. The night is young! We're headin' to Foxwoods right now!" I give Diane a sizeable chunk of my winnings and we're off to see the Wizard!

CHAPTER EIGHTEEN

...*Boy oh boy time sure passes fast when you're havin' fun! The clock is just draggin' its ass! It's only about quarter to ten. Thank God it's a Friday in the middle of February. No need to worry about a tee time tomorrow. I remember when Gannon Golf Club used to be called "Happy Valley." My weekend group tees off at first light on Saturdays and Sundays. It just now dawns on me how our group got our name. I never thought about it before but somehow the "Valley Rats" now seems quite appropriate. I can picture the logo of a little rat with big ears and a long tail swinging a golf club. My closet is loaded with hats, jackets, and jerseys with that distinctive logo.*

The thought of tee times would be innocuous enough for a normal person, but not with me. Every Thursday during golf season I would log on to Gannon's web site and sign up for the weekend. Every Friday afternoon I would log on again to learn my tee time and the names of the other three players in my foursome. I felt a strong loyalty to the league and I knew the others did also. I considered my duty to appear to be sacrosanct. I knew that my fellow golfers relied upon each other to show up and round out the teams. We also contributed to a money pool each day, which was used for a variety of prizes at the end of each round. The more the golfers the larger the cash payouts. It seems that I lived by this code of conduct from time immemorial, or at least for nearly three decades.

Diane may not have understood it fully but she recognized my devotion to the tee times. If she told me once she told me a thousand times: "The winter belongs to me and the summer belongs to you!" The compromising came about gradually. Beginning in the late 1990's and continuing to the present I started missing my tee times. It really depended upon the posture of my gambling and how I felt about two hours before a scheduled tee time. It took two hours to go from Foxwoods to Gannon.

A typical response to a query the following week would relate that I caught a bug, or I had a bad case of diarrhea, or my back was killing me. After a while no one really believed me. They all eventually knew that I was gambling. My good friend, Bobby Casper, was also a bit of a gambler and we often commiserated with each other. Rarely did we confide in our losses but we sure boasted about our hits. I think he may have inadvertently revealed the truth to the other golfers.

Not infrequently, I drop off the threesome at Donnelly Drive and pull into the Gannon parking lot less than five minutes later. I open the trunk, slip on my golf shoes, sling the bag of clubs over my shoulder, drop the bag against the stone wall near the carts, run up the stairs to the pro shop, pay for the cart, grab a cup of black coffee, run back down the stairs, put the bag on the cart, race to the first tee, grab my seven wood, note that the others have already hit, put a tee in the ground, swing the club, watch the errant ball, get back in the cart, and head down the path alongside the fairway, spot my ball in the rough on the left, and wait for those behind me to hit. I take a sip of coffee and look at my watch. It's only five minutes from the time I entered the parking lot…

…One day we're waiting to tee off on the second hole. The group ahead of us is looking for a lost ball. One of the golfers is staring at me while we're waiting. He shakes his head from side to side and says, "Jesus, Sachar, your eyes are all bloodshot. You been up all night again?"

"Yeah, just drove in from Foxwoods."

"How'd you do?"

"Did fine at Lincoln before I went to Foxwoods. The slots there were awfully tight but I managed to hold on to most of my winnings from Lincoln."

The group ahead is just climbing the hill in front of us. We can't hit yet. Another in my foursome gets in his two cents worth. Sarcastically, but jokingly, he says, " We sure as hell ain't gonna make any money today. You'll be sleepin' between shots and we gotta suffer. You suck even with ten hours sleep! How come you never tell us about losses? All we ever hear is how much you win. I think you're full of shit!"

Before I can answer one of the guys in our group is coming down the hill towards us in his cart. He's waving a hand indicating that it's safe to hit. We tee off and finish the hole. We're waiting to tee off again on the next hole. I face the group and address them defiantly.

"So you guys think I'm full of shit! Well here take a gander at this!" I reach into one of the large floppy pockets in my green army fatigues and pull out a huge stack of hundred dollar bills. I wave the stack at them. When I'm through waiving I put the wad to my ear, tilt my head to one side, and noisily flip the bills. I put the stack back where it came from. Still defiantly I say, "Well, whata you got to say about that!"

Someone asks, "How much is that, anyway?"

"It's $300.00 short of the six grand I won at Lincoln."

No one says another word about gambling for the rest of the round. I'm exhausted but do everything I can not to show it. It's a slow round and the jokes are plentiful as we wait on each tee. But I'm not hearing them. My mind is still at Lincoln. I'm actually deriving great pleasure over and over again as I relive the hit. I'm attempting to lineup a putt, but all I can see is myself at Lincoln sitting at the second machine from the end on the left. I'm playing keno at my favorite machine and my numbers are coming out often. I'm constantly praying that the numbers will fall into the configuration that I'm playing.

The top left hand corner is hot. I try a block of ten and get a few numbers. I alternate blocks in that area. Close, close, close, but not enough. I play numbers elsewhere for a few hands but come right back to that corner. I play the top two rows on the left. Numbers 1 through 5 on top and 10 to 15 right under it. I bet the max and hit the button. I watch my picks get hit. I've got eight of them for $1,500.00. There are two open numbers. The last number allowed by the machine lands in one of them. It becomes a "power ball." The $1,500.00 becomes $6,000.00.

Diane and Connie are at the other end of the row. I motion for Diane to come over. I point to the hit and the amount. She screams for Connie to come over. "Look. He did it again!" I get a hug and a kiss as I look at my watch. It's almost closing time.

"Find your mother and have her cash this for me. The cashier knows it's my hit and not hers. Tell her to give the cashier the same tip as before. We'll meet at the valet and head south!"

For some time now I've noticed that the majority of golfers are using metal woods. Their driver heads are huge. I'm one of the few who's still using wooden woods. They belong to the set of Pings which I've had for about ten years. Tired as I am, I decide that Sunday to come at least partially out of the dark ages. As soon as we come off the eighteenth hole I grab my bag and throw it in the trunk. I leave the parking lot without even going upstairs to see if I've won any money. Instead I head for Route One and drive to Revere.

Golf Day is located behind Wonderland Dog Track. I know it's open on Sundays. I find and stop at the Ping display and beckon for a salesman to come over. Without any casual chatter or wasted words I just start talking, as I point to the well-advertised $500.00 Ping driver in the display. "Have you got a left-handed one of these with a ten degree loft and a stiff shaft?"

He looks around and doesn't see one. "Can you wait a moment sir while I check our inventory?"

"Yeah, no problem."

I watch as he uses a computer for a couple of minutes. He returns, and says, "Yes. We have that model in stock but it's in our warehouse in the back. Unfortunately it's closed on Sundays. If you come back tomorrow I'd be happy to get it for you."

I deliberately take out my wad of bills. One at a time I peel off five one hundreds and lay them on the counter side by side. I shake my head from side to side, look directly into his eyes, and tell him very sincerely, "Yes. It's unfortunate that the warehouse is closed on Sunday. It's also unfortunate that I won't be back after today. It'll also be unfortunate if you stood to make a commission on this sale."

As I'm scooping up the money, I hear what I want to hear. "Wait just one moment Sir while I check with the manager." He returns in less than a minute. "Our stock boy is on the way to the warehouse. Your club should be here shortly."

In the car I shake my head in disbelief. How could I be so impulsive as to spend that kind of money for one club! It's absolutely irrational! It's insane! It's really against my grain and better judgment. I better not tell anybody. I saw the ad and just couldn't control myself. Shit, ten years ago I think I paid $500.00 for the whole set.

I try out the club at the driving range for weeks. I just can't hit it. I can hit my 5-wood farther. The club never makes the golf course. It stays in my trunk for nearly a year. I finally sell to another lefty for $150.00…

…It's about four o'clock on a Sunday morning and I have a 7:28 tee time. We've been at Foxwoods since Friday afternoon. I never made it to the room. I've been bouncing around from casino hall to hall. I'm nearly batted out and I keep dozing off while playing the slots. I make a guess that the girls are playing Keno in the casino next to the bingo hall. My knee and my back are killing me as I make the long walk. All that I want is to find a seat to rest. I enter the hall. There they are. The three of them are sitting side by side playing keno for a quarter or two per hand. I plop down in the end seat next to them. I'm thankful that there are plenty of available seats at this ungodly hour.

They look in my direction and Diane is the first to speak. She's as cheerful as a daisy as she says, "Good morning."

I look in her direction and acknowledge my presence with a nod and a grunt, as I put in a twenty. I start playing the max of four quarters with no luck whatsoever. I'm watchin' the screen with one eye and lookin' towards the gang with the other. I announce. "Hey, we gotta leave right this minute if we wanna beat the early morning trailer trucks on the Mass Pike."

Connie answers. "Yeah, we know. We were just about to go lookin' for you."

Rose adds, "Diane and Connie have already put the luggage in the trunk."

Diane chips in with, "I'm glad I told 'em you were a diabetic. Instead of the usual box of chocolates in the room they left us a beautifully wrapped package of assorted nuts and a large fresh fruit platter. They're in the trunk too."

"OK guys, let's vamoose. I'm probably gonna have to borrow money from someone at Gannon to pay for the cart and gambling. Diane, you drive as usual. At least you got a little sleep."

We make the long walk back to the casino where I had just been. Rose and I are slowing the pace. Finally we're there. Diane looks back over her shoulder towards us and says, "We're goin' to the ladies room right over there first. To save time you oughta take the escalator to the lobby and give the ticket to the valet." (The Hampton Club had not as yet come into existence).

"OK. good idea. See you there."

As I enter the casino and take a left towards the escalator I spot a whole row of machines which I had never seen there before. They're all brand new dollar machines. It's obvious that they've been installed sometime during the week. I'm tempted to play. I reach into my pocket and all I've got left is a ten and a twenty. I'm debating with myself. Save the money for golf or give it a shot?

There's something else nagging in my mind about new machines. Then it comes to me. About six months earlier I had sent away for a book entitled, "How to Win at Slots Every Time." The book advises…"Never play a machine right next to one that's winning…always try to play machines which are prominently placed in high traffic and visibility areas, since management wants customers to observe hits…"

On the same page there's also a suggestion to play newly installed machines. The rationale is that oftentimes they have not as yet been programmed by the house. They still may have the factory settings which usually produce a higher percentage of wins. That's all I needed to remember. My mind is made up.

I survey the bank of slots and decide to play the first machine in the row, which faces the highly traveled corridor and customers entering the room. I sit down and hit the menu button even though the machine has the word "POKER" at the top. There are several different types of slot games in additional to several poker game options. I insert my twenty as soon as I see the game "JOKER POKER."

The maximum bet is $5.00. The big Jackpot pays $4,000.00 for five of a kind. I look at my watch and think about my tee time, the valet, and traffic on the pike. Time is short as I bet five dollars and hit the button. I study the five dealt cards, hold my choices, and hit the "draw" button. The hand is a total loser. The next hand is no better. Shit. I picked the wrong damn machine. I have thoughts of cashing out the remaining ten bucks and playing the machine next to me on the right. I look at my watch and instead hit the button again. Five new cards appear. I'm dealt an automatic winner. I hold two Kings and a Joker and hit the "draw" button.

Instantaneously lights are flashing everywhere, as the music loudly plays, "California, here I come..." An attendant, obviously aware of the possibility of a large tip, is quickly at my side congratulating me as he places a JACKPOT card in the center of the screen for all to see. A crowd gathers. I keep looking in the direction of the entrance to the ladies room. Diane and crew apparently hear the music and see me at the same time. Diane is now actually running towards me. She knows it gotta be good news. Excitedly she asks, "What happened? What'd you get?"

I point to the center of the screen and tell her incredulously, "Would you believe it? I just caught five Kings!"

"Did you play the max? What'd you win?"

"Four grand!"

"Great! You owe me half!"

"I gotta think about that!"

"I'm absolutely broke. Lucky I've still got my bloomers. Lend me a twenty."

"All of a sudden it's a loan? When did that happen?"

She giggles somewhat sheepishly and says, "You know what I mean."

I reach into my pocket and hold up a ten dollar bill. "This is all I've got left. My last twenty went into my machine. Here, good luck!"

She remembers the rules, skips the machine next to me, and puts the ten into the next one.

I had previously told the attendant not to take out any money for taxes. He and another are now at my side putting one hundred dollar bills into the upturned palm of one of my hands. From my right I once again hear the wordless song blasting out, "California, here I come..."

I turn just in time to watch Diane jump up and down while screaming at the top of her lungs. She's now hollering to me. "I just got five threes! I can't believe it! I can't believe it!"

"That's terrific! You owe me half!"

I'm no longer dragin' my behind. I'm wide awake and rejuvenated. Gannon never sees me at tee time nor at any time that day. We stay. We play...

CHAPTER NINETEEN

...“Wanna know a secret, Machera?”

“Sure. Why not? I’m all ears. I like a bit of juicy gossip every now and then jus’ like everyone else.”

Pretending to be hurt I answer him. “Sorry to disappoint you pal. Here I am about to share my innermost thoughts with you and all you wanna hear is gossip.”

His voice has more than just a touch of sarcasm as he jokingly responds. “Shit Boss, how’m I supposed to know that you want me to put on my shrink’s hat?”

Still feigning indignation in my voice. “Forgeddaboutit. It’s too late now. Besides, I can’t afford your office visit, Doctor Shrink.”

The early morning Boston bound traffic on the Mystic River Bridge is bumper-to-bumper as usual. I’m impatiently waiting my turn to pay the toll. The banter with Joe helps pass the time.

This time I can tell he’s serious. “All right Bruce, what’s really on your mind?”

“Nothing earth-shattering. I was merely gonna tell you that every time I cross this damn bridge I have a lousy feeling in the pit of my stomach. It’s even worse when I’m heading for Middlesex Superior. Can’t stop thinkin’ of Seit, who’s in the can because he never had a fair trial.”

“Well, that ain’t your fault and you oughta realize it.”

“Deep down I know you’re right, but it’s no consolation.”

“Listen to me. I’m gonna tell ya what you should already know. It was His Nibs, Judge Sullivan, who put Barry behind bars. It wasn’t the jury and it sure as hell wasn't you! And as long as I've got the floor I'm gonna stand on a big soap box and pontificate. I rarely get this kind of opportunity."

He takes a sip of his cold coffee, clears his throat, and begins to talk philosophically. "I'm gonna be very brief. All's I really wanna say, is that whoever said that a trial by a jury composed of one's peers will guarantee a fair trial is just plainly and simply full of shit!"

"Sure, that may be so in some scattered cases, but overall it's the best system going.

Wouldn't wanna be in Russia or China using their methods. You gotta look at the big picture. It's the average results over an extended period of time that really counts. I believe in my heart that juries really ensure a fair trial. You can't just look at the results of one or two isolated cases."

"Now look who's pontificating!"

"Maybe you're right. But juries can't help but to be influenced by the Judge. It's still the Judge who runs the trial and is capable of swaying a jury one way or another. I still maintain that in many cases a jury verdict is a Judge's verdict. And that's exactly what happened with Seit. The jury never got the whole true picture. Sullivan, by his tone of voice, his inflections, his rulings on questions of law, and his overall demeanor, guaranteed a conviction for the Commonwealth."

"Joe, I never realized before, that you were such a scholar in the field of jurisprudence."

"Stop strokin' me!"

"I'm not. I'm dead serious."

I pay the toll, get into the lane on the extreme right, and follow the arrow and the sign pointing towards Charlestown. There's very little traffic in this lane. Most of the commuters have gone straight ahead towards Boston. The tension returns. It gets worse as I take a left at Bunker Hill Junior College. We're now only a few minutes from the courthouse.

"Jus' think, 'hotshot', I get to face the sunovabitch again in less than an hour from now. Ain't that jus' Ducky?"

"Better thee than me!"

We make good time. The Criminal Motion Session doesn't begin until ten o'clock. It's now only 9:15. "C'mon Joe let's go to the cafeteria. I'll buy you a cup of coffee."

We sit at a table facing the corridor. The cigarette smoke filling my lungs has a calming effect.

Somberly Joe says, "This is really scary. How many times did we sit at this table during the trial?"

"Too many. Wonder how many crossword puzzles I did while waitin' for the jury? I'd like a dime for every cup of coffee I had sittin' in this very chair?"

We're in the hall outside the designated courtroom. "Joe, please check that list posted on the wall. See how many cases there are and where we are on the list. I'll grab two seats and meet you inside."

There aren't many lawyers in the room. I easily find two seats next to each other. Before I have a chance to get comfortable and open my briefcase Joe is settling in beside me.

"There are only ten Motions on the list. We're fourth."

"OK. Thanks. We oughta be outa here in no time at all. I'll be surprised if the Judge even lets me say my name!"

A door behind the Judge's bench opens. A Court Officer walks in. He stands quietly next to Clerk's portion of the bench until the Clerk and the Judge are both standing behind their respective chairs. I look at the wall clock and can't believe that they're here this early. It's only twenty past ten!

The Court Officer booms out, "All persons having anything to do before the Superior Court within and for the County of Middlesex, holden at Cambridge in said County, draw near, give your attendance, and ye shall be heard. God save the Commonwealth of Massachusetts. Judge Robert Sullivan presiding." Before the Judge is fully seated the loud voice continue.: "You may be seated."

The Clerk then calls the cases one by one. I note that the prosecutors are permanently ensconced at the table on the left facing the Judge. As each case is called the lawyer for the Defendant takes the table on the right and quickly covers it with books and papers before addressing the Judge.

The Motions are simple and routine. It only takes a moment or two for both parties to be heard and for the Judge to announce his decision right then and there. There are really no questions of law nor are any earth-shattering decisions made. Case number three has just concluded. I've already decided that I don't need any books or notes. I know the issues cold turkey. I've even memorized the citations for the cases which I intend to use. I open my briefcase and put a clean yellow pad in my hand as I simultaneously begin to rise in anticipation of the Clerk calling my case. He calls a different case. I'm in disbelief as I settle back again in my chair.

Joe nudges my arm and whispers, "What the hell was that all about?"

"I can only guess that they wanna get rid of all the routine quick stuff first. No need to keep all those lawyers here to listen to something which could take up a good deal of time. The Court's aware that our Motion for a New Trial involves a capital crime and that there will undoubtedly be several substantial legal issues to ponder. Betcha they hold us until last."

I hit the nail on the head. The courtroom is clear, except for us. I'm already on my feet and halfway to the table when the Clerk calls Commonwealth versus Bariki Seit. I haven't reached the table yet but start speaking loudly as though there's a full house listening.

"May it please the Court, Attorney Bruce Sachar for the Defendant. Good morning, Your Honor." Similar words come from opposing counsel's table on my left.

The Judge smiles, nods his head in acknowledgement of our presence, and says pleasantly, "Good morning gentlemen." He then looks down at some papers before him. Eventually he looks at me again and speaks in a monotone. I think I detect a sense of boredom in his voice, as he says, "Oh, yes. I remember this case now. It's your Motion Mr. Sachar so I'll hear from you first."

"Thank you, Your Honor."

Before I have a chance to open my mouth and begin my argument the Judge looks direcly at me and asks, "Isn't this the case where the Defendant incredulously claimed to have been working as a CIA Agent?"

I'm in a state of shock with that opening question. Is this gonna be a replay of the trial? The trial is over. He can't hurt me any more. I'm now totally pissed as I answer his question. The sarcasm in my responsive voice leaves no room for conjecture in anyone's mind as to how I feel about the subject matter of his question.

"Yes, Your Honor, you have a good memory. This is indeed the case in which my client made that assertion and I think that your disbelief of the same was clearly conveyed to the jury. And incidentally, that issue probably goes hand in hand with my ultimate contention, that a new trial should be granted, since the jury never got the whole picture of the facts, as I shall attempt to point out momentarily."

His cheeks are becoming redder. Before he can speak I add with the same sarcasm as before, "Oh, Yeah, before I forget Judge, it turns out that he was in fact woking for the CIA. It was confirmed by Senator Ted Kennedy's Washington Office on the last day of trial. The earliest that we could have produced a corroborating witness was two weeks. I didn't think that the court would look favorably upon a two week continuance at that point in the trial, so I never made the request."

I thought that he was about to have a stroke right before my eyes. Nevertheless I saved the best for last. "One last thing Judge. I believe that I would be remiss, if I failed to inform the Court, that according to a spokesperson from Kennedy's office, the prosecution in this case knew of the CIA connection prior to the commencement of the trial. Doesn't it seem strange to you, Your Honor, that in spite of that knowledge, which they hid, they nevertheless attempted to portray him as a liar during cross-examination on the subject.

I hadn't intended to argue this issue today so it is not contained in my Memorandum of Law. Had I known that the issue was to be raised, I certainly would have argued that what the prosecution did in this regard was tantamount to withholding exculpatory evidence, which constitutes sufficient grounds alone to warrant a new trial."

I'm about to begin my argument on the Motion when the Judge turns to the prosecutor's table and asks, "Is what Mr. Sachar has just told the Court true?" The three prosecutors at the table begin to look frantically in their files. After a couple of minutes one of them stands and sheepishly tells the Court, "Your Honor, neither one of us was actually involved in any way with the trial of this case. In fact, I wasn't even in the District

Attorney's office at the time. Therefore, we can't respond to Mr. Sachar's allegations, other than to say that there is nothing in our files, which would allow us to either confirm or deny the allegations." He sits down. The Judge announces that there will be a fifteen minute recess.

In the hallway Joe asks, "Where the hell did you get the nerve to talk to the Judge in that tone of voice? I think that he's really pissed off at you now!"

"Good, because I'm pissed at him too! Why hold back? He ain't gonna give us anything anyway. Just as well that he brought it up. Finally got it off my chest. And you know what Joe? I feel a hundred percent better now about the trial than I have since it began!"

We're back in the courtroom. I'm on my feet and begin. "Your Honor, I would like to call the Court's attention to the fact that Motions for a New Trial are equally present in civil as well as in criminal cases. In both areas of the law it's not uncommon to request a new trial on the ground that the verdict is against the weight of the credible evidence, and that it would, therefore, be unjust to allow the verdict to stand. But in this case I cannot make such an argument. Although the verdict may be unjust in my mind, it is certainly not against the weight of the credible evidence. The evidence before the jury was certainly sufficient for the verdict of second degree murder.

But I respectfully submit, Your Honor, that therein lies a part of the problem. There should have been more credible evidence for use by the jurors during deliberation. I think that several of your rulings prevented just that. Your ruling which prohibited our ballistician from testifying about the potential impact power of a bullet being discharged from a 357 magnum was crucial to our defense of self-defense. Equally crucial was your exclusion of evidence from him regarding the phenomenon known as an "involuntary firing reaction."

I'm relieved that there are no questions. "Begging the Court's further indulgence I think that an analogy can be made between my Motion for a New Trial and a Motion for Judgment Notwithstanding the Verdict, which is often used in civil cases. I believe that they're definitely related and perhaps even second cousins." I pause a bit with a faint smile and hope for a little laugh from somewhere. The reaction is total silence.

"I would again submit, Your Honor, that the failure of the jury to hear all the evidence has resulted in a miscarriage of justice, which can be corrected by ordering a new trial. .Lastly, Judge, I have a request of you which may be somewhat novel. There are no cases directly in point. I'm asking the Court to set a precedent."

I take a breath and continue. "As the Court is well aware, Massachusetts General Laws, chapter 278, Section 33E, confers the power directly to the Supreme Judicial Court to vacate a verdict in a criminal case, and in the interests of justice to reduce the verdict to a lesser crime. I am quick to point out, Your Honor, that it is a power seldom invoked by the Court. The statute says, that the power arises only in cases entered in that Court."

Before I can continue it speaks! Holy shit he's alive! Has the renowned author of "The Strange Disappearance of Dr. Parkman" been listening?

"Mr. Sachar, are you asking me to reduce the verdict of murder in the second degree to the lesser crime of manslaughter?"

"Yes, Your Honor, that's precisely what I'm asking."

"Even if I were inclined to do it I simply haven't got the power. As I remember the statute the power to reduce is strictly reserved to the SJC."

"It would appear that way at first blush, Your Honor, but the statute definitely says, that the power is given over all cases entered in that Court. My argument is simply that this case has not yet been entered in that Court, so it cannot yet act under that statute. At this point in time the SJC simply doesn't have jurisdiction. You on the other hand, should be able to do it if you were so inclined. The case is definitely entered in this Court. After all, if you have the power to order a new trial or even to set aside a verdict, why shouldn't you be able to reduce a verdict to a lesser crime? It seems only logical."

"Well, Mr. Sachar, that's a novel approach. First time that I've heard it. Do you wish to be heard further?"

"No. Thank you for your indulgence. I'm quite finished. Anything else that I might say would be redundant. I'll rely upon the Memorandum of Law which was filed simultaneously with my Motion."

He turns his head to the prosecutors and asks, "Does anyone at your table wish to respond?"

A young prosecutor stands and addresses the court. "May it please the Court. If your rulings as to the admissibility of certain testimony, and or, the testifying of certain witnesses, was good enough at the time, and in the heat of battle, then they should be good enough today. Nothing significant has happened since then to cause you to believe that your rulings were then incorrect. Insofar as the request to reduce the verdict is concerned, the case will soon be entered in the SJC. I believe that even Mr. Sachar would agree that they can handle his request at that time. Thank you, Your Honor."

He sits. I whisper to Joe. "Great argument. Short, sweet, and right to the point. He's smart beyond his years."

"Thank you gentlemen, I'll take the matter under advisement."

The trip back is quiet and uneventful. I'm not feeling queasy anymore. Joe breaks the silence as we cross the Mystic. "When do you think we'll get a decision?"

"Usually within a month. In this case it's probably already being delivered by pony express. What the hell difference does it make? We both know the result. Let's start with the full appeal to the SJC. One never knows what can happen in those lofty hallowed halls. It's a crap shoot"...

CHAPTER TWENTY

...Except for Steph's call earlier this morning I've been hanging around all alone in these three rooms. It's hardly a comforting thought that all of the other conversations have been with myself. The cable box clock flips to three minutes after midnight. I become painfully aware that I've been up for almost twenty-four straight hours. My only company has been my crosswords, my music, and of course my thoughts.

I get up and head for the bathroom to take the pills which I forgot to take earlier. I open the medicine chest. The top two shelves contain my daily dosage of pills. As I reach for and open the bottle of Mirapex I can think only of the horrors which have been visited upon me because of these little white pills. I put my nightly dose of pills into the palm of my left hand. My right holds half a cup of water. I close the medicine chest and stare at my reflection in the mirror, as I hold the cup of water up high and make a toast out loud. It's as if I'm referring to a groom or my closest friend in a hall full of people. As the unrehearsed words are spoken it becomes a roast and not a toast...

...''Here's to you Mirapex! Because of you I have no wife; I have no job; I have no friends; I have no house; and I have no money. I feel obliged to add that I have also been disbarred as an attorney and thrown out of the Masons. To top it all off I'm now impatiently waiting for the other shoe to drop. You know, the one that will bestow upon me the honor of becoming a Defendant in a criminal case. It's the same shoe which will bring me closer to my new residence—the jailhouse!

Just think, Mr. Mirapex, that were it not for you none of these wonderful things would have been bestowed upon me. I would have been forced to lead my dull and unexciting life trying to keep innocent people out of jail, and putting money into the hands of injured victims. Ladies and gentlemen, I can even remember the day when Mirapex and I first met about twelve years ago. Our relationship from then to now has been like a ride on a roller-coaster. I want you all to know that he has a very unique personality. He has allowed both calmness and aggression to live side by side within me at the same.

It's not for publication, but I recently tried to go it alone without my dear friend, Mirapex. It just didn't work. Something was missing. So here we are again. Buddies to the end. Would you all please rise to join with me in a salute. Thanks again, Mr. Mirapex. Just think. I owe it all to you!...

...The "oldies" are playing as I take a cup of tea from the Keurig to my desk where the crossword book patiently awaits. My reading glasses are on and I have pen in hand as I look down towards the book. Once again the music interferes with my intended purpose. Is there some hidden meaning in the words of the songs I've programmed? Maybe the titles have a clue? Is there some mysterious relationship between the titles or the words of a particular song and my personality or my life? What determines whether a song or certain music is appealing or not?

The little voice within me points out that I've got plenty of time on my hands these days. "Look for the answer to your questions. Play the damn songs and listen to the words. Do it now! Why wait, Dummy? Anyway, what else you got to do? You talk too damn much. How come you're not hoarse?"

I reset the music selections, turn up the volume, and listen to the songs being played indiscriminately. After a few songs are played I come to the conclusion that I'm all wet. I'm unable to correlate the music with anything. Then I decide to cheat a little in order to try and prove my initial feelings. I hand-pick the songs that I want to hear. Since Al Jolson was my father's favorite all-time vocalist, I start with him...'I'm sittin' on top of the world, jus' rollin' along, rollin' along...glory, glory hallelujah...and jus' like Humpty Dumpty, I'm goin' to fall..."

Bobby Darin sings...'I want a Dream lover, so I don't have to dream alone..."

He follows with...'Somewhere, beyond the sea, I'll go sailin'...happy I will be...if I could fly like birds on high..."

Hank Williams adds...'Hey, hey, good lookin', what ya got cookin'? How's about cookin' somethin' up with me?...I got a hot rod Ford and a two dollar bill..."

Hidden meanings? Don't see an awful lot. Maybe if I were to stretch things a bit? I can't help but think of Jolson...'I'm sittin' on top of the world, jus' rollin' along…and jus' like Humpty Dumpty, I'm goin' to fall…"…

…During the 80's the BCU sends me hundreds of mortgages to do every year. In one year alone I open close to a thousand new files for the BCU. Bank lawyers are generally charging between $500.00 and $750.00 per mortgage closing. I'm not bound by their policy. I follow in the tradition of now deceased, Arthur Levine, former attorney for the BCU. I charge one percent of the loan. If someone borrows $100,000.00 my legal fee is $1,000.00. The maximum loan then allowed by the BCU is $150,000.00.

It's a glorious time for the BCU and all the local banks. They're getting back at least one point (one percent) of the mortgage loan right at the closing. Business everywhere is thriving. Consumers are rewriting their old mortgages at low rates and paying off the high interest loans of the 70's. New homes are springing up everywhere. I'm working on files at home in order to keep up with the closing dates.

The women in the office are all behind in their duties. They work even during coffee breaks. The new $10,000.00 CPT computer sitting on Melinda's desk is a monstrosity. It appears to be about three feet by three feet. Melinda is a perfectionist. She has virtually every document needed for a closing on a labeled disc and located where she can retrieve it instantly.

I'm still punchy as I enter the office and gather my messages from Melinda's, Bernice's, and Florence's desks. I'm scanning the messages as I walk slowly in the direction of my office. Melinda asks, "Bruce, what happened? You look terrible. How did those back-to-back closings go at the Registry?"

I stop in my tracks, and turn around slowly to face her. "You don't wanna know how it went. I scheduled the first closing for nine o'clock sharp and the second one for ten.

I also had a nine o'clock criminal arraignment in Peabody from a phone call at home last night. They wouldn't bail him so I had to appear. I went to Peabody before I went to the Registry. I saw the Clerk, Russ Craig, and he agreed to hold the case for me until I arrived. OK? So far so good, No problem, right?"

I pause to take a sip of the cold coffee which I brought with me. I continue. "And then it started. The attorney for the first closing shows up a half hour late. He's supposed to be representing the buyers, a pleasant couple, who obtained a loan from the BCU to buy a new house. They're already pissed because they're supposed to meet the movers at quarter past ten. Introductions follow and everyone shakes hands. The sellers then announce that they have to be in Boston at the Suffolk Registry of Deeds at ten thirty. They're buying a condo at a new development in Winthrop and are using the proceeds from this closing in order close."

I take another swig, sit on the couch, light up a cigarette, and continue. "Now, when I hear all this I tell everyone not to panic. I'll do the closing ultra fast. I'll paraphrase the contents of the documents which you will have to sign. Most of the papers pertain to the buyers. There are only a few for the seller. The most important papers for the buyers are the deed, note, mortgage, and HUD Statement. They all appear to look at their watches at the same time. All I hear is, 'go, go, go!'

I pick up the HUD first and am about to give a quick synopsis of the money part of the transaction, when the buyers' lawyer says that he would prefer to explain it to his clients. I'm peeved to say the least, as he begins using a copy which was in the package I had handed him shortly before. Now I take a good look at this guy for the first time. He looks too young to be a lawyer. I think he must have got out of law school yesterday.

Then it starts. Oh, shit. Of all the luck. I catch a guy with what I call, "the young lawyer syndrome." Bernice interrupts. "What's a young lawyer syndrome?"

"That's a lawyer who feels the necessity to impress his client. He wants to show his erudition. He also feels a need to justify his fee. At a real estate closing he wants to read virtually every word on every document to his client. He then offers his own explanation of what he has just read and invariably he's usually totally wrong. The sad thing is that I'm not allowed to change a comma anyway in the vast majority of the documents.

Fifteen minutes later he's still trying to interpret the HUD Statement. He absolutely has no idea whatsoever as to how one arrives at the tax adjustments. He even questions the fact that his clients have to pay for the recording of the mortgage, deed, and Municipal Lien Certificate. Not only doesn't he understand the figures on the Lien Certificate but he wants the seller to pay for recording the deed. I point out the law and closing practices in this State. I tell him that it would be quicker for me to explain the various documents. I remind him that both parties have time commitments. Nevertheless, he continues with what he's doing and at the same slow pace.

Everyone at the table shares in my uneasiness. They merely shrug their shoulders and shake their heads in disbelief. Finally I grab my copy of the HUD Form. I interrupt him in mid-sentence. 'Excuse me Counsel, but I believe that you have inadvertently given some improper interpretations of the numbers on this form.' I don't wait for a response. In less than a minute I'm through correcting and am passing the forms around the table for signature.

I then pick up the promissory note and before he has his copy in hand, I tell the buyers that this is a fixed rate note for $125,000.00 calling for interest at 6% per year. I tell them the monthly payment, inform them that it's a thirty year loan, and that they have the right to prepay at any time after three years without a penalty. I tell them the penalty for prepayment before the three year period, and that if the note goes to collection they will be obligated to pay reasonable legal fees and costs. The buyers quickly sign.

He's still looking at the note and I know he wants to put in his two cents worth. Before he has a chance I'm already explaining the mortgage. We don't finish until quarter after ten. I had to wait in a long line to record. No one is happy. Especially the new buyers and sellers who are waiting for the next scheduled closing, which I previously told them would commence promptly at ten.

The participants in the next closing have similar time commitments. I start at twenty past ten and at quarter to eleven I return from recording and give out the checks. Fifteen minutes later the Clerk calls my case in Peabody and announces that both Judges are tied up. Come back at one o'clock. I get a coffee from the Dunkin Donuts across the street and bring it to my car. I sit like a jackass for the next two hours doing crosswords and napping.

First Justice of the Peabody District Court, Santo J. Ruma, is on the bench. My good friend of many years, Mary Coen, is his Clerk. The client is pleased that he's free. The big problem becomes obvious when I look at his record. There are numerous past defaults. He doesn't know how lucky he is. We both light up. I tell him to call in a week or so for an appointment to start preparing for his trial date. And you wanna know why I look so terrible?"

I stand up and head for my office with messages in hand. "Melinda, please gimme about fifteen minutes to return some calls, and then come in."

"OK."

My door is partially open and Melinda can see that I'm on the phone. She's about to turn around but I waive her to come in. She puts a cup of coffee on my blotter and opens up her shorthand notebook just as I'm in the process of hanging up. We both light up.

"Melinda, I've got a big problem. It's been on my mind for a long time. My experience today in Peabody really highlighted the dilemma. I wanna run it by you and get your opinion."

"OK. *No problemo.* What's buggin' you?"

"Several things I guess. Really don't know where to start. Look over here at these two large stacks of files. These are all cases that need my immediate attention but I just can't seem to get to them. I have to bring suit in some of them immediately, before the Statute of Limitations runs out. A couple of the criminal cases need me to prepare and mark up some assorted Motions including at least one Motion to Suppress. There are also a couple of cases which have already been given trial dates, and I gotta find the time to prepare the clients. Everyone in the office is so busy with the real estate closings, that I just don't know what to do to solve the problem. Any suggestions?"

Without a moment's hesitation she says very calmly. "I think you're really makin' a mountain out of a mole hill. We oughta be able to clean up those two piles quickly. All we gotta do is stay late or come back after supper to put in an extra few hours on two or three nights. Just in case you've forgotten I've got the CPT out there just sittin' on my desk. All you gotta do is just give me the tort and contract files which require that suit be brought immediately. You don't have to be concerned with them. Don't even give 'em a second thought. There's no need to even dictate. I've got sample Complaints saved on discs for almost every type of tort or contract case."

She takes a last large drag on her cigarette before snuffing it out in the ashtray. She continues without missing a beat. "Gimme some credit here! I've got a little more than just air between my ears! Remember those two huge white three ring binders in the library? You should, you put them together. Let me remind you that they contain every conceivable type of letter imaginable, as well sets of Interrogatories and Requests for Production of Documents for either a Plaintiff or a Defendant. Heck, there's even some form eviction notices, statutory letters in snow and ice cases, and assorted letters to doctors. Well, the good news is that they're all in the computer. So are all the Trusts, Wills, Codicils, Powers of Attorney, Health Care proxies, and Living Wills.

All you really gotta do is go through the remaining files while I'm workin' on the files which require that suit be brought. Just make some brief notes telling me what you want on each file. If I can't figure it out, I'll ask. Your biggest task will probably be in the drafting of an Affidavit and a Memorandum of Law in support of the Motion to Suppress. But don't forget I've got several Memorandums. The cases are probably the same. All right, you asked for my input and I've just given it. What do you think?"

"I think that you're just great! You've solved a big part of my dilemma. I'm now gonna tell you how I intend to solve the other, and why."

Pretending to be critical, I shake my head from side to side and I tell her, "Incidentally, my dear, the plural for 'Memorandum' is not 'Memorandums', it's 'Memoranda'.

She knows that I'm only toying with her but gives an answer in spades. "I'm truly sorry, sir, that you find my language skills to be so deficient, but regretfully I'm only a paralegal. I am also deeply ashamed that I never had your five years of Latin classes, which you once told me about. The bottom line is, that you can just take your 'Memoranda' and shove it!"

"*Touche!*"

We both laugh. Another sip of coffee and another cigarette, are all that I need to continue.

"The episode in Peabody today merely confirms what I've known now for quite some time. I can't serve two masters at once anymore. It's simply impossible for me to continue doing the volume of work coming from the BCU and represent criminals at the same time. The mortgage work requires precision in determining and coordinating a closing date. We have to compute per diem rates for mortgage payoffs and add an extra few days to allow for the mail to reach a prior mortgage holder. The closing dates are really etched in stone. The exact time of a closing is equally important because of prior routine commitments of buyers and sellers.

On the other hand a Court appearance in a criminal matter is almost always unpredictable. I can never tell what time a Judge will hit the bench. I can't tell if a case will actually go to trial on the assigned date. Calls often come to me at home during the night, which require my attendance in Court the next morning. You haven't the faintest idea, Melinda, as to the number of times that I've had to turn down such a request because I have a scheduled closing, which could be held anywhere between Cape Cod and Rockingham County in New Hampshire.

From a purely economical and perhaps even selfish point of view I get paid right away at a closing. There's no hassle and no waiting for my fee. I just cut a check to myself from my Trustee's Account right after the closing. On the other hand, it's usually quite different in criminal cases, as you should be well aware from all the letters you've typed requesting all or part of a fee which is long overdue.

You, above all people, should know how much I really enjoy the criminal work. If it weren't for you, whom else could I tell? I'd like to think that you listen because you're interested and not because you're on my payroll. The bottom line is that I will no longer be accepting any criminal cases. I realize, that every rule has an exception and this one is probably no different. Time will tell. I really hate to give up the Hell's Angels. See if you can set up an appointment for me with 'Hoppy'. I'd prefer to tell him face to face. In the meantime, as far as new criminal cases are concerned, I have in mind a couple of guys to whom we can refer cases."

"It's too bad, that you can't do what you want, Bruce, but it may be a blessing in disguise. At least there won't be a conflict as to which master to serve. The bright side of the coin is that you should be thankful that you have the option to make the decision yourself."

"I guess you're right. Wait a sec." I quickly run through one of the stacks on my desk and pull out four cases. Without missing a beat I hand them to her and jokingly say, "Here big mouth! Serves ya right!"...

...*My practice is getting stronger every year. I'm making good money, but I always believe that next year will be even better. I spend, as though I have no fixed obligations, and consequently I'm never able to accumulate* substantial savings...

...What the hell just happened? Did someone hit a switch by mistake? Headlines and news broadcasts announce the closing of a popular new bank in Lynn; Comfed, one of the largest mortgage lenders in the State for nearly a decade is forced by Federal Authorities to close its doors under a cloud of suspicion; bank directors everywhere are being indicted for fraud, conflicts of interest, and a wide assortment of conspiracy allegations; lawyers are being indicted and disbarred. As quickly as it had started, the mortgage business suddenly comes to a screeching halt, as banks and credit unions everywhere are being investigated by Federal and State Auditors.

In spite of all that's happening right before my nose I am truly convinced, that it's all only a temporary inconvenience or set-back. Everything will be back to normal in a couple of months. Suddenly the office is eerily quiet. The old mortgage discharges have been returned by the Registry of Deeds, as well as the mortgages from my last closings. Files have been closed and missing documents in open files have been requested again. The secretarial desks are all neat and uncluttered for the first time that I can remember.

The well has run dry, There's nothing of any significance producing income. No-Fault has taken its toll. There's very little new criminal business, which I now no longer refuse.

I made a bad choice which appeared to be correct at the time. *I put all of my eggs in one basket and lost.*

I just don't have the heart to let Florence and Bernice go. It's only a temporary thing. I'll carry them for a while until the economy and the mortgage market return. When it bounces back I'll be prepared. I won't have to look for new skilled people. They're both getting on in years and I'm their only source of income. Layoffs are unthinkable. The word is not even in my vocabulary.

How can I pay them, the rent, all other fixed office expenses, and my personal obligations, which simply don't go away just because the mortgage work has dried up. The answer is quite simple!

I'll use those credit cards with the zero balances. Why, I've got some for 25K, 10K, and 5K. As Melinda would say, *"No Problemo!"*...

It's also *"No Problemo,"* when Melinda obtains a divorce and we start dating...The market never bounces back. Melinda and I are alone. I use one credit card to make a payment due on another until they are all finally maxed out, and I'm being besieged by phone calls looking for payments. Gone also are my stocks, bonds, and retirement funds. I'm in arrears with my alimony payments to Phyliss and child support payments with Chris. I'm behind with the office rent and my house mortgage with the BCU. Uncle Sam and the Massachusetts Department of Revenue are also after me for non-payment of taxes.

Thank you, Charles Dickens!...If this is not the best of times, then it certainly must approach the worst of times!...

I guess my father really liked Jolson because he apparently knew what no one else seemed to recognize. Jolson was not merely a singer. He was also a philosopher and a genuine soothsayer. Sachar, just listen to those words again..."I'm sittin' on top of the world, jus' rollin' along, jus' rollin' along...glory, glory, halleluja...and jus' like Humpty Dumpty, I'm goin' to fall..."

CHAPTER TWENTY-ONE

...The harsh ring of the phone startles me. I must have dozed off again. The clock on my desk indicates six o'clock. There's only one person who would call me at this hour in the morning. Sure enough the caller ID indicates it's Michael. "Hello Michael. Good afternoon!"

"It's much too early. Don't be such a smart ass! I think you and I are the only people awake and possibly alert at this ungodly hour." He knows, that I'm about to say something sarcastic, but without waiting for my retort, he starts talking . "Thought you'd be interested to know that yesterday Karen and I had our best Friday yet at Karmichael's."

"Terrific! What'd you gross?"

"Almost two grand."

"Considering you've only been open a couple of months and never did a stitch of advertising, it's kinda mind-boggling to me."

"Yeah, me too."

"Any particular reason for the exceptional night?"

"We had an order from the old age home down the street. Besides a few breaded veal cutlet subs and a couple of spaghetti and meat ball dinners, they ordered 79 lobster rolls. Oh yeah, we also sold them a few orders of our macadamia encrusted chicken dinners."

"Just think what you coulda taken in if you charged more per item. I keep tellin' you, compared to the prices around here, you're just givin' it away!"

"Yup. And I keep playin' you the same damn song. This ain't Lynn! This is Augusta, Maine! Besides, I have no intention of rippin' people off. I give large portions and charge very reasonable prices. We've got a gourmet menu, use the best

quality food products, and coincidentally the food tastes good. We gotta be doin' something right, 'cause our business has been generated solely by word of mouth."

"Can't argue about anything you said. Between your cooking and Karen's desserts you seem to have a good operation."

"Right. Gotta turn on all the pilot lights for cooking and start preparing for the day. Just thought you'd like the good news. Gotta run. Speak to you later. So long."

"Ok. Regards to Karen."…

…What exactly is it that causes a word or a thought to conjure up a seemingly unrelated subject in one's mind? I'm sitting here thinking that perhaps Michael has finally found his niche. Let's see, there were the comic book stores. He was forced out of business because of his back operation which left him with serious physical deficits. Then he was a stockbroker. Then a certified numismatist. I loved going to all those coin shows. The operation and a bad knee abruptly stopped his bowling. From a strictly selfish point of view I have to be content with remembering the bowler that he was and what might have been…

…I'm thinking about all the bowling on weekend and holiday visitations. They ultimately led him to glory and a place in the sun, albeit briefly…

Similar thoughts are focusing in my mind regarding the visitations with Steph and Matt. When Matt was about five I cut down a driver and an eight iron to fit his size. We're at Dilisio's Driving Range in Swampscott. I remember the speech as though it were yesterday. "Look at this book, Matt. It's all in color. It's 'Tee to Green' by Jack Nicklaus. Now you pay strict attention to the pictures. This is what the grip looks like. These are pictures of what you should look like from the front and back when you finish the swing. Be sure you don't watch me 'cause it's all wrong. You have to do what I tell you, not as I do!"

By the time he's in the sixth and seventh grades he draws crowds of onlookers at every range we visit. "Matt, fade the next drive to the second light pole from the right at the far end of the range." He was long for his age and deadly accurate. "Matt, draw the next drive to the last pole on the left." And he does. In high school he's a captain of both the golf and hockey teams. He gets awards for MVP and Scholar Athlete. I have the money as he's growing up for the best clubs, baseball bats, and hockey equipment. I coach his baseball team.

"Look, Matt, why don't you go to college somewhere down south, or to Wakeforest, or to Stanford in California, or to the University of Arizona, where you can play golf all year. All you gotta do is take a few strokes off your cap and join

the tour after graduation I'll quit my job and be your caddie!" Little does he know, that I'm more than a little serious.

"I'm gonna go to Bentley. I wanna be near my girlfriend and close to home."

"Matt, I keep getting phone calls from coaches. They tell me you're ignoring them. My sources tell me that you didn't bring a hockey stick, a golf club, or a baseball mitt to school with you. That true?"

"Yeah, it's true. Dad, I'm here for an education."

I'm shut off at the pass, there's no possible answer from me...

...I look forward to Matt's monthly invitation to join him as his guest for golf at the Tedesco country Club in Swampscott. As much as I love the company and the golf, it's secretly demoralizing to play with someone who has such a talent for the game. Needless to say, I'm no longer consulted for advice if he becomes a little erratic...

...I've decided that I won't be hurt if the invitations stop. I know many of the members. It just might be too embarrassing for both of us given the recent adverse newspaper articles. Those articles are replete with candid references to my taking money from my Trustee for Clients' Funds Account. How could I of all people committed such a dastardly crime?...

...We're in a private dining room at Bishop's Restaurant in Lawrence. Two large tables nearly fill the room. There's very little space for the waiters and waitresses. The tinkling of a spoon hitting a water glass subdues the idle chatter. When the room is completely silent, the President Nick Decoulos speaks: " May I have your attention please. The meeting of the Executive Committee of the Essex County Bar association is now called to order. Will the Secretary please read the minutes of the last meeting."

"A meeting was duly called to order by the President at which a quorum was present. It was held at...on.... Under the topic of Old Business there was a further discussion regarding the request by the Board of Bar Overseers. They want us to forward the name of the person selected to serve as a Hearing Officer in lawyer disciplinary cases. By Motion duly made and seconded, it was voted that names of volunteers be solicited from the general membership and that the election and appointment be made at the next meeting. In accordance with that vote Mr. President I caused the request of the BBO to be sent to all active members of the ECBA. We have seven volunteers and each of you has been given a list of the names…there being no further business to come before the Committee, the meeting was adjourned at quarter past ten by unanimous vote."

"Thank you for such a comprehensive and detailed report. Do I hear a Motion?"

"I move that the Minutes be accepted as read" comes from behind me. Just as quickly I hear, "Second."

Decoulos says, "All those in favor please raise your hand." He looks around and announces, "The Minutes are accepted as read by a unanimous vote."

The same ritual follows with regard to the Treasurer's report.

The portly Nick Decoulas is in his mid-fifties and is probably the oldest among us at this particular meeting. He's a well-known and respected trial attorney from Peabody. The bespectacled lawyer has fringes of whitening hair just above his ears and below his otherwise bald head. In addition to his legendary prowess as a champion for the rights of the "little guy," he is also a real estate entrepreneur in his own right.

Most people would agree with my perception and assessment of our President. But I for one appreciate his other qualities. He has a great dry wit and is the master of sarcasm, especially when he's knocking big business interests and the powers that be in State Government. Sometimes it's difficult to know what he really means. He's a very tough read. But when he speaks, I listen.

Another clinking of the glass. When absolute silence is achieved Nick begins with a combination of sarcasm and jest in his voice. "For those among you who were not present at our last meeting, I take great pleasure in welcoming all of you to this fine restaurant located in the boondocks of Essex County" After some laughter and snickering he continues. "If the location and or the food is not to your liking please do not complain to management. Kindly direct any and all complaints to Mr. Sachar who's sitting directly opposite me. Bruce, would you please raise your right hand so everyone will know just where you are." More laughter as I rise, turn around, and waive at everybody.

"It must be his Jewish upbringing because he laid a measure of guilt upon most of at the last meeting. He noted that attendance at our last couple of annual meetings, as well as most of the meetings of this committee, have not been well represented by members from northern Essex. He pointed out that perhaps we southerners were too complacent and too lazy. All we ever suggested were places in and around Salem for our monthly meetings. He had the colossal and unmitigated gall, I think he would call it *chutzpah*, to suggest that our next meeting actually be held in northern Essex.

The guilt must have been overwhelming because the vote was unanimous to come here tonight. Sachar is never right about anything, so I find it rather disconcerting to announce, that maybe he was actually right just this once. There are about eight of you here tonight from this remote part of the world and I bid you welcome."

Everyone recognized his candor and promise. The sarcasm was gone. "As long as I have any say in the matter regular meetings will be held in both southern and northern Essex." There's heartfelt applause from around the room. In an instant his voice unmistakably returns to the prior mode. "I really don't know how he got the vote. He said we might be too lazy to make the trip and that we might be getting too selfish and complacent in our ways. We should think of others. It's difficult to imagine the results. I have it on good authority that the very traits which he attributes to us are now discussed at length in a mandatory freshman course in the law schools. They now offer a course called 'Dilatory Tactics'. It's worth three credits." Laughter and applause follow.

"Just as a point of interest Sachar suggested this place to have our meeting. He told me that it's his favorite restaurant and that he's been coming here since high school, when it was located elsewhere and didn't have the trappings we see today. Notwithstanding the fact that when Sachar was in high school we were still the dark ages, I would now like to call upon him for enlightenment on the menu. Bruce, would you be so kind before our orders are taken?"

Ham that I am I position myself in the aisle between the tables in a spot where everyone can see me. I fold my right arm across my waist and drape my linen napkin over it. In my left hand I hold a menu. I clear my throat and begin. "Ladies and gentlemen, and I use those terms cautiously, I would like to suggest that two large Arabic appetizer platters be ordered for each table. You will find to your palate's delight an assortment of rice pilaf, baked kibee, grapeleaves, stuffed cabbage, and baked lima beans made with a secret gravy which has been a Bishop's family secret for generations. I might add for the benefit of the neophytes that kibee is ground baked lamb. Any entrée from the menu will satisfy your wildest dream. I would caution the bold among you to be wary of the baked lobster with our famous walnut stuffing. It could very well lead to a culinary orgasm!" I sit down amidst laughter and cheers.

Coffee and dessert are being served as the now familiar tinkling is heard again. Total silence comes more quickly than before. Nick stands for the first time. "The last item on the agenda is Old Business which I deliberately deferred until now. You all have before you a list of seven volunteers for the vacant position with the BBO. I have some very strong opinions about this which I would like to share with you. Please bear in mind that these opinions are mine and mine alone and not necessarily the opinion of the ECBA.

There is nothing like a certified letter from the BBO. It can put fear into any lawyer even before opening the envelope. For those among you who have never had the pleasure, count your blessings. As far as I'm concerned the BBO is like the Gestapo. Lawyers have little or no rights whatsoever. When they schedule a disciplinary hearing the only goal is to stick it to the lawyer. The vacancy should be filled by someone who's been around the block once or twice. It should be filled by someone who's been in practice long enough to recognize the pitfalls inherent in the running of a law office. It should be someone with common sense who's not afraid to take strong action, if it's really required. Look over the list carefully. I'll now entertain questions. Are there any?"

Not a peep is heard. "OK then, I'll now take nominations from the floor."

Nick barely stops talking when a loud voice from the other side of the room booms out, "I nominate number three on the list, Bruce Sachar."

All at once several people are shouting "Second."

Decoulas stands again and asks, "Are their any other nominations?"

After about fifteen seconds with no response he speaks again. " If there is to be any discussion on the nomination I will ask Mr. Sachar to vacate the room. Does anyone wish to be heard?"

A couple of seconds later someone says, "I call for the vote."

There are several seconds.

Nick speaks again. "All those in favor of sending Bruce Sachar to the lion's den, please say 'Aye'."

The response is loud and clear...

...A committee of three sits at each hearing. Majority rules; however, a minority opinion may also be submitted. The vast majority of the cases deal with infractions involving the misappropriation of clients' funds. I can't fathom or understand how a lawyer can dip into a Trustee for Clients' Funds Account. That account is sacred. To take from it is stealing. How can a lawyer be so stupid as to take funds from an account which is constantly being monitored by the BBO? Fear of the punishment alone should be a deterrent to any lawyer.

Knowing what I know it would probably be the last thing which could ever happen to me. The thought of doing it is so absurd, that I don't have to make an oath or promise myself, that I would never misappropriate clients' funds...

...Then how and why did I? What set of circumstances could possibly drive me to steal funds belonging to a client, especially since I know that the account is monitored by the BBO and that disbarment will follow?...

CHAPTER TWENTY-TWO

...I spot a couple of fingerprints on the glass covering my desk. In two seconds the desk top is clear. A quick trip to the closet and I return armed with Windex and paper towels. I know from past experience that Windex works on brass, the telephone, the copier, the fax machine and leather blotter. The glass is left spotless. I look around the room looking for another Windex target. Mirrors, pictures, porcelain pieces in the bookcase, clock dials, and the television are done in a jiffy.

It's just about seven on Saturday morning. I'm in a semi-isolated corner apartment on the first floor. I decide that everyone should be up by now and that the noise of the vacuum won't disturb a soul. In minutes the carpeting in the three rooms looks as though it was just installed. I spot a slight scratch on the side of the desk. Old English for dark wood does the job. I hunt for scratches on the tables and bookcases. A daub here and there puts my mind at ease. Hey, what the hell. As long as I'm in the mood I grab a spray bottle of orange Pledge furniture revitalizer. First the desk. Wow, what a gloss! Shit, the rest of the furniture looks absolutely drab in comparison. In no time at all every piece of furniture in the living room and bedroom are absolutely gleaming.

As I'm lighting up and surveying my efforts I conclude that the leather couch and arm chairs look pale next to the polished furniture. Another trip to the closet and I've rearmed myself with Armoral Leather Wipes. I stand back to admire my efforts but am forced to retrieve the damp Pledge rag. I should have polished those wooden legs on the wing chairs before. In less than two minutes they're all done. I'm content...at least until I think I see a bare spot on one of the mahogany-stained closet doors. Naturally, I cover the whole door with my friend, "Agent Orange." When I finish the door I can see that it outshines the rest of the woodwork. There's only one cure for this dilemma. I'm absolutely forced and obliged to do all the closet doors, as well as the matching doors to the bathroom and bedroom.

I'm absolutely obsessed. I feel like I've just swallowed a bottle of amphetamine pills. I sit at the kitchen table to take a breather. The cabinets in the kitchen now seem out of place. The whole apartment is shining except for them. It's an intolerable situation which I can't allow to exist. By the time I finish them the orange bottle is nearly empty. It was worth the effort. I haven't had any strangers visit me yet, but one can never tell. Better to be prepared...just in case...

...I'm back at my desk listening to music and admiring my work. I really have to admit that I did a much better job today than I did on Wednesday!...

...If I had some money I'd leave for Foxwoods right now! What kind of a person are you! You're here because of Foxwoods! Haven't you learned anything? You dumb jerk! Didn't the loss of your house a couple of years ago teach you anything? Obviously not. You continued to gamble. Now look at what it cost you! How in God's name did it happen?...

...Somehow in my haste I must have accidentally polished Aladdin's Lamp. No need for three wishes. I need and use only one. I'm no longer seated behind my desk. I'm sitting behind the steering wheel of my car and making the turn into Foxwoods as I pluck my Hampton Club card from my wallet...

...The car is safely parked in the reserved Hampton Club area; I make a stop at the VIP registration room; I use my Hampton Card and buy a carton of cigarettes; I grab two packs for myself and give Diane and Connie a few packs; I pass out room keys to the other three; the last two digits of the room number are 14; I throw my gym bag and the rest of the cigarettes on top of their luggage; I hand Diane two or three c-notes; we make tentative plans to meet later...

Jesse Owens is no match for me. I leave his records in the dust as I bolt up the moving escalator towards heaven. My strategy and plan of attack for today was well thought-out and planned during the two hour ride from home. As I enter the Pequot Casino I know exactly where I'm going first. I refuse to be sidetracked by the sea of humanity or by all the lights flashing around me. I'm a robot on a mission. I'm a horse wearing blinders to keep my vision focused dead ahead. I'm like a general in the army. I have a predetermined second plan of attack if my main objective is blocked.

All roads lead to slots! I follow the aisle for about two-thirds the length of the room, and all the while hoping and praying that there's an empty seat in the circle of the six "Quick Hit" machines. My favorite machine is the one right in front of me as I approach the circle. I start taking fast extra-long strides towards the machine as I see that a woman is about to leave my seat. She stands up and pushes the button to play her last two remaining credits. *Nada!* I've already got a twenty in one hand and my card in the other as I outrace two others for the seat.

In goes my card followed quickly by the twenty. Ritualistically, I move the ashtray to the shelf on my left and put my cigarettes and lighter on the right. I light up and inhale deeply. It's not often that I can start the day playing one of my favorite slot machines, and in my favorite seat to boot! I totally ignore the scowls from the two guys that I beat for the seat. I nod my head to the familiar faces playing on either side of me. This has all the makings of being my lucky day!

The "Quick Hit" machines are very simple three reelers which afford a wide variety of winning possibilities. The maximun bet is two dollars. The top jackpot prize is five thousand dollars which can be won if three oval-shaped balls containing the word "Quick Hit" appear on the center line. It can also be won if the center line has any combination of 2's, 5's, and 10's. If one happens to catch a triple bar which is worth thirty credits,combined with two tens the payoff is $3,000.00. Likewise, a red seven has a value of fifty, but in the company of two tens the payoff would be $5,000.00.

The best part of the game is a mini-progressive jackpot. The amount goes up every second that the machine is being played. The minimum payout is $1,000.00. All one needs to win the progressive amount is to have three "Quick Hits" appear anywhere on the screen. They do not have to be on the center line. Two of them pay twenty credits. I prefer to hit the progressive jackpot when the payoff is less than $1,200.00, so that Uncle Sam doesn't become my partner. It's not uncommon to see "regulars" stand between two machines and play them both at once.

In the event of a disaster my second objective is right behind me. The multi-reel slots can pay twelve times a normal payoff, or 144 times a normal payoff if two 12's show up in a winning combination. My mind is on these machines even as I play the Quick Hits.

I hit the max bet button for a two dollar bet on the Quick Hit machine. As the reels spin my mind is concentrating and trying to take control of the results. I'm zeroing in on and attempting to visualize three center line hits for 5K. One Quick Hit appears above the center line for two credits. The twenty is gone quickly and the progressive is just over eleven hundred dollars. It's overdue. It's usually hit before it reaches twelve hundred. In goes another twenty which quickly disappears. As I'm reloading the girls are at my side. "Where're you guys headin'?"

Diane answers. "We'll be in the Keno room over there. Any luck?"

"Not yet. Just sat down. Gotta give it a fair shot. We'll meet for supper at seven in the VIP lounge. Don't panic if I'm not there. Eat without me. If this machine and the 12's are both cold I may go to the Cedar's Casino for a while. Catch up with you later somewhere."

"Well where do I find you if I run out of money?"

"I'm not sure. Just told you where I'll probably be."

"In that case gimme another hundred so I won't have to chase you all over the world."

"I can't. I'm playin' on short money as it is. If I make a score I'll find you. I've got a few blank checks just in case. Hope I don't need 'em. Not sure I can even cover 'em. OK, now leave me alone, I gotta concentrate."

Sarcastically, she comes back with, "Yeah, yeah, yeah. I know. I'm a jinx!"

A good-natured response follows. "Now that we fully understand each other I'll see you later. Bye!"

I'm catching a lot of double Quick Hits. It's usually a good sign that I'll soon get a triple for the progressive. Bells and lights go on next to me.

I get up and take a fast look at the three Quick Hits. Payoff is a thousand something. I tell the player: "Good job! Hit it again! Beat the bastards!"

"Gonna try like hell. Good luck to you!"

"Thanks. Need all I can get!"

That hit is another good sign. Other machines in the circle are sure to follow. I catch a hit for $100.00. Good sign. Only a matter of time. Another machine in the circle hits. I'm chain smoking and just waiting my turn to cash in. Soon the hundred is down to twenty bucks. Now it's gone. What to do? Maybe the machine is just waitin' for a fresh twenty.

In it goes and the second play gives me another $100.00. I'm short of cash and breathe a sigh of relief. At least I've now got some playin' money. The progressive is approaching $1,200.00. The hundred is gone and I've gotta make a decision. I'm debating. Just my luck if I leave, 'cause some sonovabitch is gonna put in a sawbuck and make a score. I turn around and see that the corner 12 machine is open. I leave reluctantly and wishing I had a larger starting bankroll.

The twelve machine has nine possibilities of winning horizontally, vertically, and diagonally. The machine can be adjusted to play for nickels, dimes or quarters. Gotta play 180 coins at one time to hit big jackpot. The payoff is $144,000.00 for quarters and 144,000 coins for nickels or dimes. One twelve in a winning combo pays twelve times the win. Likewise, two twelves multiplies the win by 144. I've noticed that the majority of people who play these two machines play all nine lines betting two nickels for a total of ninety cents. The quarter players usually play two quarters for $2.25. There are very few dollar players. Rare is the player who plays 180 coins in any denomination.

Oftentimes, I may be losing my shirt when playing a slot machine for a certain denomination. A sudden switch from quarters to dollars can suddenly turn a losing machine into a big winner. I'm thinkin' of the big hits which I've made on this machine. Most involve the IRS because they exceed $1,200.00. With ashtray and cigarettes in proper position, I begin. I gotta catch up from the bad beginning. I put a Franklin into the machine. I start conservatively playing nickels. A few plays at fort-five cents produces nothing. I graduate to ninety cents and still nothing. Now debating whether or not to play quarters. Opt to stay with nickels for a while.

I curse out loud as I hear music coming from my right. A woman who just sat down at the machine I vacated caught three Quick Hits for just under twelve hundred dollars. Sachar, what kind of a schmuck are you? You stupid shit! You knew it was only a matter of time. All the signs were there. I'm furious when the purple jackets arrive to give her the winnings. It shoulda been me!

Piss on it! Worse comes to worse, I'll cash a check and worry about covering it later. I expect a retainer in a new criminal matter on Monday morning. Only been here about an hour. How the hell am I gonna last 'til tomorrow? Still fuming over what could have been I decide to play the max in nickels. Five cents times 180 or $9.00. What the hell I've bet a lot more in the high roller rooms. My hundred dollar investment dwindles quickly at nine bucks a pop. And then I catch two twelves with something else. The loud music plays as people gather around. "What'd you win?" I point to the bottom left of the screen and look at the tiny numbers. I turn to crowd and quite calmly announce: "$6, 237.50."

As I hand over my license I tell the purple jackets not to take out taxes. It seems like an eternity before I'm paid my winnings. Meanwhile, I just sit there waiting and wanting to play something, anything at all, but I'm stuck here and forced to wait for them. The machine is cooling off and time's being wasted. The machine on my left becomes open. I slip in my card and three twenties. I try the same $9.00 bet. The money is gone and I'm still waiting for my payoff. Finally it comes. I give the attendant a huge tip and he thanks me profusely.

"That's quite alright. Come again soon, please!"

"My pleasure! Please hit the machine again in my presence."

I hit the repeat button as I speak to the machine. "Ok you sucker hit it again back to back!"

He leaves after my first attempt and failure.

OK, Sachar. It proves, what I've said before and have always believed. You always have to play the max allowed in any game on any slot machine. With that thought firmly entrenched in my mind I change the denomination in the machine to dimes. I hit the button for 180 coins.

YOU BE THE JUDGE

The total bet is $18.00. So what? Means nothing! I'm playin' with their money! I know that this is my lucky night!

The dimes become quarters. In a heart-beat I give back well over a grand. I get up and head for the Keno room. I find my associates in crime and tell Diane what happened, including the woman who took my seat and made a hit. After a little scream and a kiss on the cheek I hand her a grand. "Is this all? Where's the rest of my share?"

"I'm here to gamble too. Maybe I can double or triple it. I'm our only hope. I'm luckier than all of you put together. If you run out I'll probably be at Cedar's. Meanwhile, I'm gonna try my luck at that open Keno machine. It's almost seven. You guys wanna eat? I'm not hungry."

I watch as Diane switches from quarters to dollars. "Not hungry right now. Maybe later."

"OK."

I sit down at the open Keno machine and play for dollars. I make a few hits to keep playing but nothing significant. The two machines that I'd prefer to play are both taken by people who never leave. I drop a couple of hundred and take off without a word to anyone. I know they'll find me if needed.

I leave the Keno room and take a left towards the corridor leading to Cedar's. As I pass the circle of Quick Hits there's an open chair. I'm in it without hesitation. The progressive is over seventeen hundred dollars. Gotta get hit soon. It's rarely that high. Another ace from my pocket finds its way into the machine. Jesus, is this sonovabitch cold! I recognize the woman playing on my left. "How're you doin'? Any luck here at all?"

"Yeah, I got luck. It's all bad, Bruce. How about you? That machine doin' anything?"

"I've got news for ya. This machine will give you ice in the winter! Oh well, I'm just a glutton for punishment. Good luck."

"Thanks. Same to you."

I'm compelled to play. I feel like I'm in an hypnotic state. I stare at the progressive payoff at the top of the machine which is increasing every second. It's gotta hit soon. If I leave now someone will just sit down and get an immediate hit. It always happens. But not this time. I'm not gonna give up hope and just walk away.

Every once in a while I get a little hit which gives me some playin' money. How can I walk away now? I can't afford to. Got five hundred dollars already invested in this sucker. One hit gets me even and a profit to boot. I'm having the same thoughts $300.00 later. All I need is three little Quick Hits and I get my $800.00 investment back plus a profit of a grand.

The progressive is now over $1,800.00. Nobody's looking this way. I vow that it's the last hundred from me. I bend down low to count my money. How come there's only $3,500.00 left. Oh, yeah. I forgot about what I had given Diane. Why wasn't someone sitting here when I was on my way to the other casino? I know what I said before but this is definitely the last hundred that this machine gets outa me. I just can't get myself to walk away. This damn machine is still the best chance for me to get my money back. My bankroll dwindles to $3,000.00. I finally remove my card and continue on my journey to Cedar's.

The order of which games I intend to play in this room has already been preordained. There's no point in deviating from the ritual. It's been lucky before and I see no sound reason to change now. *Ergo*, I walk down the aisle to the left of center and stop about a third of the way into the room. There's a row of six machines on my left. The one at the aisle at the far left and the two closest to my aisle are dollar machines which feature all sorts of poker games. I'm only interested in Joker Poker. The maximum bet is $5.00. The luckiest machine for me in the past has been the second one in from the aisle. It's vacant. I sit down and put in an ace. I now have $2,900.00 left from the earlier big hit. This machine pays a bundle for a royal straight flush and $14,000.00 for five of a kind.

The best hand I ever got on these machines is four of a kind for $600.00. When I catch a hot machine it's not uncommon to get several of these hands within a short period of time. By the second hundred a moron can tell that the machine is ice cold. An investment in the machine to my right on the aisle and the machine at the aisle on the far left both prove to be of no avail. Time for the next order of battle...

...Every casino has the next type of machine in quarters, halves, dollars, and five dollar denominations. It's a very simple three reel machine which requires a maximum bet of three coins. Amidst the usual bars and numbers there are 2's, 5's and 10's, which appear as round balls with painted circles around the numbers. A two and a five in a winning combination, multiplies the payoff by ten. Two tens multiply a win by a hundred. Three twos pays $1,000.00 and three fives pays $2,500.00. Three tens earns the big jackpot.

This room has only three of these machines. They're located in different rows and areas although two of them are in the same aisle opposite each other. The hottest one is located across the aisle from the joker machines which I am now leaving...

...*I've been inserting hundred dollar bills everywhere as though they're dollar bills. Money has no meaning or value. It's only a tool to be used to reach an end result. It never enters my mind to take the 6K and go right home. I could have got even with the office rent and still have something left over for other past due bills including my home mortgage with the BCU. I'm convinced that the illness is not so much the winning, as it is the playing in anticipation of a big win. But no matter what it really is I just can't stop. I forego trips to the rest room, eating at regular hours, and sleep in order to get the maximum play at the slots. I'm no different than a junkie hooked on dope. I'm in need of a continuous fix. My needle in the arm is whatever it takes to keep me at the slots. Nothing can stand in my way...*

...The 2, 5, 10 machine that I want is taken. The one at the opposite aisle is just opening. I sit and arrange the ashtray and cigarettes. I look at the bottom left and learn that the previous player cashed out $120.00. Good sign. Maybe something hot left for me. Another hundred given back to the house. At three dollars a pop it doesn't last long. A couple more Benjamins make the journey from my pockets to the slots. I keep looking behind me and to the left for the other machine to open up. When it becomes available I can't cash out and get there fast enough.

What difference does it make that the other player probably left because the machine gave him nothing. I'm a new player with fresh money. All the other guy did was to prep the machine for me. Another wasted half hour before I head for the last machine of this type. I catch a fast $250.00. No way do I take it and run! The big hit is just around the corner! A half hour later I cup my hands to count my money. I can't believe it. I've only got $1,100.00 left.

I head back to the Joker Poker machines looking for a fast $600.00. Instead it cost me $200.00. OK. I head for the high roller room. Against the wall as one enters are about eight Quick Hit machines. They're all taken. I wait impatiently for someone to leave. I keep checking everyone's credits. I stand behind the machine with the least credits showing and hope the player doesn't put in another twenty when it reaches zero.

I finally grab a seat, make the usual adjustments, put in a hundred, light up, and take a big drag. I've already gone through one pack of butts.

I keep putting in c-notes as a couple of other machines hit the progressive jackpots. My turn is surely coming. It's definitely gonna be on the next spin. Eventually, I get a series of small hits which allow me play without adding money. I can't believe how the slot gods are treating me. Not much money left. Time to visit my old standby the Keno machines. I leave reluctantly because I know that whoever sits here is gonna win.

I exit the high roller room and enter the casino. I take a sharp left towards the rows and rows of slots. No matter how they're labeled they all have a couple of Keno game choices. I find a machine to my liking, light up again, and put in another hundred. I play a few dollar games. Maximum bet is $8.00. Absolutely *nada*. Can't last at this rate and I cut bet to $4.00. An occasional hit gives me nothing but a little more playing time. I change machines several times. A peek at what's left in my pocket and I start playing eight quarters. My last twenty is a total bust. I'm absolutely wiped out clean. It's only 9:30. What am I gonna do between now and tomorrow? I'm certainly not gonna go to the room and sleep.

I reach into another pocket where I have several blank checks from my personal account. I know I've got a $6,000.00 a day line of credit. All I gotta do is write out a check and give it to a cashier in exchange for cash. Only one problem. My account has less than $100.00 in it. OK, Sachar, think! You've been in this predicament before and everything has always worked out...

...Lemme think. I'm waiting for a settlement check in a tort case. Check shoulda been here a few days ago. Got a healthy fee comin'. Was gonna use it for back rent and other pressing bills. It's illegal. If I get caught I'm done. I'm sittin' on some clients' funds in my Trustee Account which are not yet scheduled for distribution. I can borrow from the Trustee Account to cover any checks that I cash tonight. When the tort money comes in I'll put the money back in the Trustee Account. Nobody has to know. It's foolproof. Besides, I could just get lucky again and use my winnings to cover the checks. This is a weekend so I'll have a few day spread before the checks from here reach my bank...

...."Here's my license, Hampton Card, and check in the amount of $1,000.00. I'll take the cash in large bills please." I oughta go back to the 12's and give 'em another shot. After all that's where I made the big hit. If I did it once I can certainly do it again. How come I have such stamina and will-power in the casino? I can play all through the night and I'm rarely hungry. Just think, if I lived here I'd be as skinny as a rail...

CHAPTER TWENTY-THREE

...It seems like it was only yesterday...It's a Thursday afternoon in the late winter of 1988 when Melinda buzzes me on the intercom. "Bruce, there's a Joe Furnari on the phone for you. Line One." She hangs up before I can answer her. Line One is flashing red. I didn't know it then but it was a call which was destined to breathe a breath of fresh air into the courts in Essex County and especially in Lynn. It was a call which was to change the way that civil cases would be treated in the future. It was a call which would restore the faith of lawyers and litigants alike in the judicial system.

Before I answer the call I buzz Melinda. "Did he say 'Joe' or 'Judge' Furnari?"

"Definitely 'Joe.'"

"OK. Thanks." I hang up.

I quickly mull over the fact that the only person I know by the name of "Furnari" is Judge Joseph Furnari who's the First Justice of the Ipswich District Court. Why in the world would he be calling me? How do I answer this call without putting my foot in my mouth?

I push the flashing button and speak. "Hello. This is Bruce Sachar."

"Bruce, this is Joe Furnari. How're you doing?"

I immediately recognize the slow and deliberate words being spoken with a slight nasal twang. It's Judge Furnari. I instantly picture the tall husky frame with the short black and somewhat curly hair with only a hint of gray. I visualize his almost ever-present smile. I also remember that he likes to hear a good joke.

"Fine Judge. Just fine. To what do I owe the honor of this call? What'd I do wrong now?"

"Oh. No, no, no. *Au contraire*, you haven't done anything wrong. Judge Joe Dever suggested I give you a call. You probably haven't got the word yet, but I've just been appointed the Chief Regional District Court Judge for Southern Essex. I've got a lot of ideas for programs which I would like to implement in the civil area. My boss, the Chief District Court Administrative Judge for the Commonwealth, has pretty much given me *carte blanche* authority to try out some of my theories."

"That's great Judge. Congratulations."

"To be honest with you I can't do it alone. I need some help from the local lawyers because my first project will be in the Lynn Court. I can't go to the Lynn Bar Association because it's non-existent. It's virtually defunct and has been for several years. Sachar, I've known you ever since I became a Judge. I can even remember George Cole introducing us when I was initially assigned to the Lynn Court for training."

"Oh, yeah! I remember that day too! I was putting on George's carpet when you walked in with your robe folded neatly in your hands. You never commented about the golf club in my hands. All you wanted to know was if you could have a cup of coffee from the pot brewing behind George's desk."

"You've got a good memory, Sachar, and so do I. I can remember one particular case which you tried in Ipswich involving a nefarious character charged with illegal possession of a firearm, which at that time called for a mandatory one year commitment. Remember that case?"

"Will never forget it, Judge."

"Did I take care of you then, or what?"

"You sure did. Never thought I'd be leaving the courthouse with my client. The night before I told him not to forget his tooth brush!"

"Well, the truth of the matter is that your cross-exam of the two cops left me with some reasonable doubt. It made your Motion to Suppress right on point."

We both laugh and he finally says, "This is not something that we can do on the phone. Are you willing to help me out?"

Sarcastically, and with a thick Yiddish brogue I answer him. "To a Furnari I can say just as qvick az a vink, dat dere's no vay! But who can say 'no' to a Dever?"

After laughing a little he replies. "Cana you meeta me tomorrow ina da Thirda Session Lobby ata ten o'clocka?"

"I have a small matter in the Salem District Court but I shouldn't be too long. If worse comes to worse I'll only be a few minutes late. That OK with you?"

"Great! See you tomorrow, Sachar."...

...Sometimes I have difficulty remembering yesterday, but the distant past is often as clear as a new digital television set...Motions are heard every Friday morning at nine o'clock in the Lynn District Court and the trial list is called at ten. It's been this way from time immemorial. It was no shock when Judge Furnari asked me yesterday to see him today at ten. He knew what I, and every other local lawyer knew. At ten sharp a Clerk would call the trial list and, go through the ritual of seeing how many and which cases were ready for trial. Shortly thereafter an announcement would be made that there are no judges available and that we should obtain new trial dates. We both knew he'd be available to see me at ten in his lobby...

...I step out of the elevator on the second floor a little before ten and take a left in the direction of the Third Session. I open the door to a full house. Lawyers and clients are everywhere. SRO is the usual scenario on a Friday at ten. The lawyers with cases ready for trial are praying that there are enough judges to hold a civil trial.

I'm inside the room and standing near the door in the rear when Court Officer Marty Cloonan approaches. He's short in stature, has a thin waist line, and a full head of straight black hair parted on one side. He's in his forties and the shape of his nose is a dead giveaway that he's Irish. I surmise that he's about to go into the hallway and announce that the trial list is about to be called.

"Hi Bruce. You ready for trial?" He's laughing as he asks the question. Before I can respond he gives me a playful tap on the shoulder. He's still laughing when he adds. "Fat chance!"

"To be honest with you I stopped marking cases up for trial. It always ends up being a colossal waste of time and energy. Actually I've got an appointment with Judge Furnari. Any chance you could peek in his chambers and see if he's ready to see me?"

"Yeah, no problem, just let me make an announcement in the hallway first. Be right with you. Hang loose right about where you are."

"OK, thanks."

Assistant Clerk Billy Casey has already started calling the "make-believe" and purely fictitious trial list, when Marty exits the Judge's lobby at the front right of the courtroom. He gives me a thumb's up and points to the Judge's door. A couple of seconds later I'm facing the Judge who's sitting behind a desk a few feet from the door. He stands up to shake hands and with absolute sincerity says. "So glad you could make it, Sachar. I really appreciate it and want to thank you personally. Let's sit down over there at the large folding table which I had brought in." With a smile on his face he adds, "Don't panic at the sight of all of those piles of paper. I'll eventually explain what they're all about." He sits on one side of the table and points to a chair for me opposite him.

The Judge appears to be thinking about what he's going to say when there's a knock on the door. He says, "Enter!"

"You sent for me, Judge?"

"Yes, Ms. Burke. Please have a seat. I assume that you know Mr. Sachar."

The tall thin figure adjusts her glasses and moves closer to me. She bends down and squints at me. Our noses are almost touching when she speaks. It's obvious that she's joking. She can hardly contain herself as she says, "What'd you say his name is?"

Barbara Burke is an Assistant Clerk in charge of civil cases. It's a very difficult and challenging task. She has many masters to serve but her pleasant personality, tact, and brainpower, make her the best choice for her job.

Before Judge Furnari says a word I interject with, "Hi 'BB'. How's it goin'?"

She's now standing tall again and addresses the Judge. "Your Honor, I apologize for my actions. Just couldn't resist the temptation. Actually, I've know Bruce ever since I first started working here as an assistant in small claims."

"Delighted. We're gonna be working closely together for quite some time to come. Your boss, Charlie Flynn, says it's ok. That alright with you?"

"Yes, Judge."

"Mind if I call you, 'BB'?"

"Not at all, please do!"

"It's difficult to know where to begin. I have so many thoughts running through my head. I want you to know that I've also had some sleepless nights. The problem in this Court as I see it is two-fold. The first is the inability to get a case tried. The second is the backlog of open unresolved cases. What's your best recollection BB? Where are you regarding backlog?"

"Judge, there are a few cases that are still open and unresolved which go back a full decade to 1978. After that there are a few stragglers still open in almost every year. But I think it fair to say that the bulk of open pending cases starts around five or six years ago in 1982 and 1983."

"What's your best guess volume-wise? How many cases are we really talking about from that 1978 case to the present?"

"I can easily give you an exact figure Judge if you let me check my records downstairs. It'll only take a few minutes"

"No need for that right now. How about ball-parking it? Are we talking about hundreds or what.?"

"I hate to be a 'party-pooper' but we're talking in the thousands. Don't forget this is one of the busiest District Courts in the entire Commonwealth. Thousands of civil cases are filed here annually."

"I can address the second problem regarding the inability to get a case tried. As you both know I was just recently appointed and given the title of 'RAJ'. In English it means that I am now the District Court Chief Regional Administrative Judge for Southern Essex. My boss is just simply tired of receiving complaints from lawyers and litigants alike about the inability to get a trial in this Court. He's tired of reading newspaper editorials directed at his office and innuendos regarding his incompetence. He's tired of answering BBO inquiries when clients complain that their lawyers probably settled their cases and absconded with the funds.

As a result of all this I have been given a directive. It's a direct order from my boss to clean up the mess no matter what it takes. With your help I intend to do just that. In all fairness I'm the first to point out and acknowledge that there are certain mitigating factors in play here. The fault doesn't lie with the able and competent Judges and Clerks assigned to this Court. As I see it there are at least three major problems which must be addressed.

The first problem is the constitutionally-mandated directive from the United States Supreme Court stating that criminal cases are to be given priority. They get top billing. They get preferential treatment in all the Courts of the Commonwealth, and I might add, in the entire country. Too many serious criminal cases have been dismissed because of the failure to afford a speedy trial to a defendant.

The second and third problems are closely related to each other. My boss and my able predecessors have been stymied. They've been effectively check-mated. There are just not enough Judges to go around. Usually the only Judges who appear here on any given day are the two Judges who are already assigned to this Court. Sheer volume requires that they must both sit on criminal cases irrespective of their personal feelings.

At first blush it might seem that my boss is at fault for not sending in more Judges to this very busy Court. The reality of the situation is that there simply are not enough Judges to go around. There are presently a host of District Court judgeship vacancies. If these positions were filled then some headway might be achieved. The Executive Branch of our government just turns a deaf ear to our requests. The Governor's Office is just sitting on its ass and for whatever reason will just not fill the open spots.

As you know, I'm the presiding Justice in the Ipswich District Court. Quite frankly we just don't have the volume of cases which the other local District Courts have. I have already implemented and taken it upon myself to change the opening of the Court from nine o'clock to eight-thirty. Beginning next month I am personally assigning myself to this Court every Friday to hear Motions at nine and to sit on civil trials at ten. And since it's my office which assigns Judges in my District to a particular

Court, I have likewise designated Judge Bob Cornetta to sit here on civil trials. No matter where I might be obliged to assign myself on a given day I will hear trials from this Court in the afternoons. Any comments or suggestions?"

The ever affable and pleasant BB comments as I would have expected. " Your Honor, my office will do everything in its power to help the cause. Quite frankly it's about time that something be done."

"Thanks, BB. Well, Sachar, what've you got to say for yourself?"

"I agree with BB Judge. I also think that we should meet again in a couple of days. I wanna give some thought to addressing the backlog situation. There are a couple of statutes and maybe even a particular obscure Rule of Court that I want to research. With your permission I would like to invite Attorney Anne Carrigan to our next session."

"I have no problem with your suggestion. I know Anne. She's a fine and capable attorney; If you think that she can help the team by all means bring her along. When is it convenient for our next meeting? I don't wanna drag this out."

"Well BB is available any time. How about this coming Wednesday at ten?"

"Kinda tight. Don't forget I've still got Court in Ipswich in the morning."

In an attempt to lighten up the session I answer with a false air of seriousness. "Aw c'mon, Judge, let's face facts. By your own directive that poor imitation of a Court in Ipswich now opens at eight-thirty. I would estimate that you oughta be done by eight thity-five at the latest. That'll give you plenty of time to get here by ten. You can even stop somewhere along the way for a full course breakfast and still be early!"

They both laugh a little but it's Furnari who answers. He now emulates my tone of voice and shakes his head from side to side as he speaks. "Sachar, have you no respect for this robe? You are undoubtedly the most irreverent s.o.b. that I have ever had the displeasure of meeting!"

"Thanks for the compliment, You Honor!"

As he stands to shake our hands, he merely says, "See you on Wednesday at ten."...

...The tone of the meeting is set by my playful sarcasm. "I brought some coffee, Judge. Knowing how busy you probably were in Ipswich I didn't think you'd have the time to stop."

"Thank you for the sentiment and the thought. Actually, I consider the source from whence it comes and feel obliged to just humor you at this hour of the day."

"As always, Your Honor, I'm honored by the obvious confidence placed upon me by a member of our esteemed judiciary!"

"Ok. Enough of these pleasantries. Let's get down to business. Good morning Ladies. As for you, Sachar, the word 'gentleman' just sticks in my craw. Can't seem to get it out. But good morning anyway. Have you briefed Anne on our lofty aspirations?"

"Yes Judge. We have some suggestions as to how we should proceed initially regarding the backlog issue. Several statutes and Rules come into play here. Lemme throw out a couple for starters. There's a provision in our laws which gives a Judge and/or a Court the power to dismiss any case in which there has been no significant activity over an extended period of time. No time is given with exactitude. It's purely a matter of discretion.

Equally important for our purposes is District Court Rule 4(j). That's the Rule which gives a Court the right to dismiss any case in which the Summons is not returned to Court within ninety days of entering the case."

"I'm familiar with them both. What do you propose?"

"Anne and I feel that we should emulate the Superior Court practice of having a 'cattle call'. We set up a series of dates giving about a month's advance notice to both counsel involved in a particular case. The notice from the Court should contain a list of at least thirty to fifty of the chronologically oldest open civil cases. The notice should advise that the following cases will be called on such and such a date at nine o'clock in the Third Session. It should also state that the cases on the list will be Dismissed either for inactivity or due to the failure to return a Summons within ninety days following entry of the case. A further caveat should appear advising that failure of counsel to appear will result in an automatic Dismissal. Lastly, there should be the usual proviso that counsel must appear on that date and be prepared to address the Court if they oppose a Dismissal.

Simultaneously with that list of cases a separate list should appear on a different notice. As long as each backlog case must be looked at individually to ascertain if Dismissal is appropriate, there are bound to be many cases in which service has been made and in which the Summons has been returned to Court in a timely fashion, but no answer has been filed by the Defendant. In those cases the notice will advise that dates will be assigned for an Assessment of Damages hearing. Likewise, the failure to appear, will result in Dismissal.

The results of these 'hit lists' will dictate the procedure which we should probably follow with respect to getting rid of the remaining live cases. That procedure will obviously depend upon the number of live cases remaining after the 'cattle calls'."

Judge Furnari is obviously intrigued with the proposal. "Just how often do you propose to schedule a list call?"

" We would like to have a weekly call of the lists until further notice."

"What do you propose with respect to those who appear and object to Dismissal.?"

"We give 'em ten days to mark up a Motion objecting to the Dismissal, which then has to be heard before you some Friday at nine."

Enthusiastically Furnari declares. "I like it! I like it!"

BB is immediately on her feet. She's visibly upset. "Now just hold on a minute here!

Aren't you guys forgettin' somethin'? I'm only one person. I don't have any staff. How in hell am I supposed to do my regular duties, have the time to go through every backlog file, inspect it, determine what has to be done, create lists, do mailings, keep track of results, and enter everything in the master docket entry book? Hey, gimme a break!"

I interject, "Judge, can we take a ten minute break? I'd like to talk with Anne alone for a bit?"

"Sure, no problem."...

...Anne is the first to speak. She addresses BB. "What if Bruce and I can chip in and give you a hand? What if we help pull the old files and determine what has to be done. We'll also be responsible for creating the precise language that we want in the notices, subject of course to Judge Furnari's approval. Would that ease your burden and help to make it a viable plan?"

"If you guys are willing to donate the time from your busy schedules we can give it a go. Only one other problem. We don't even have enough postage budgeted by the State to do our monthly obligatory mailings"...

...The silence is ominous as Furnari, Anne and I stare at each other in disbelief. Furnari is the first to speak. "I'll talk to my boss and see if he can arrange for a special dispensation for us for postage. In the meantime I suggest that we forge ahead with all that has to be done short of mailing."

I catch Anne's eye and she nods in agreement to my unspoken question. "Your Honor, Anne's office and mine will temporarily foot the postage bills. Chalk it up as an addition to our 'pro bono' contributions."

"All I can say, Sachar, is that Dever was right when he touted you. I'll still see how fast I can get some additional postage. There oughta be some attached to my new job. How about another meeting in about a month to check on progress? I have to check my calendar."

"Done. Just leave me a message as to date and time and I'll notify Anne."...

...*I don't have a clue, a hint, or the slightest inkling as to the ramifications of these seemingly innocuous meetings. I'm totally unaware of their true significance. The law has been good to me and I feel obliged to reciprocate...little did I know...*

CHAPTER TWENTY-FOUR

...My watch has me about five minutes early. "How long have you guys been waitin' in the hall? You all look frozen to death!"

Boots answers for the three of them. "Not long. Only about five minutes. A resident from upstairs let us unto the hall."

As I insert the key into the lock I make an obviously stupid statement in an attempt to lighten up the meeting. "Well this is one helluva way to spend Christmas night. Was Santa good to you earlier?" *I want to take back the words even before they're all out of my mouth. How can I be such an ass? I'm waitin' for a response to put me in my place. I hope it's harsh. I deserve it.*

Quite calmly and without any apparent emotion Jim Said," No Christmas at our place today. Too morbid. Santa must have sensed it. The atmosphere was too thick."

"I think we'll all be more comfortable in the library on the right. Go in and make yourselves comfortable. Rest rooms are downstairs. Gonna grab a yellow pad and put a pot of coffee on downstairs. Be with you in a jiffy."

I join the Monico family in about five minutes and begin. "How're you feelin'? Any better than last night? What'd they do for you at the hospital?"

"Yeah, I feel a lot better than yesterday but am still a bit spaced out. My memory seems to be all shot to hell. My father keeps tellin' me about all the different versions which I told the police. They cleaned me up at the hospital, put a couple of stitches in my head, and took a bunch of x-rays. They also gave me some medication for pain. I suppose you wanna hear what I can remember about yesterday?"

"Yeah, I wanna hear from you at length but I have my own style in this type of case. Before I hear anything from you I'd like to tell you a little bit about the law and how it applies to this case."

"OK. You're the boss. Shoot!"

" I'm gonna give you a broad brush lecture without all of the possibilities or ramifications. There are many exceptions to what I'm about to tell you, but basically you should be aware that a conviction for Murder One carries a life sentence with no possibility of parole or early release. A Conviction for Murder Two also carries a life sentence, but allows for the possibility of a possible parole after first serving twenty years. A conviction of Manslaughter can mean a sentence which has a range of from a continuation without a finding, calling for no served time and all the way up to twenty years in the can.

Murder One really means that you killed someone with malice aforethought. It's a premeditated crime. The premeditation need only be a few seconds. There are really no extenuating circumstances. On the other hand, Murder Two lacks the malice aforethought ingredient. Manslaughter has many forms. It can be a crime committed in the heat of passion. The classic example is if you happen to walk into the bedroom and catch your wife in the act. Your blood boils and you blast away. Manslaughter can also occur if you originally start acting in self-defense, but use such force as is unreasonable under the circumstances. In other words the force used is excessive. Can't use a gun if a fist will suffice. Can't use excessive force to defend yourself if there is an avenue for you to retreat.

There is also a defense based upon the theory of temporary insanity. In other words, what you see has so roused your passions that you are unable to control your actions. A true insanity defense, however, means that you either didn't know the difference between right and wrong, or that you were unable to conform your conduct due to some mental defect which could have been temporary or permanent."

I give it a little time to sink in. After a lecture on the law it never ceases to amaze me how a client's story usually seems to weave its own defense without any prompting from me. "Jimmy, it's the day before Christmas. I want you to tell me everything from the time you got up until I came to the station."

"I'm a security guard for Wells Fargo and had the day off because of the holiday. Got up around ten and went to meet my buddy. We had made arrangements to go Christmas shopping and then we were goin' to the dump to shoot rats. We finally got to his house for a holiday party and I put my gun in a closet. Then I called my wife and told her to keep the twins up until I got home. I got my gun from the closet and left around eight o'clock. I stopped at the White Eagle Café for a drink. Music was playing and I asked a girl to dance. Some dude said not to bother his girlfriend. He came over and shoved me into the wall. The back of my head hit a metal wall lamp and broke the globe.

Then it starts to get hazy. I left, and am told that two guys follow me out to the sidewalk. They both come after me using karate kicks and chops. I tell 'em to go away and back off. They keep comin' so I warn 'em that I'll shoot. They still keep comin' and I fire a bunch of warning shots into the sidewalk. I get kicked in the face and can taste the blood. The cops come and I give 'em the gun. Then they take me downtown for statements. My father said you showed up but I don't remember you being there. The cops told me that I killed two guys. That's about it."

"After you guys left the station I got copies of some of the police reports. Interesting stuff in these reports. They indicate that some guy in the bar knocked a knife with a six or seven inch blade out of your hands and put it in his belt. There's an inspection of the wall lamp and besides the broken globe the metal frame is bent. Some witnesses claim that you were told to leave. You're seen on the sidewalk as the two guys approach you. You tell 'em to back off or you'll shoot. You fire a warning shot into the sidewalk. They keep coming and hitting you with karate-type kicks. Three more shots are fired and the two guys get killed. A witness claims that before shooting you said, 'Keep away. I've got a gun and I'll shoot!' One of the victims falls to the ground and the other is on top of you wrestling.

The reports written by officers at the scene claim that you said, 'Here's the gun. I shot *him*. Here's the gun!' After being read your Miranda warnings you ask if you killed *him*. At the station you keep referring to one person who kept charging after you. You claim that he reaches for a gun and you have no choice. You name your assailant by name and claim that he has a .32 revolver. The guy you named wasn't there. Later you claim that a black guy was coming after you, and still later it was a member of the Hell's Angels. Witnesses in the bar claim that you had $15.00 in your pocket and was looking for sex at the bar. You also made statements indicating that you were being attacked by baseball bats. None were found at the scene. Then you ask, 'Did I kill *him* or what? I hope the f…I did. I wanted to kill the mother……,and put that in your report!'"

I wait for a few obligatory moments before I ask, "Any comments Jimmy?"

"Yeah. I never had a knife. I still don't remember much after my head hit the lamp."

"Judging from your version of what happened and what the reports claim there is obviously a great disparity. It is quite possible that your recollection as to what really happened was impaired as the result of a possible concussion. I'm no expert but your symptoms seem to imply a concussion, which can cause a temporary or permanent loss of memory."

"Hey, that's right! I fell off an oil delivery truck a couple of years ago and hit my head on the sidewalk. I was totally spaced out. The x-rays showed a fractured skull and I was diagnosed with having had a concussion. Lost my memory. According to others I was talkin' ragtime. Then there was the automobile accident. Same damned thing. Fractured skull in a different spot. Same symptoms. I was kept as an in-patient because I was off the wall."

"Well folks, this history kind of sheds new light on the subject. I want you to see the doctor who treated you before. Know who he is?"

"Yeah. He's my family doctor. Knows me since I was a baby. Told me he's very familiar with concussions since he's the high school football doctor and concussions are rather common."

"Great. Make an appointment to see him asap. Give me his name and address before you leave so that I can contact him. In addition we're going to need a well-qualified expert in the field of neurology who will

YOU BE THE JUDGE

have to testify in Court. See if your doctor can refer you to one. If not, I'll check around and find someone. We can't wait. "

Jim the father finally speaks. "Well pal, whaddaya think? Any hope here?"

" I honestly don't know at this point. It's much too early. But I think I know what the DA should say in his opening statement to the jury. If I were the DA I'd be very short and sweet. I'd probably say something like: 'Ladies and gentlemen of the jury, just ask yourselves, why would a married father of two young twins go into a bar looking for sex after eight o'clock at night on Christmas Eve instead of being at home with his family?'

Then I'd just simply sit down!"

"Yeah, I hear you. What's the next step?"

"Make the medical appointments. Next time we meet I want to interview your son's rat-hunting buddy. Call me in a couple of weeks if I don't get in touch with you first."

I obtain the names of the hospitals where he was previously treated for concussions and have him sign authorizations for me to obtain his medical records.

"C'mon, I'll walk you guys out to the parking lot."

...Great press coverage. High profile case. I'm at the top of my game. It's a bubble which can never burst. Ah, but little did I know! Would that I had a crystal ball or the powers of the Oracle of Delphi. As I now reflect, I wonder if I could have altered the course of history? Does anyone have such power or are we all living a preordained existence? Does man really ever have freedom of choice or are we all living according to some predestined divine plan?...

CHAPTER TWENTY-FIVE

...I've been resisting all attempts and suggestions urging me to go to Gambler's Anonymous. It's early spring and following a successful result for a Hell's Angel in a criminal matter in the Chelsea District Court I confide in my good friend and client.

I tell him that I'm about to be disbarred. I explain all the gory details. He listens carefully without interruption and finally says, "Shit Bruce, I had a similar problem in the past. I can relate to your dilemma. How about letting me be your escort to a GA meeting? You don't have to face anyone you know. There are meetings in Salem, Peabody, and Boston. They're all over the place. You don't have to confine yourself to Lynn."

"Thanks Larry, but I really don't see how GA can help my special situation. Just picture this: I go to GA to learn all about the evils of gambling and what steps I have to take to try and stop. At the same time I'm taking that damned Mirapex which causes me to gamble. I think it's an exercise in futility, but thanks for the offer. I really appreciate your concern."

I use the same rationale to all who suggest that I go to GA. Steph and Matt are persistently insistent. Matt goes on line and tells me where the meetings are. Nevertheless, I ignore any and all suggestions. It was several weeks following Larry's suggestion that I go on line. The closest place is the Union Hospital on Lynnfield Street in Lynn. They meet at 7:00 P.M. on Friday nights. With great trepidation I reluctantly take the plunge...

The hospital receptionist directs me to the ground floor meeting room. I take a deep breath and walk in. It's a large room with four tables forming a square. There are comfortable looking chairs situated on the outside perimeter of the square. There are about fifteen people in the room. I surmise that the officers are seated on the leg of the square at the far end of the room. There's an assortment of literature in front of each chair. I sit down to the pleasurable aroma of fresh coffee brewing. I turn around and spot the coffee maker behind me. I get up and head for the coffee table. As I'm filling a paper cup one of the officers is suddenly at my side.

He offers his hand to me and says, "I'm Bill and I'm a compulsive gambler. Welcome.

What's your name?"

"I'm Bruce."

"It's a pleasure to meet you, Bruce. Why don't you have a seat and get comfortable."

"Thanks. I'll try."

I look around the room and see familiar faces but can't put a name to any. I definitely recognize a woman sitting across the table from me. I've seen her on the Horizon's Edge gambling boat and at Foxwoods Casino. She looks at me and I sense that she also recognizes me. *Is this a good idea or should I have gone to another city where I wouldn't be recognized?*

A treasurer's report and minutes of the last meeting are read. Bill stands up and announces: "My name is Bill, and I'm a recovering compulsive gambler."

In unison everyone responds with, "Hi Bill."

Bill continues. "I'd like to introduce you all to Bruce. This is his first visit with us."

All respond with, "Welcome, Bruce."

Each person chooses and reads from one of the books or pamphlets located in front of each chair. When it's my turn, I'm directed to page 15 of the yellow book and asked to read the twenty questions. When I finish reading each question there's a resounding "yes" from all in attendance. I suddenly find myself also responding in the affirmative to each question.

Did you ever lose time from work or school due to gambling?

Has gambling ever made your home life unhappy?

Did gambling affect your reputation?

Have you ever felt remorse after gambling?

Did you ever gamble to get money with which to pay debts or otherwise solve financial difficulties?

Did gambling cause a decrease in your ambition or efficiency?

After losing did you feel you must return as soon as possible and win back your losses?

After a win did you have a strong urge to return and win more?

Did you often gamble until your last dollar was gone?

Did you ever borrow to finance your gambling?

Have you ever sold anything to finance gambling?

Were you reluctant to use "gambling money" for normal expenditures?

Did gambling make you careless of the welfare of yourself or your family?

Did you ever gamble longer than you had planned?

Have you ever gambled to escape worry or trouble?

Have you ever committed, or considered committing, an illegal act to finance gambling?

Did gambling cause you to have difficulty in sleeping?

Do arguments, disappointments or frustrations create within you an urge to gamble?

Did you ever have an urge to celebrate any good fortune by a few hours of gambling?

Have you ever considered self-destruction or suicide as a result of your gambling?

MOST COMPULSIVE GAMBLERS WILL ANSWER YES TO AT LEAST SEVEN OF THESE QUESTIONS.

Holy smoke! I've got a perfect score and I never studied for the damn test!

Each person volunteers to say a few words about the facts and circumstances which brought him or her to GA. Everyone's dissertation welcomes me and acknowledges the great difficulty which I had in taking the first step into that room. I'm advised that the true test of my sincerity will be evidenced if I come to the next meeting.

Bill announces a short recess. I go into the outside patio to have a cigarette with others. The woman whom I had recognized earlier comes over to me. She shakes my hand and says that we often played the same "Quick Hit" slot machines at Foxwoods. She's also quick to point out that she's been "clean" since last October.

The meeting resumes. The remainder speak of the trials and tribulations of gambling and how it affected each of them. I listen intently to losses of businesses, incarcerations, stealing and embezzlement, tax woes, losses of spouses, maxing out of credit cards, writings of bad checks, losses of homes, losses of reputations, and attempts at suicide. I become painfully aware that I'm not alone. Utterly destroyed is my preconceived notion that I'm unique.

After everyone had spoken Bill turns to me and advises, "Bruce, if you'd like to say a few words now is the time. We recognize that this is your first meeting and that there's no obligation to say anything at this time. I think I came to about six or seven meetings before I gathered up enough courage to speak. Now they just can't shut me up."

"Yes. I feel as though I'm with kindred spirits and I'd like to say a few words with your indulgence." I hold nothing back and make a complete revelation as to what brought me to this meeting at this stage of my life. When I'm through I feel entirely naked. I have bared my soul and innermost thoughts and feelings. It's a complete catharsis. I'm profusely thanked for being so honest and candid at my first attempt. I'm applauded for my efforts but no one is in shock.

It's now a month and four meetings later. I've come to some rather significant conclusions. It's apparently a human frailty which causes each of us to think that he or she is rather unique. Nothing could be further from the truth. Insofar as gambling is concerned, nothing that I have experienced in my life was mine and mine alone. Whatever feelings possessed me were also shared by others in the room. Factual circumstances which fell upon me were shared by others. If there exists any differences among us it is only a question of degree. If I were a scientist I could easily postulate that everyone in this room, as well as every compulsive gambler in the world, has the same DNA.

I have come to learn that the GA credo is analogous to that of AA. One must undertake the cessation of gambling "one day at a time." GA espouses the doctrine that in order to recover one must put the past to rest. Guilt or remorse can come to cripple us. It's analogous to self-pity. GA doctrine mandates that the book must be closed on the life I led, and that the void caused by the lack of gambling must be filled. I'm convinced that my Friday night meetings are the right step in that direction. My visits to the casinos almost always started on a Friday.

The biggest problem I have in GA dogma is its suggested treatment of the "guilt" concept. I can certainly recognize the crippling effect of guilt feelings, but at this stage of my GA career feelings of guilt are still overwhelming. I have done such bad things and have caused grief to so many people, that it's just simply impossible for a few sentences in a book to wipe out the past. The fact that my slate simply cannot be wiped clean by a few well-chosen words may eventually prove to be my undoing. The "guilt" issue is undoubtedly the biggest hurdle to cross in my attempted recovery.

I can perceive a certain contradiction on the "guilt-remorse" issue. There's no question in my mind that these very feelings are the ones which have contributed most significantly to thoughts of self-destruction by GA members. I dare say that it's also these very issues which has driven people to become GA members. How is it now possible to simply say: "forgeddaboutit. Such thoughts will deter your recovery?" Perhaps forgiveness from those who were hurt the most may be a more important factor to those of us who have succumbed to human frailty.

GA literature is also quick to point out that compulsive gambling is neither inherited nor environmentally caused. I'm not entirely convinced with that position. Each of the compulsives sitting around the table were exposed to gambling activities at an early age, and usually from a family member or members. I think that in many cases the settings and the foundations were there to create a later predisposition for gambling.

I haven't a clue as to what the future will hold, since GA teaches that "compulsive gambling is an emotional illness which can only be arrested but never cured..."

CHAPTER TWENTY-SIX

...I really can't pinpoint the exact time that my obsessive-compulsive behavior began. It was a gradual metamorphosis. Perhaps it was most vividly displayed while playing slots. What rhyme or reason always compelled me to place the ashtray to the left of the machine and my cigarettes and lighter on the right? At one time I thought it was because I had once made a good hit with that arrangement. Upon further reflection I've determined that the reason is not that simple. Apparently there's some inner driving force behind my illogical behavior.

My bizarre behavior is certainly not confined to the casino. For several years I have felt obliged to dress in a certain way, and I don't necessarily mean the style or color combinations of my attire. I am referring directly to the order or pattern of getting dressed, irrespective of the articles of clothing which I might be wearing.

Whenever I put on any kind of pants, whether it be part of a tuxedo or underwear, I must put my left leg in first. The pecking order for my daily dressing must be followed without deviation lest something terrible will occur during the day for violating the rules. My left sock is followed by my right, which in turn is followed by my left shoe and then the right. Any attempt, or even a thought of a change in the batting order, is immediately rejected by my inner-self...

...It's about six-thirty on a Saturday morning about four or five years ago. I'm playing golf at Gannon with the Valley Rats, as usual. We're playing the first hole. I hit a nice but rare tee shot in the middle of the fairway. I'm just about level with the end of the sand trap on my left and have about 120 yards to the green. I have a choice of hitting either a wedge or a nine iron. I decide to go with the nine since the pin is at the back of the green and there's a slight wind in my face.

I wait for the others on my team to hit first. While waiting, I remind myself that this is the fifth handicap hole on the course and that I get two strokes. I have a chance to get our team off to a good start. A par will result in a net two and a bogie five will result in a net three. As a lefty I take my stance to the right of the ball. I line up my hips and shoulder parallel to the club face which is lined up with the flag ahead. I take a slow back-swing and mentally tell myself to follow through with the club to the target.

I shank the ball. It hits off the end of my club. The ball lands about 50 yards to my front left on the fifth hole in the heavy grass in the rough. I find the ball and have an opening between some trees, so that all I have to do is punch the ball to the green. I can still make a par. I get over the ball and line up the club face with the pin. I'm concentrating on the space between the trees. I bring back the club and swing towards the ball in an attempt to punch a "bump and run" chip shot. I scuff the shot and the ball moves about a foot. It's now hidden behind a tree. I finally make a triple bogie seven. No one says a word but I'm seething and cursing myself.

I address the ball for my tee shot on the second hole as the team captain says, "OK Bruce, put that first hole behind you. There's plenty more to come." I hit a fairly good drive near a rock on the left side of the fairway about fifty yards from the green. I approach the ball with a wedge and sand wedge in hand. The next shot requires a lob over a sand trap to get to the green and to the pin in the back...

...What the hell happened on that last hole? I still can't get it out of my mind. I realize what went wrong. I sit down on the rock and take off my shoes and socks. I then put on my left sock followed by the right, which is followed by my left shoe and then the right. I knew I had earlier put on both socks first and then my right shoe before the left. They were closest to me in that order as I dressed in the dark at home. It was on my mind when I entered the store for coffee and during the ride to the course.

The captain spots me and asks, "Hey, Saitch, what's the problem?"

"No problemo. I got a stone in my shoe."

As soon as the footwear is put on properly an inward calmness and serenity betakes my being. I'm relaxed physically and mentally for the first time since I dressed for golf at home.

I make par...

...I've come to believe that obsessive-compulsive behavior subjectively comes in many shapes and forms and ultimately preys upon its victims. In 2006 and 2007 my entourage and I are gambling frequently. At a minimum we leave for Foxwoods, Mohegan Sun and/or Twin River every Friday afternoon. Not infrequently we pay visits to two or more of them on the same day. I'm also gambling on line. Slowly but surely I'm maxing out my credit cards, which proves to be to my detriment when I visit an ATM machine at a casino.

When the ATM refuses my requests for cash I start writing checks from my business account. The bottom line is that I must gamble no matter what the cost or the risk. I write checks well-knowing that there are insufficient funds to cover the same. I neglect my home mortgage and nearly all routine office expenses. I'm compelled to rewrite my office lease due to arrearages. In order to keep the Brotherhood Credit Union as a client I authorize it to withhold my legal fees and to apply the same to my mortgage.

We're enjoying the casino enticements and perks which are offered in order to secure my regular attendance. Little did they know, but I would have been there without any of the "free" benefits. Whenever I wrote checks which I couldn't cover, it was in anticipation of money which I expected to be receiving.

There must have then been a convergence of all my negative astrological signs. Checks to honor had been presented to my bank but fees to cover them were delayed due to Court scheduling problems. At the same time, the IRS and the Massachusetts Department of Revenue decided, that the time was ripe for them to force a sale of my house and to recoup at least some of the money which I owed them.

I had a first mortgage with the BCU and a second mortgage for $25,000.00, which secured a loan from my good friend and now deceased Attorney, Charlie Cronis. The BCU mortgage would have first priority upon a forced sale at auction. The IRS and the MDOR, would take the difference. There would be nothing left in this scenario for Cronis, since his mortgage post-dated the various tax liens.

Matthew prevailed upon his mother and stepfather to come to my aid. They certainly did. They stepped up to the plate and hit a home run! My good friend and colleague for nearly half a century was Attorney Loring Paul Fluke. He negotiated a deal with all the lien holders. He pointed out that it would be advantageous to them and all others concerned to allow an arm's length private sale of the property to Matt's stepfather. The BCU would receive every penny due it as the first lien holder by virtue of its mortgage. The IRS and the MDOR compromised their positions and agreed to take less than what was due each of them. They each agreed to discharge their liens so that a sale could take place. Fluke convinced them that something was better than nothing. He told them that if the BCU were to foreclose it would wipe out their liens.

The only detriment to the impending sale was the Cronis mortgage. There were insufficient funds to repay the same with interest, which was insisted upon by Cronis's son. Consequently, my buyer had to come up with an additional sum of money to pay him off. It was his intention to sell the property as soon as possible in order to recover his money. In the event that he was unable so to do, I named him as a beneficiary on some insurance policies.

Just prior to the sale taking place Matt decided to purchase the property from him. In early 2007 the transactions were concluded. Matt owned the house with his bride-to-be and his stepfather was repaid in full. The Cronis loan was paid. I still owed the IRS and the MDOR well over $100,000.00 for unpaid taxes.

While all this was going on Diane and I needed to find suitable quarters to live in. After much disagreement and debate we finally rented a place at the Dearborn Highland complex in Peabody.

The loss of the house was heart-wrenching and a bitter pill to swallow. The bright side of the coin was that I was not disbarred and was still able to practice law. I certainly learned an expensive lesson! It could never happen again! Right? Wrong!!! In less than eighteen months of continued lying and deception It happened all over again. Disbarment and the loss of my wife followed my compulsive gambling, while engaging in the same routine as before in order to feed my habit.

The only people who expressed no surprise regarding my repetitious conduct were my compatriots at GA. Apparently, as I soon learned, taking and spending other people's money, as well as committing crimes, is a common thread running in the veins of compulsive gamblers. In order to feed the habit anything is considered fair game regardless of the consequences.

CHAPTER TWENTY-SEVEN

...I feel proud of myself as I drive on Route 114 West on my way to the Market Basket in Danvers to do some light food shopping. The food isn't any better or cheaper than the stores closer to home, but there's less likelihood that I'll bump into someone I know. I can't believe that I actually have some cash in my pocket for food. How'd this happen? I'm only about six weeks into the GA program.

I stop for gas on the way home at an Exxon/Mobile station. I insert one of the gas cards which I bought with Wampum points at Foxwoods. As I stare at the moving numbers on the pump GA is foremost in my mind.

One of the biggest burdens which I had to carry while gambling was my "unsharable secret." The onus of this heavy burden on my mind and what I was doing in order to continue my gambling certainly changed my persona. I had become a "loner" even though I was never alone. I was devoting much of my time and energy into attempting to maintain my so-called image and in trying to keep it intact. I was not pleasant company for anyone. I had convinced myself that I was the worst person on the face of the earth.

Suddenly the pump stops. I know the tank's not full. It then dawns upon me that the balance of available funds on the card was exhausted. I'm now driving south on Route One and still have gambling on my mind. I'm now aware and admit for the first time that my gambling was done with reckless abandon without regard for the consequences. GA hit the nail on the head again. I had the typical compulsive gambler's grandiose dreams of providing my family with untold riches and luxuries. Why couldn't I figure this out before?

Just what the hell is it with GA? What's goin' on at those meetings? The very first meeting made me painfully aware that I was not unique. My great "unsharable secret" was in fact common to all. To deny its existence would be like trying to make an apple pie without the apples. Are we all psychiatrists for each other?...

"...My name is Charlie and I'm a recovering compulsive gambler."

The rest of those in the room respond in unison. "Hi Charlie!"

Charlie tells of his past and present problems. We all listen even though his tale of woe may be somewhat repetitious. I'm left with Charlie's forthright and somewhat philosophical conclusion, when he says, "We are gathered here tonight to listen and to feel each other's pain."

...Now that's really deep food for thought. Can this be the key which unlocks the secret to the success of GA?...

..."My name is Gloria and I'm a recovering compulsive gambler."

"Hi Gloria!"

There are tears coupled with a broken voice as she describes the destruction of her life brought about by gambling.

"I'm in my sixth month at GA. It's difficult to believe, that I actually have a few bucks left in my check book each week after paying bills. I had grandiose dreams of winning untold fortunes when I was gambling. I tried to protect my image and keep my big secret hidden from those I loved the most.

Membership and attendance at GA meetings has actually worked for me. It's amazing and virtually impossible to believe that GA can accomplish so much. Just think about it folks. We're a fellowship of cheats, liars, and thieves, sitting around a table listening to each other's problems and giving advice and encouragement!"

She speaks with such clarity and an obvious command of English, that I naturally wonder what her background is. I can't help but laugh at her comical description of what is obviously and painfully the truth. Are we allowed to practice this amateur psychology without the benefit of a degree or some kind of formal training?

Sachar, stop thinkin' so much. If it ain't broken, don't fix it!
I put up my hand and the Chair recognizes me to speak.
"My name is Bruce and I'm a compulsive gambler."
The words "Hi Bruce" fill the room.
"Ladies and gentlemen I'll be very brief. I've previously made certain revelations to you about my bizarre conduct and my obsessive-compulsive behavioral patterns. I've also told you about the side effects which Mirapex attributes to itself. I'm trying to discover what role Mirapex actually played in my compulsive behavior. I'm anxious to learn whether or not you people have experienced the same behavioral patterns without the use of Mirapex.

In short, is obsessive-compulsive behavior a common trait among gamblers? I'd really appreciate it, if each of you would comment upon the same when it's your opportunity to speak. It might make interesting reading in the book I'm writing and previously told you about. Thank you."

There are no less than five responses to my question. The race track enthusiast reveals that he never uses the same door to enter or leave the track. Whatever door he uses to enter will not be used to exit.

The indulger in craps shooting claims that he can never win, if any part of his left hand or arm touches the left side of the table.

The slots player says that she must always use the same parking spot in the garage if available, and even though it's in a row which is located farthest from the entry door. The rationale is that she once had a winning night when her car was in that spot.

The sport-betting player uses only a bookie. If he has a win, he will call the bookie on the following day at the exact time and from the same place as the previous day.

One gambler reveals that his compulsive behavior is strangely enough related only to labels. He promptly removes all labels from bottles brought home by his wife following her food shopping. He claims that he also has an uncontrollable urge to advise people, when he becomes aware of a label which sticks out of a shirt at the back of the neck.

...The meeting adjourns. I feel much better about left sock, right sock, left shoe, and lastly my right shoe...

199

...The weekly meetings had moved from the Union Hospital on Lynnfield Street to the Sacred Heart Church on Boston Street. For no rhyme or reason following the meeting I'm deeply in thought. I pay little attention to the quickest route home. I've apparently driven down Market Street and then onto Lynn Shore Drive. I wonder why my car has taken me here as I pass the Port Hole Restaurant. It's certainly not the shortest way home for me. But It surely was in another lifetime.

I make a u-turn around the Nahant-Lynn-Swampscott rotary. Now I'm on Washington Street heading back towards downtown Lynn intending to get a tuna salad at Broad and Silsbee Streets. I notice the sign on the pole as I pass Amity Street. It's a street full of memories for me. It once was the residence of Frankie McCarthy, a co-worker at the chicken store whom I often had to pick up for work. Renowned criminal defense attorney and a former Assistant District Attorney, Joe Casey, lived there with his brother Attorney Billy Casey(later an Assistant Clerk/Magistrate at the Lynn District Court). In earlier days they often came to Singer's Poultry with their mother.

Amity Street also brings to mind that almost twenty-six years ago my client, Bariki Seit, lived there in a two-family house with his wife and three small children. It was in July of 1977 that I argued his appeal from a conviction of Second Degree Murder at the Supreme Judicial Court before a panel consisting of Chief Justice Hennessey and Justices, Quirico, Braucher, Kaplan, and Liacos.

I'm so preoccupied with Seit that it's not until I pass my office, when I realize that I'd forgotten about the tuna salad...

...I vividly remember returning to the office from Court and being handed my mail.

There was a letter from the SJC. I knew it could only pertain to Seit. It might be years later but I'm there again now.

I'm right. I quickly scan the decision and run into the secretarial area and announce loudly, "Seit's conviction set aside. Reduced to Manslaughter. Resentencing to take place."

Machera comes running out of the library screaming, "No shit! Lemme see the decision!"

"You will Joe, but I think that for the benefit of all here concerned, I oughta first paraphrase the results."

"Right on! Shoot!"

"It's a long and well-written opinion by Justice Kaplan. He discusses all the issues raised on our appeal. He begins by reciting the evidence presented by the Commonwealth, which includes Barry's statements to the Lynn police, that he had just killed his partner and wanted to be locked up. The Commonwealth then introduced evidence showing that he escorted an officer to his car and handed over a .380 Remington semi-automatic and a Smith & Wesson .357 magnum revolver. Seit informed the police that he and the deceased had an argument over a missing gun, and that Seit believed that the deceased, Pagoni, had stolen it. Kaplan also recites the fact that Seit wanted to kill himself but couldn't muster up the courage.

Based upon info furnished by Seit the Cambridge Police found Pagoni lying face down with his right cheek to floor in the storage area at the rear of the store. Pictures taken by the State Police indicate that the entire front of the store was in good order and appeared to be undisturbed, despite Seit's later testimony about a violent struggle with the decedent in that very area.

Judge Kaplan describes in detail the results of my running battle with the State pathologist. The opinion refers to the pathologist's original opinion on direct exam in which he concluded, that there was a superficial bullet wound to the forehead with the exit and entry points less that an inch apart. The doctor also testified on direct, that the fatal blow was caused by a bullet entering the back of the neck and severing the carotid artery. The doctor opined that that both shots came from the victim's rear, and that the wound to the neck was the fatal blow.

Kaplan's apparently reluctant to say that the pathologist lied during his direct testimony. He's very polite in his treatment of the doctor. He merely says that during cross-examination the doctor 'retreated' from those opinions. Although he still maintained that the forehead wound was not disabling, he now admitted that the victim could have been facing Seit at that time. He further admitted on cross that the wound to the forehead could have caused the victim to spin around and then receive the fatal shot to the rear of the neck.

The opinion then goes into Seit's lengthy testimony regarding the defendant's long-standing relationship with him. It began in Albania when Seit was about ten and Pagoni about twenty. The opinion at this point recites in detail those factors which may have had some bearing on Seit's state of mind at the time of the shooting, as a result of Pagoni's history of violence. Kaplan, who of course is speaking for the entire Court, recites in detail Seit's testimony, which obviously portrays to the jury a very plausible theory of self-defense.

On the other hand the opinion affirms the trial Judge's rulings regarding the admissibility of evidence, and exactly what a ballistician and a pathologist could say to a jury. The bottom line is that 'the trial judge has broad and wide powers' in making such rulings. You all recall that we claimed in our brief, that if our ballistician was not allowed to testify about the spinning effect of the bullet to the forehead, since he was not a pathologist, then the pathologist should not have been able to testify to the contrary because he was not a ballistician. Well, the Court disagreed, and said that the trial Judge was correct in ruling that the pathologist was better qualified to render an expert opinion on the subject matter.

We all know that every word in the entire written transcript of the trial was read by each of the SJC Judges. Judge Sullivan, who heard the case is now deceased. The opinion is entirely devoid of all of those snide remarks by the trial Judge. It is also silent on my argument regarding the Judge's derogatory voice inflections while addressing the jury on matters pertaining to the defendant.

Finally the Court reasoned that there was enough evidence before the jury to warrant its finding of Murder in the Second Degree, but in reviewing the entire record the Court felt that a verdict of Manslaughter 'would be more consonant with justice'. The Court then adopted our argument and invoked its seldom-used power Under Chapter 278, Section 33E, and remanded the case back to the Middlesex Superior Court for re-sentencing.

OK folks, that's the whole ball game. You're all free to make copies and read the decision itself verbatim instead of relying upon my analysis."

A round of shaking hands and applause follow and someone asks me what happens next.

"The murder conviction afforded him the possibility only of a release on parole after serving a minimum of twenty years. Manslaughter on the other hand carries no such requirement. It's a new ball game. What happens next is absolutely dependent upon the Superior Court Judge, who happens to be sitting in the Middlesex Superior Court on the day when our case is scheduled.

I'll anticipate the next question. There's no way of telling who the Judge will be. Superior Court Judges are rotated from County to County on a monthly basis. In a large County, such as Middlesex, several Judges will move in on any given month, and there will undoubtedly be more than one assigned to criminal business. As a purely practical matter I just hope it's not some former Assistant District Attorney. With our luck it'll probably be some distant cousin of the victim. Lastly, I believe that Pagoni's family members will be invited to appear and make comments regarding sentencing.

Ok. That's enough love-making!

Everyone back to work!"

CHAPTER TWENTY-EIGHT

...It's shortly before noon when I enter the office. I had just completed a real estate transaction at the Registry of Deeds in Salem, and delivered a package of the closing documents to the BCU. Melinda is on the phone and holds up her hand indicating for me to wait before going in to my office. I scan my messages as I wait for her to finish the call. She's laughing and obviously enjoying the conversation. I can't imagine who's on the other end.

Finally, she states matter of factly, "Joe Furnari's on the phone and would like to talk to you."

"Since when do you call the Judge by his first name? I wouldn't have the nerve!"

"Well, he introduces himself as 'Joe' so I only reciprocate. Besides, he's a really funny guy. He's got a great sense of humor and is a real down-to-earth person."

"Accurate analysis. I'll take the call in my office."

"Hi Judge, how're you doin?"

"Fine, Sachar, just fine."

Pretending to be hurt, I ask, "To what do I owe the honor of this call? We were bosom buddies for a while and then silence. What am I chopped liver? Haven't heard from you in nearly three months. How'd you remember my name and number?"

"Thanks to you guys I've really been as busy as hell sitting on all the Motions opposing the dismissal of cases. I've also been hearing civil trials together with Judge Cornetta. I think it's time for a meeting of the committee to see exactly where we are."

" Sounds good Judge. Today is Tuesday. How about a week from today at 8:30 in the morning. It's a regularly scheduled date for Anne and I. All you gotta do is make sure BB is there."

"It's a date. See you all then. I'll bring the coffee this time."

"Holy smoke! Do my ears deceive me? You buyin'? We'll definitely be there!"

"OK wiseass, see you all next week."

In addition to the coffee there's a dozen donuts from Marty's. It's a famous place around the corner from the main drag in Ipswich and near Zabaglione's Italian Restaurant. Diets be damned. We all partake. Judge Furnari is the first to speak on the subject matter at hand.

"Well, it's been about six months since our last meeting and I'd like to have some sort of an analysis or update. I'd like to know if we've accomplished our purpose, and besides, I have to make a progress report to my boss."

The three of us look at each other. Anne Carrigan responds. "Well Judge, as you know we scheduled a call of cases twice a month since our last meeting. Bruce, BB and I went through each an every open pending file in order to determine what action had to be taken. We began with the oldest cases and worked forward by date chronologically. Notices were prepared by us and sent to lawyers or litigants on both sides of every case advising them that their case would be dismissed for various reasons at the call of the list.

It's absolutely amazing that very few lawyers actually appeared to contest dismissal. Apparently, many of the cases had been settled previously but never reported to Court. Others just couldn't find or make service upon a defendant. I'm pleased to report that we have disposed of thousands of cases and that as of this moment, we have a backlog of only active cases. The oldest cases are about five years old.

We're astutely aware that you've been sitting in the Friday Motion Sessions at nine. However, the most important event is that you and Judge Cornetta are both actually hearing civil cases, which have been marked for trial at ten on Fridays. This hasn't happened for years and I'm pleased to report that the local lawyers are absolutely delighted. We're no longer hearing the gripes and whining about the fact that 'justice delayed is justice denied'.

Bruce and I footed the postage bills until the Court was able to step up to the plate. We're not looking for reimbursement. Consider it part of our *pro bono* contribution. We've also discussed what needs to be done next. Bruce will give you that report."

Judge Furnari is absolutely delighted. "Thank you, Anne, for such a comprehensive report and a for a job well done. OK, Sachar, what's next on the agenda for our committee?"

"I think that we should adopt a conciliation plan similar to the one in the Superior Court. I envision a monthly call of the open pending cases beginning with the oldest by docket number. I will put together a team of local trial-seasoned attorneys, who will volunteer their services each month as conciliators in order to try and settle the backlog of cases short of an actual trial.

The monthly list should have between 25 and 40 cases. In order for this program to work there must be certain hard and fast criteria, which must come from you. The list of cases to be called in any given month should be accompanied by a Notice signed by you. The Notice should state, among other things, that failure to appear will result in Dismissal or Default, as the case may be. The Notice should also state that insurance company adjusters must be present, or in the very least, reachable by phone. Failure to negotiate 'in good faith' may be subject to sanctions including fines, Dismissals or Defaults. Lastly, the Notices should advise the parties, that in the event the cases do not settle, a firm trial date will be assigned, and that the assigned trial date will be etched in stone. Only a Motion to be heard by you or Judge Cornetta can change any such date. That's about it in a nut shell, Judge."

"Sachar, I think it's a wonderful plan but I have certain reservations. I'd be delighted to prepare a Notice as suggested, but let's be realistic about this project. Just where in hell are you going to find these skilled lawyers, who'd be willing to devote so much uncompensated time?"

"Judge, with all due respect I think that you misjudge the lawyers in Lynn's trial bar. This program will serve to move cases and expedite

207

settlements. Cases merely sitting and languishing in file cabinets don't do anyone any good. The moving of cases will be a great boon to the public at large. A prompt resolution will put money in the hands of the litigants where it belongs. They in turn will feed the economy. The incentive for the lawyers is that they too will finally have a pay day."

"Sachar, I really hope that your vision is truly prophetic."

"Judge, the biggest aid to settling on a conciliation date is the assignment of an early trial date. The litigants must be under the gun and feel the pressure of a relatively quick trial date. In addition, your notice should clearly and unequivocally state that no case will be tried unless it has first gone to conciliation."

"I approve wholeheartedly and you all have my blessing."

"The best for last, Judge. In anticipation of your support I've already received full or promised support from a cadre of Lynn trial lawyers, who will volunteer to sit as conciliators every month on a *pro bono* basis."

"Who've you got lined up? I'm really curious."

"In addition to Anne and myself, you can add Anne's husband, Jim Carrigan. Also, Billy O'Shea, Charlie Cronis, John McGloin, Joe Sano, Loring Fluke, and Eli Mavros."

"I can't believe it! I'm really impressed! Those lawyers are among the finest trial lawyers in the County, if not the State. I have a feeling that all of you guys are gonna make me look good!"

"I certainly hope so, Judge. I'll send you a draft Notice for you to alter as you deem fit. In the meantime BB will start scheduling dates and preparing cases for the Conciliation Sessions. We'll be in touch as needed if that's all right with you Judge?"

"Perfect. Talk to you all soon."

"If there's no objection I'll take the rest of the donuts!"...

...The program is implemented and proves to be a great success thanks to the tireless devotion and efforts of the conciliators. They often take cases back to their offices to further meet with the parties in an effort to resolve the disputes. In less than a year there's no longer a backlog of cases at the Lynn District Court. It's now probably the most efficient District Court in the Commonwealth insofar as the disposition of civil cases is concerned.

Joseph I. Dever, former Acting Presiding First Justice and later Presiding First Justice of the Lynn District Court, was undoubtedly the one person most responsible for the program's success. He worked closely with us and removed every impediment and obstacle which appeared in reality or on the horizon, and which might have posed a threat to the success of the conciliation program...

...The Lynn Bar association had long been dormant. The once vibrant organization had virtually ceased to exist for almost ten years. In former times we met often at Anthony's Hawthorne Restaurant in downtown Lynn. Colorful speakers often addressed the body. It was a time of great camaraderie among its members.

At coffee following our conciliation sessions it was not uncommon to reminisce of days gone by. It was often suggested that an attempt should be made to restore the Lynn Bar Association to its once proud status in the community.

In 1991 notices were sent out by my office calling for an organizational meeting and election of officers in the Second Session of the Lynn District Court. I was elected President and sworn in by Judge Furnari. The Board of Directors was comprised mostly of the conciliators in addition to John Vasapoli from Saugus, Mary Ann Calnan from Lynnfield, Joe Sano from Lynn, and Frances Weiner from Swampscott.

The original Bylaws required that membership be limited to lawyers who either lived or worked in Lynn, Saugus, Nahant, Lynnfield, Swampscott or Marblehead. We soon changed the name to 'The Greater Lynn Bar Association' and we were off and running.

Educational seminars and lectures were held frequently at the Port Hole Pub in Lynn. Guest speakers were drawn from the plethora of legal talent in the community. Judges throughout Essex County often served as lecturers on a panel. The Annual Meetings resumed at Anthony's General Glover in Marblehead. I had the pleasure of serving two terms. In 1995 I was succeeded by Anne Carrigan, who became the first woman President of a Lynn Bar Association.

Requests came from everywhere seeking my advice in establishing a conciliation program, which could be tailor-made to meet the needs of a specific Court. Soon we established a conciliation program in Lynn for Small Claims. I brought the matter before the Essex County Bar Association Board of Directors and that organization has continued to monitor it.

One day I happened to be in the Essex County Probate Court on an uncontested matter. While waiting to be reached a recess was called. Judge Edward Rockett was on the bench. While waiting for Court to resume a Court Officer approached me in the hallway, and advised that Judge Rockett would like to see me in chambers.

His secretary said, "Go right in Mr. Sachar, he's expecting you."

"Thank you."

I open the door and am greeted with, "Hey, good to see you. Come on in and pull up a chair."

"What'd I do wrong now?"

"Nothing. Just felt like reminiscing."

"Well, it's certainly been a long road from the time when we first met. I was a struggling new lawyer and you were a claims adjuster for Liberty Mutual. You've risen from the ranks. From an Assistant Probate Clerk to the First Justice of this Court."

"Bruce, I wish I knew where the years went."

"You know, Judge, I've been meaning to talk to you about the possibility of a conciliation program in this Court. I think it possible that such a program could significantly reduce the trial backlog, and afford the litigants a much earlier trial date."

"Amazing that you should bring up the subject. It's been on my mind a long time. I've been meaning to call you after I heard about the success of the Lynn Program. The thing that bothers me most is that I'm not sure that conciliations can work in this Court. We deal with issues usually far more sensitive than a breach of contract or trying to work out a settlement in a personal injury case. We're talking custody, support, alimony, will contests, visitations, and a host of other issues not particularly suited for conciliation. What do you think?"

"I've got mixed emotions with that analysis. I've been doing domestic work and other cases germane to this Court for over 30 years now. I believe that I've now come to some inescapable conclusions."

He sips his coffee and smiles as he says, "I'd be very interested in hearing those conclusions. Please enlighten me."

"Delighted to have the opportunity, Your Honor. As I see it, the bottom line in the vast majority of cases is money and only money. The rest is only a smoke screen. When a husband seeks more visitation rights it's often a subterfuge. What he really wants is a break on support issues or the right to claim the children as exemptions for tax purposes. It's usually a smoke screen. It's no different with the wife. Her overt complaints and allegations about the conduct of her former spouse and/ or his relationship with the children are simply her way of bringing well-concealed money issues to the surface. Let's face it Judge. How many cases seem to resolve themselves when more money is put on the table?

Now that I'm on a soap box I really have to take exception to your 'highly sensitive issues' analysis. I'm gonna try and reduce your feelings *ad absurdiam.* In other words, to the ridiculous if you'll bear with me. Try this one on for size. I think that settling or conciliating a divorce case is virtually no different than trying to settle a routine tort case. We're talking money and only money. Once that issue is resolved to everyone's satisfaction, generally all the other problems suddenly disappear.

A conciliator needs only a piece of paper and a calculator. Once the parties agree on a division of pension plans, equity in a home, and payment of bills, all other issues just seem to go away. Isn't it usually true, that a wife who receives a larger percentage of the total assets, will suddenly waive her request for alimony? A self-employed husband who gets exemptions for the kids can suddenly find that a slight increase in weekly support will not be to his detriment.

Likewise, a Will contestant has only one issue. Money and only money. So, contrary to your belief, I think that a group of highly skilled probate practitioners can be put together for conciliation purposes. The big difference here, is that you have no space for these conciliations in the Court. The sessions will have to take place in a lawyer's office."

"We can't allow the files to leave the Court House. How can you call a list for conciliation in a lawyer's office?"

The program would require each Judge to have a list of conciliators together with his or her field of expertise. The cases would be referred out individually from the bench and not in a massive 'cattle call' gathering. Once a case is referred to conciliation, it will be up to the conciliator and the litigants to pick a time to meet. In lieu of the file from the Cour, each litigant should be obliged to forward a current Financial Statement and a Pre-Trial Memorandum together with copies of any other relevant documents to the conciliator."

"Sounds pretty good in theory but who's gonna do all the paper work? Our staff is so far behind in docketing that we can't do it. And besides, where in hell do you think that you can get *pro bono* volunteers to be conciliators?"

"I'll check with Pam Surette, Executive Director of the Essex County Bar, to see if her office can accommodate. It may help in our annual requests for grants. Insofar as staffing is concerned don't sell the Essex County lawyers short. I'll bet there are 100 out there willing to devote their time and effort. Give me the go-ahead and I'll write solicitation letters to the Essex Bar Members requiring resumes from them, if interested. You then do the picking."

"If Pam can do the paper work, and you do the solicitations, you have my permission. Come see me if you get any responses with resumes."

"Done deal, Judge." We shake hands. I reenter the courtroom and wait for the recess to conclude. I later head downstairs to see Pam.

The resumes come and Judge Rockett hand-picks the chosen few. At Judge Spencer Kagan's request I explain the procedure and the success of our probate conciliations to a committee at the Middlesex Probate Court, which was chaired by my classmate, First Justice Sheila McGovern. Apparently, the Middlesex Bar fails to step up to the plate at that time.

Judge Furnari dies unexpectedly, but his good works are continued by Judge Cornetta, and later by Judge Wexler, and then by Judge Conlon.

I eventually serve as President of the Essex County Bar Association from 2000 to 2002. In 2004 The Greater Lynn Bar Association presents me with its highest honor. I become the recipient of the John Jennings Advocacy Award. The Essex County Bar Association also presents me with its highest award on May 27, 2007. The silver bowl commemorating the Ronan Family Jurisprudence Award is engraved with words

YOU BE THE JUDGE

indicating a "dedication and devotion to the quality and administration of justice."

   ...This is certainly a bubble which can't burst...but lurking somewhere in the background are the words of Al Jolson... "I'm sittin' on top of the world...and just like Humpty Dumpty, I'm gonna have a fall..."

CHAPTER TWENTY-NINE

...It's the first week in April 1983. I know that the leaves on the trees are slowly turning green and spring is in the air, but on this day I'm totally oblivious to the surroundings. The ride on Route 95 North from Lynn to the Superior Court in Newburyport would otherwise have been a pleasant trip, but today young Jimmy Monico is about to start a trial in which he is facing two life sentences. I'm totally absorbed in thought and barely remember the ride. I'm mentally rehearsing my opening statement to the jury, which is often interrupted with the line of questioning that I intend to use for the cross-examination of the witnesses for the Commonwealth.

In my reverie I become aware of the duck pond on my right which is located just before the Superior court. I have no recollection of the ride from Lynn. There are no facilities for parking unless one happens to be the Judge, a Clerk, or a Court Officer. I finally find a spot on a side street, and with my extra large briefcase in hand I start walking up a slight incline towards the court house.

The building itself has a fairly new coat of white paint on the wooden surfaces surrounding the red brick and other masonry. A bronze plaque indicates that it was originally constructed in 1805 and has been designated as an official Federal Historic Edifice. The building was designed by Charles Bulfinch, who was also responsible for the State house and Fanueil Hall in Boston.

I walk up the few cement stairs and open one side of the huge twin doors. The highly polished wooden floor creaks with every step. I wonder how many times the floor had been refurbished to some degree over the years. In front of me to the left is a small office used by the District Attorneys, a jury/conference room is directly in front, and a jury deliberation room to the extreme right. A stairway to its right leads downstairs to the rest rooms. A narrow staircase on the left leads upstairs to the courtroom. Two people are unable to pass each other at the same time. I'm alone at 8:30 in the morning except for some Court Officers. Court isn't due to start until ten o'clock but I instructed the Monicos to meet me about nine.

I start up the stairs which creak as badly as the floor below. My briefcase gets heavier and heavier with each step. At the top of the stairs there's a small conference room to the left, and on the right an even smaller office for a Court Clerk. Just as I'm about to enter the courtroom, an assistant clerk looks up from her typing and says, "Good mornin', Bruce. Guess the early bird gets the worm!"

"Good morning to you too, but in this case I get the feeling that I'm the worm, and am about to be devoured by the bird!"

A polite laugh is followed by, "Good luck!"

"Thanks, I'll need it!"

The entry into the courtroom is always awe inspiring when one thinks of its history. Huge windows surround both sides of the room. The bottoms are about waist high and reach almost to the ceiling. Old chandeliers hang from the ceiling, which in another era were probably fueled by whale oil. To the front right, as I face the bench, is the jury box. Uncomfortable dark-stained wooden pews are located at the back for litigants and witnesses. In front of them is the customary railing followed by individual chairs for the lawyers. Most of the chairs are covered in worn and torn black leather, and appear to have been untouched since the grand opening of the Court.

In my mind, however, the most significant thing which adds to the aura and mystique of this ancient courtroom, is the knowledge and awareness of what has previously transpired within these same confines. Even though the thought is trite I nevertheless wish that these walls could talk. They would bespeak of an unheralded history of laws, lawyers and Judges.

Essex Superior Court Judge, Robert Welch, penned a brief history of this Court on September 16, 2005 in honor of the occasion of the 200th anniversary of its opening. He reflected that on opening day Thomas Jefferson was starting his second term as President of the United States. But of more significance to me was a reminder by Welch of what I already knew. That great legal luminaries, such as John Quincy Adams, Daniel Webster, Rufus Choate, and Caleb Cushing, all argued cases in this Court.

...I am humbled by these thoughts. Just who the hell am I to even have the opportunity to try a case within these hallowed chambers? Am I about to make a mockery of myself and exhibit my incompetence and ineptness in the presence of the spirits of Webster and Adams, who must surely be here to listen to my every stupid comment and witness my every action...

I put my briefcase on the floor next to the table reserved for defense counsel and head downstairs looking for the Monicos. I spot them on a bench at the foot of the stairs in front of the large windows facing the street. We exchange greetings. Jimmy, the elder, is the first to speak. "Hey, Bruce, where are all of our witnesses?"

"I've had them all served with subpoenas and put them on telephone notice. No sense having everyone here at this time. I have no idea as to when they'll be needed. Besides, the prosecution has to go first."

"Oh. I understand."

"First things first. We now have to make a serious decision. As you know, Tom Niarchos, is the ADA in this case. We had a phone conversation late yesterday afternoon which I initiated. I asked him what the Commonwealth would recommend for a sentence, if we opted to plead guilty. He said probably 15 to 18 years. I then made a call to his boss, Kevin Burke, the County DA, who confirmed the same. Claimed that he would like to accommodate and make a lesser proposal, but foremost in his mind was the fact, that this was a double homicide.

You will all recall my earlier statements about the sentencing parameters in the event of a conviction of murder. You've got to weigh the possibilities of a finding of guilty with never a chance for parole on Murder One, and a possible parole after twenty years for a Murder Two conviction. You must balance these facts against the offer made yesterday, and the possibility of verdicts of Not Guilty based upon our twofold defenses of temporary insanity and self-defense. I'm going outside for a smoke while you guys talk about the options. Come get me when you're ready. Take your time."

I leave the front steps as the individual jurors arrive. Eventually, the Monicos join me and I'm informed that the father wants to accept the offer and enter a plea. There's always a chance that the Judge may give him less. He has tears in his eyes as he speaks with a cracking voice that's barely audible.

"I've been a cop for most of my life and a prosecutor for more years than I care to remember. I don't trust juries. It's a crap shoot. I think jurors are prone to believe the cops. At least a plea will guarantee that young Jimmy will see the light of day sometime down the road. In my mind the alternative is too bitter to think about. The problem we have here is that Boots and Jimmy both want to go to trial. I'm outvoted."

I look to the other two and ask for confirmation. Young Jimmy says, "Hell, why did I spend all that time with the doctors and clinical psychologist, if I intended to plead guilty. They tell me I had a concussion and didn't have control of my faculties. Besides, this was two on one for a good self-defense argument."

Boots adds, "I agree with my son all around. The jury will have two grounds to find him not guilty. We should try the damn thing! What do you think, Bruce?"

"In matters such as this it's not for me to decide. I can only advise as to the consequences of any choice which you may make. The decision is not for me to make. It might be different, if we had no semblance of a defense, and that a Murder One conviction was a foregone conclusion. In that kind of a case I would probably stress the importance of a plea. I'm going to prepare a written statement advising of the offer and your majority rejection. I want you each to sign it. I'm protecting my ass. I don't want any ramifications in the future claiming that I failed to advise you properly."

Boots continues. "How well do you know Judge Linscott?"

"Not that it really matters, but I've known him and his father before him ever since I became a lawyer. They had an upstairs office on Monroe

Street at the corner of Washington. The Judge represented Employers Mutual Insurance Company as a defense counsel in motor vehicle accidents. We've tried several cases against each other and have also settled some. He was also a former member of the Swampscott Board of Selectman. He served long before me."

A Court Officer approaches and advises that the Judge wants to see counsel in chambers.

The tall lanky Judge, Andrew Linscott, rose to greet us. He was a handsome figure of a man. His physical condition and full head of blondish/gray tight curly hair hid his age well. His robe was partially open and his reading glasses were perched on the bottom of his nose, as he said, "Good morning gentlemen. Have a seat anywhere in this crowded office. Well, where do we stand? Let me hear from you first, Tom."

"Thank you, Judge. This is a double homicide in which the defendant is charged with two counts of Murder One. We have about a dozen witnesses and the case will go approximately two weeks."

"Tell me a little about the factual allegations which the Commonwealth intends to prove."

Niarchos states his best picture and summarizes the most favorable expected testimony which he anticipates from his various witnesses.

"Thank you. Bruce, I'll now hear from you."

I give a similar recitation from our point of view including the defenses of temporary insanity and self-defense. I recite evidence, which I believe will offset the testimony expected by the prosecution.

"I anticipate calling six witnesses. My client, his father, a friend, and three medical witnesses. I agree that the case should last about two weeks."

"Has there been any discussion about a plea?"

"Yes, Your Honor. The recommendation is 15 to 18. My client and his family have rejected the same after I fully explained the ramifications of a conviction. Maybe a lesser sentence proposal from the Commonwealth might cause my clients to have second thoughts."

The Judge looks in the direction of Niarchos, who matter-of-factly states, "The offer is etched in stone, Your Honor. After all, he killed two men."

The Judge responds. "I tend to agree with Tom given the circumstances. I can certainly tell you, Bruce, that it's been my experience to perceive that insanity defenses are seldom listened to by juries. You should prevail upon your client to rethink his position."

"Believe me, Judge, it would be a waste of time and effort."

"OK, then we'll start to empanel and pick a jury in about 15 minutes, which will be followed by opening statements. I would hope that this will be accomplished by lunch and that testimony will begin following the luncheon break. See you all in the courtroom."

The shocker of all shockers. At the proper time in the proceedings the Judge absolutely refuses to instruct the jury on the issue of insanity. He makes this ruling despite abundant evidence of the Defendant's erratic behavior and statements, as recited by the police, as well as defense witnesses. He makes the ruling despite medical evidence from two doctors. He also absolutely refuses to allow our clinical neuro-psychologist to give an opinion as to insanity, simply because he is not a medical doctor.

I point out to the Judge that his rulings are contrary to the law in the Commonweaalth, and I give him the names and citations of the key controlling cases in this area. *Commonwealth vs. McHoul, Osborne vs. Commonwealth, Commonwealth vs. Mattson, and Commonwealth vs, Laliberty.*

It's all to no avail. The jury has no choice but to convict. He's found guilty of one count of Murder One and one Count of Murder Two on April 14, 1983. I argue the case on appeal at the Supreme Judicial Court on December 8, 1985. The panel consists of Chief Justice Hennessey, and Justices Wilkins, Liacos, and Nolan.

On February 20, 1986 Justice Nolan, speaking for the Court in a lengthy opinion sets the tone in the very first paragraph. "...We accept the defendant's argument that the trial judge committed reversible error in refusing to instruct the jury on the issue of the defendant's criminal responsibility in accordance with *Commonwealth vs. McHoul...*"

Justice Nolan recites the several inconsistent statements made by the defendant to the police at the scene, and later to others at the station regarding his assailant or assailants. The statements were replete with serious incongruities. The Court reflects upon the lack of credibility of patrons at the bar following my cross-examination. Of great significance was the fact, that when one of the victims shoved the defendant against the wall, his head struck a wall lamp and not only broke the globe, but bent the metal frame.

The Court then went on to explain the rationale contained in the various cases which we cited in our brief. Quoting from *McHoul*, Nolan writes that a person is not responsible for criminal conduct, if at the time of such conduct, as a result of mental disease or defect, he lacks substantial capacity, either to appreciate the criminality of his conduct, or to conform his conduct to the requirements of the law.

Nolan then cites *Osborne*, which stands for the proposition, that expert psychiatric testimony is not needed to raise the issue of insanity as a complete defense. The opinion then references *Mattson and Laliberty*, and states that an insanity issue may be raised from the facts of the case, through the witnesses for the Commonwealth, or any combination thereof. In fact, an insanity defense may be raised by the admission of any evidence, which, if believed, might create a reasonable doubt concerning a defendant's criminal responsibility at the time of the crime.

The opinion then quotes directly from *Laliberty*…"Once the defense has been raised by the evidence, the judge must instruct on it, if requested to do so…"

A recitation follows of the observations, diagnoses, and conclusions of the medical witnesses regarding the defendant's past and present injuries. Explanations of how a concussion can be caused, typical symptoms following a concussive injury, and areas of the brain affected. For the first time in this State the Court authorizess a clinical neuro-psychologist to testify and to render an opinion. The Court finds that such a person submits a patient to a wide variety of written, oral, and manual tests, which are aimed at confirming or rejecting the findings of a neurologist, and pinpointing the exact affected area of the brain.

The upshot of the entire decision is to reverse the convictions, and order that the case be remanded to the Essex Superior Court for a new trial in conformity with the law, as set forth in Nolan's opinion.

On the eve of the second trial the Commonwealth offers something like 8 to 12 with credit for time served. This time my client opts to enter a plea. I have no doubt in my mind that his twenty month incarceration pending the decision of the SJC, has much to do in influencing his change. The thought of a life sentence must have played heavily in the decision making process.

The issue was never raised in The Monico Case, but the ruling in McHoul also has great significance to me. Massachusetts is one of the few states, which holds that an insanity defense may also be raised, if a person commits a crime which is the result of an irresistible impulse caused by some external force, such as a drug. This is so, even if the perpetrator is aware of the difference between right and wrong and knows that his conduct is a crime.

CHAPTER THIRTY

…"My name is Robert and I'm a recovering compulsive gambler."
Everyone responds. "Hello Robert."

Robert speaks for almost an hour without interruption. We learn that he's a business college graduate, who eventually obtained a position of trust as a loan officer in a local bank. He was the new "fair-haired boy" on the block, and was well-respected by all of his colleagues, peers, and superiors.

He claims that he was first introduced to gambling while a student in high school. A fellow student was running a weekly pool for the selection and betting on the results of certain professional sports games. Robert claims that he was very naïve about such matters and didn't know how the pool worked. An explanation followed together with a request for a $3.00 wager. He was off and running from then on because he won.

He speculates, that if he had lost on that first bet he might never have gambled again. It just became too easy.

The saga continued with revelations of continued betting with bookies and on line. Eventually his credit cards were maxed out. He became a cheat and a liar, as he made every effort to hide his addiction and expenditures from his wife and family. When all funds were exhausted, he arranged for a bank loan to cover his expenditures. It worked. He managed to pay back the loan and make a substantial dent in his otherwise precarious financial situation.

His gambling continued and subsequent borrowing went awry. The first time was the toughest. He dipped into bank funds over which he had control in order to cover his losses and debts. He managed to replace the funds without anyone from the bank being the wiser. Subsequent "borrowing" didn't work out as planned. It was only a matter of time before he would be exposed.

His conscience finally forced him to reveal his covert actions to his superiors at the bank. They were all in shock and disbelief. Naturally, he was discharged. His family life was destroyed. His children became estranged. His wife left him and filed for divorce. He lost his house. He also wrote suicide notes to his wife and each of his children.

The Federal bank authorities brought criminal charges against him. He was sentenced and served two years in a Federal prison even though he had made restitution. He claims that a two month stint in a half-way house prior to release was worse than the entire prison term.

Robert started attending GA meetings several nights a week at different locations. He's been clean now for a couple of years. He became involved in GA to the point where he now holds some sort of regional title. He has a new job where he earns a modest income. It's a far cry from his former job and earnings. There's a gleam in his eye, as he proudly boasts, that there's usually a little surplus in his checking account after the payment of his monthly bills.

I listen intently to his and everyone else's story. It's absolutely amazing. The tales of woe are all the same. There's a profound commonality among us all. Instead of saying, "Hello, I'm Robert…" He could just as easily said, "Hello, I'm Bruce…" If he did, his recitation would still be 99% correct!

The chairperson calls upon each of us at every meeting to read a portion of the materials furnished by GA. Not only do I then and there try to understand the recitations, but I've become an avid reader of the literature at home. I've come away with some truisms. For instance, one simply cannot stop gambling because of the feeling that one *has* to stop. That person will undoubtedly be doomed to failure. The innate feeling must be that one *wants* to stop. There's a world of difference between *"has to stop"* and *"want to stop"!* The desire to stop must of course be coupled with a recognition and open admission of one's illness.

The little yellow book entitled, *Gamblers Anonymous*, states on page 9, "…To recover from one of the most baffling, insidious, compulsive addictions will require diligent effort. HONESTY, OPENMINDEDNESS, AND WILLINGNESS are the key words in our recovery."

There are other similar passages in that little yellow book, which make me feel that it was written with me in mind. In paraphrasing other passages, I deduce that one need not be a psychologist nor a rocket scientist to realize that a compulsive gambler lives in a dream world. It's a world in which one is able to escape from reality. In fact I never felt more comfortable than when I was gambling. The casinos afforded me a haven and a venue without constant phone calls. There were no external demands being made upon me.

According to GA studies have shown that most compulsive gamblers have an inner urge to feel like a "big shot" or "all-powerful." Apparently, it's all part of the syndrome in which a compulsive gambler will use any and all means at his or her disposal in order to create a certain image which he would like others to see.

In retrospect, I've now come to the conclusion that casinos are fully aware of the image which compulsive gamblers would like to portray to the others. Why else would they cater to us? Why give us free rooms? Why give us reserved parking spaces? Why leave gifts in the free rooms? Why create VIP Lounges exclusively for us? Why give us free meals? Why give us the best seats for shows?

The answer to all these questions is really quite simple. Casinos apparently agree with GA and recognize the need of a compulsive gambler to feel like a "big shot'!

The greatest anomaly is that although I felt secure and comfortable while gambling, I still had a minimal amount of sense left to realize that I was subconsciously bent on a course of self-destruction. A feeling, which I obviously suppressed.

I'm certainly convinced that I'm no different than a "junkie" or an alcoholic. Rock-bottom must first be hit. The self-destruction must be nearly complete before the road to recovery may begin. It's about as axiomatic as, "apple pie and ice cream." I'm presently ultra-careful not place myself in an atmosphere which would be conducive to making that first bet. Listening to my compatriots sitting around the table sends me a clear message. Relapses are the rule and not the exception. In this instance I'm striving to be the exception and not the rule. Only time will tell.

This is all ludicrous. I must be the biggest hypocrite in the world. Here I find myself extolling the virtues of GA and its good works and teachings. But there's only one place that I really want to be even as these words are being written. I want to be at Foxwoods right now, and if I had the funds I think that I might make the trip. I miss the atmosphere and aura of the casino. I miss the highs with the blood rushing to my head in anticipation of a hit. I miss the surges of adrenalin and the quickening of my pulse. I miss the challenge of trying to outsmart the slot machine programmed chip. I miss the sounds of the machines and the songs which accompany a big hit. I miss it all and it really wouldn't matter if I won or not. If I did win, I'd probably give it all back in vain attempts to win even more.

Just what good does it do me to have been blessed with an analytical mind? One would think that I could have and should have stopped my gambling before total disaster struck. After all, I think that I have more between my ears than just plain air.

"...Aye, therein lies the rub..." A compulsive gambler is unable to take curative measures. It's part of the addiction. Even common sense has no role to play. The subconscious desires for self-destruction and the maintaining of desired images are just too strong to overcome in a normal manner.

Given all that I have experienced, witnessed, and now understand, I here and now throw the proverbial gauntlet into the cauldron containing a witch's brew, which has all the necessary ingredients used in the making of a compulsive gambler. Will my challenge withstand the heat? Acting alone can I combat or interfere with the intended goal of the boiling pot? The answer is a resounding "no"! And that's because a compulsive gambler's addiction is a true and genuine incurable illness. Anyone who denies this concept is just a plain fool.

Compulsive gambling is an illness similar to cancer. Sometimes a cancer can be cured by excising it before it has the opportunity to consume one's entire body, spirit and soul. But not so with compulsive gambling. It's an incurable disease which cannot be excised. The only treatment for one suffering from this addiction is to attempt to place it into remission. The GA meetings and teachings have become my chemotherapy. They've put my compulsion into remission, but I still report every Friday evening for my weekly dose of chemotherapy.

...*I'm still besieged and perplexed as I search for an answer to the all-important question. What role, if any, does Mirapex have in this equation?...*

CHAPTER THIRTY-ONE

...It's a humid summer day in the beginning of August 1977. Joe Machera and I are passing through the toll booth on the Mystic River Bridge. We're on our way to the Middlesex Superior Court in Cambridge.

"Joe, this is certainly strange. I never got a formal written notice from the Court to appear today on Seit's case. All I got was a call from some clerk late last week telling me to appear today for a re-sentencing hearing. I asked him who the Judge was going to be, and he simply said that no one knows yet. It was too early to predict. Assignments for the new group had not as yet been made."

"I really hate to knock a dead man, but at least that s.o.b. Sullivan wont be there. He's really the one most responsible for Barry's incarceration in the first place."

"Yeah. I'm glad too. The Rules provide that it's the trial Judge who must preside over this kind of a proceeding. The Sullivan Family misfortune allows us to luck out on that score. Now it's up to the luck of the draw. Remember what I told you before. Superior Court Judges are on circuit and they usually sit in a different jurisdiction monthly."

Neither of us talks. Joe is reading some notes and reviewing cases. I'm mulling over in my mind the pitch which I intend to use to any Judge we happen to catch. We've already passed Bunker Hill Junior College. We've also turned right at the bottom of what used to be Prison Point Bridge in an era before the Charles Street Jail was demolished...

...It seems as though there's a memory attached to almost every street I see...I smile to myself remembering that my uncles Bob, Phil, and Al

229

Singer, always took this long and circuitous route to Boston. My father and I were often their passengers enroute to Fenway Park. In those days one could virtually choose any seat in the park. This was their route of choice in order to avoid the ten cent toll at the Sumner Tunnel. Today I wonder how much more than the toll was used up in gas, while waiting in the heavy traffic near all of the Everett and Chelsea factories...

We've circled the blocks twice when Joe breaks the silence. "What a travesty this is. It's really a crime. The powers-that-be spent all that money in order to erect this huge new building, which even provides space for some sessions of the Cambridge District Court. They probably had to take some land by eminent domain to accomplish this feat. Apparently none of those idiots had any foresight, or even the hint of a brain! Didn't any of those morons realize that people in this day and age actually drive automobiles?"

Finally, we grab a spot next to a meter just as a car pulls out.

"OK. Good sign, Boss. This is gonna be your lucky day!"

"We're still early. How about a cup of coffee in the cafeteria?"

" Sounds good. Haven't been in there since the jury came in with the verdict on Seit. How long's it been now?"

"Just about eighteen months. In fact almost to the day. It was difficult explaining to the Seits that the long delay was caused by some snafu in the Clerk's Office. We never got to enter the Appeal until May 19, 1977. I was given excuses ranging from Sullivan's illness to a loss of the stenographer's notes.

Things were different once we got to the SJC. They held oral arguments ninety days after the entry in that Court. Now look at us. The SJC rendered its opinion and in less than three weeks from that date we're here on a re-sentencing hearing. That, my friend, is efficiency!"

The courtroom is packed. I wave to Barry's wife and kids. They listened to me and got there early enough to obtain seats in the first row directly in front of the Judge's bench. I keep looking for my two character witnesses. Father Mihos from the Greek Church in Lynn is spotted easily because of his collar. I finally see Anthony Athanas, owner of the Pier Four Restaurant in Boston, the General Glover at the Salem/Swampscott/Marblehead line, the Hawthorne By The Sea in

Swampscott, the Hawthorne in the Cape, and The Hawthorne in Lynn. He was Barry's former employer. He also lent Barry money with which to start up his own business.

Joe asks some guy to move over so that we have seats together in the back row. It's a good move. We should at least be able to whisper from there. Minutes later a door behind the Judge's bench opens and the usual entourage enters led by a uniformed Court Officer.

The only words I hear are, "Hear ye, hear ye..." I'm oblivious to the rest of his littany as I stare at the Judge. He's standing next to his chair. I can't believe who I see standing there high above the rest of us peons. I'm stunned! No, I'm really in shock! What the hell are the odds of such a draw? Holy smoke! We catch *him* of all people, when the judge's pool includes every Superior Court Judge from Essex County in the East to Berkshire in the West to Barnstable in the South.

Joe senses that something is amiss even though I haven't uttered a sound. He whispers anxiously, "Hey, Bruce, what's the matter? Do you recognize this guy? Who the hell is he?"

"Who is he? Who is he you ask? I'll tell you who he is. He's the greatest thing since they stopped hangin' pickpockets! That man sitting up there is none other than an old friend, Judge John Ronan, whom I've known ever since I became a lawyer. When I first opened my office seventeen years ago, he was makin' his bones as a trial attorney in Phil Sisk's office at the Lynn Daily Evening Item Building on Exchange Street. Sisk represented Liberty Mutual Insurance Company at the time and I had some cases with his office.

Ronan eventually left Sisk and teamed up with Mike Harrington. Ronan & Harrington opened an office on Federal street in Salem located diagonally across the street from the Probate and Superior Courts. He managed to get some Liberty Mutual cases on his own because of his prowess as a defense lawyer in civil cases. It was a great combo. Mike Harrington was well-known locally. His father was Joe Harrington, who was the former First Justice of the Salem District Court. He was the best friend of every plaintiff's lawyer in a civil tort case where an insurance company was on the other side.

Mike Harrington eventually got elected as a Congressman to Washington. The firm changed names several times when Ronan was appointed to the bench. The firm at one time was Ronan, Harrington & Segal, when Jake Siegel became a partner. The Judge's brother, Jim Ronan, also became a member of the firm. He was no slouch as a trial lawyer and continued to fight for Liberty Mutual. By the way, their sister, Marie Williams, is the chief probation officer in the Superior Court. All in all, it's quite a family deeply entrenched in the legal world.

When the great schism took place in my former partnership, and Fred Pearlmutter was not amenable to a division of assets based upon each lawyer's capital account, he hired John Ronan to represent him. We hired another great trial lawyer, Tommy Dolan, to represent our interests. The case eventually got settled at one of the Lynn Bar Association's annual meetings at the Hawthorne in downtown Lynn. I've appeared before Ronan on many occasions in the Superior Court and have never been hurt by any of his rulings."

It's now about 11:15 and the room is nearly empty. I surmise that our case has been held intentionally for last because it may be a time-consumer. No need to keep the lawyers waiting who have matters not requiring too much time to resolve. I'm right. Soon the room has only those involved in our case.

The case is called. Joe and I take seats at the table reserved for the defense. There's one person sitting at the prosecutor's table. Seit is in the prisoner's dock to our right front. He's chained hand and foot. His family is in the front row directly behind us. Our two witnesses are seated in the back of the room. The stage is set. I'm waiting for a directive from the Court for the Prosecutor to begin his presentation. I expect him to recite a version of the facts most favorable to his position, which will then be followed by a recommendation of twenty years, which he previously conveyed to me on the phone.

The awesome presence of Judge Ronan is on the bench. He still has a full head of black wavy hair. He's tall in stature and barrel-chested. He's a big man but doesn't appear to have gained any weight since I saw him last. His face is somewhat roundish and he has a ruddy complexion. He has a thin nose and an overall appearance which cannot be taken for anything other than Irish.

What happens next is totally unexpected. If I didn't witness it, I'd have a difficult time believing it. The Judge is reading and sifting through some papers. His glasses are perched low on his nose. There's no customary request for the parties to identify themselves. The room is absolutely quiet except for the noise of the papers being shuffled on the Judge's bench.

Suddenly and without any prior warning he stands up. He's holding some papers in his left hand which he extends high in the air above his head. The booming voice of Judge John Ronan fills the room. He's now looking down directly at me as he speaks in an all too familiar tone of sarcasm. Waving the papers above his head he begins. "Mr. Sachar, I have read and reread this decision several times. As I see it, the bottom line is that Justice Kaplan and the rest of the gang at the SJC have decided to cut your client some slack. Wouldn't you agree?"

I'm in the process of standing up to answer but he never gives me the opportunity. Instead, he lowers his outstretched hand and puts the papers back down on the bench. His other hand motions me to keep my seat. He continues with a mixture of sarcasm and boredom. "Let me guess, Mr. Sachar. I suppose that you've brought some character witnesses with you today. Am I correct in that assumption?"

This time he lets me stand. I finally get the opportunity to speak more than one word at a time. "Yes, Your Honor, your assumption is quite correct. I have Father Mihos from the Greek Orthodox Church in Lynn." I turn sideways and point in his direction. "He's expected to testify about the defendant's reputation in the community for non-violence."

Still standing sideways I point to my next witness. "May it please the Court, I also have Mr. Anthony Athanas, who was my client's former employer. He is expected to..." I never get to finish the sentence. The Judge interrupts. He simultaneously waives his hand at my witness and says, "Hi Tony! How're you doing?"

"Fine thank you, Judge. And how've you been?"

"Fine. Just fine. Thank you."

"Mr. Sachar, I know both of your witnesses. I could probably tell you right now what each of them will say word for word. So with that in mind, I believe that that we can dispense with calling them to the stand. Don't you agree?"

"Absolutely, Judge." *(I'd have to be a damned fool to respond differently!).*

The Judge then turns to the Prosecutor and says, " Sir, I'll hear from you now."

"Thank you, Your Honor. This is a case in which the defendant…" Before he can finish the sentence the Judge interrupts him and asks, "Have you read the decision which caused this matter to be retransferred to this Court for further action?"

"Yes, Your Honor."

"That's Good, counsel. And as I previously indicated I've also read the decision. Wouldn't you agree that the SJC has recited all of the relevant facts in this case. Facts which are both favorable and unfavorable for both the Commonwealth and the defendant?"

"Yes, Judge."

"Well then, do you have any relevant facts to tell me which are not contained in the opinion?"

"No. Your Honor."

"All right. I believe that we all have an understanding and knowledge of the relevant facts in this case. We can now dispense with that portion of your argument to the Court. Why don't you just tell me your recommendation for sentencing on the charge of Manslaughter."

"The Commonwealth is asking for twenty years committed."

"Thank you, counsel. I will give your recommendation the weight which I think it deserves."

The Clerk, who's been sitting quietly in his chair below the level of the Judge, now rises, turns around, and converses in hushed tones with the Judge. I can see that a search is being made in the official Court folder. The Clerk then returns to his own desk and makes a phone call. Simultaneously the Judge announces. "There will be a short recess of about a half hour." He leaves the Bench. The Clerk hangs up the phone and follows him out of the courtroom.

Joe and I are joined in the hallway by Barry's family and our witnesses. Everyone starts talking at once. They all want to know what's going to happen. I tell them that I haven't the faintest idea, and am really surprised that I wasn't asked for a recommendation. When quiet is restored I announce: "Joe and I are going to the cafeteria. You can all join us, use the rest rooms, or just hang out. We'll see you all here in about a half hour."

Joe says, "I'll get the coffee and you grab a table."

"As long as you're buying bring me a grilled blueberry muffin."

"Done."

I'm relieved that only Joe and I are in the cafeteria. He's the first to speak. "Well Boss, whaddaya think?"

"Damned if I know! I'm delighted no one joined us. They'd probably ask the same question and I'd be at a loss for words. There's nothing worse than revealing your ignorance to a client. I'm trying to rehash what just happened in there. I'm lookin' for some clue or a hint of what his intentions are. I certainly believe it's a plus that he knows our character witnesses. I would think his opening remarks are also a plus and that he won't follow the prosecutor's recommendation."

"You just lost me. What's that about his opening remarks?"

"Don't you remember what his opening gambit was? He said, 'Mr. Sachar, I think that Justice Kaplan and the rest of the gang at the SJC have decided to cut your client some slack'. If that's not an exact quote it's still pretty close."

"Oh yeah. Now I remember. I just hope you're not reading too much into it."

"Yeah. I can only hope I'm right. Got nothin' else to go on at this point. Meanwhile, it's time. Let's get our behinds back in the courtroom."

Joe and I take our seats. Everyone else is already seated. Within seconds the Court Officer announces that the Session is reconvened. The Judge and the Clerk take their respective positions. The Judge doesn't look in my direction. Instead he faces the center of the room. He speaks in a commanding tone as though he were addressing a full house.

"The Clerk and I have thoroughly examined the docket sheet in this case. I have also read and digested the letters from the Wardens and chefs from our state prisons at both Walpole and Norfolk. Apparently the defendant is well-liked. He's been cooperative with the authorities and has no record of disciplinary actions taken against him. He worked as a chef at both Walpole and Norfolk. In short, he's been an exemplary prisoner."

The Judge then looks at me for the first time since entering the room. The unique combination of both sarcasm and wit are in his voice. I recognize it immediately from the many times I've heard it while sitting in his courtroom at Salem. I think I see him fight to restrain a smile and maintain his composure.

"Mr. Sachar, the record in this case indicates that your client was found guilty of Murder in the Second Degree in this Court almost eighteen months ago. Would you agree with that assessment?"

Before I'm fully standing I answer, "Yes, Your Honor."

He swivels his chair to his left and looks at some papers at the sidebar. The Clerk leaves his station and joins him. I can see the Judge pointing to something on the paper, which he calls to the Clerk's attention. The two of them are having a conversation. The Clerk keeps shaking his head up and down apparently in agreement with whatever the Judge is saying.

I remain standing in anticipation of further questioning by the Judge. He speaks to me again in the same tone of voice as before. "Mr. Sachar, today is Monday, is it not?"

"Yes, Your Honor."

"Well, the record and my calculations clearly demonstrate that in three days he will have served exactly eighteen months. Do you also agree with that assessment?"

"Yes. Absolutely, Judge."

There's a further conference with the Clerk. Then he returns to his seat and makes another phone call. No one says a word as we wait for the Clerk to finish. It seems like an eternity. The Judge apparently senses the tension in the courtroom. He looks at Athanas and breaks the silence. "By the way, Tony, how's business these days? Got room at Pier Four for dinner for me and my wife tonight?"

"Business couldn't be better. Yes, I always have room for you."

"OK. It's a date. Thank you."

The Clerk finishes his call and turns around to speak to the Judge, who's continuously nodding his head in apparent agreement. The Clerk then resumes his seat as the Judge looks towards me. I know a question is coming. I jump to my feet in anticipation of responding.

I'm right on target. In the most somber voice of the day he speaks to me in a tone of impending doom. "Mr. Sachar, it is the final judgment of this Court that your client be sentenced to serve eighteen months in the State Prison at Walpole."

There's a stifled cry from Seit's wife loud enough for all to hear. The Judge continues. "It is the further order of this Court that the defendant be given credit for time served."

For the first time the Judge breaks out with a full and unrestrained smile. He looks directly at me and asks a question. "Mr. Sachar, do you have any objection if your client is released from custody on Thursday of this week?"

In total shock I answer. "Nosiree, Judge!"

He's now actually laughing, as he says, "I thought not!"

Mrs. Seit is sobbing convulsively as the Clerk faces Barry in the prisoner's dock and reads the judgment of the Court. When he finishes, the Judge looks in Barry's direction and tells him that he was lucky to have such a competent attorney.

Then come the final words from the bench. "Mr. Sachar, please advise your client's family that I have made arrangements for them to be with him until he is returned to Norfolk later in the day. Just have them report to the Court Officer, who will take them to him."

A smiling Clerk says, "Court is now adjourned."

Ronan takes a military about-face and leaves the courtroom followed by his still smiling Clerk and Court Officer.

CHAPTER THIRTY-TWO

...Will this day never end? It's only a little after six and it's already dark. I've been up for almost sixteen hours. I've eaten only an omelet during that time but I'm not in the least bit hungry. I've been moving around all day from chair to chair just trying to get comfortable. Now I'm back at the desk again contemplating my plight and wondering when the news will hit the papers. Then what do I do? I'll never be able to face anyone again. I reach for the crossword book.

Maybe if I just concentrate on it for a while I can stop feeling sorry for myself. I go back to where I left off earlier...a six letter word for a Fund Raiser's Target. Let's see...begins with an "F" and ends with a "T." The answer jumps off the page. As I write in "FATCAT." I wonder why the answer didn't come earlier. The next step is to fill in the vertical words stemming from my answer. I never get there. My eyes focus on the letter from the SJC, which is partially exposed in front of the puzzle book. I pick it up...

"...disbarred from the practice of law...and the lawyer's name is forthwith stricken from the Roll of Attorneys..."

...I just can't fathom the thought or believe that this is to be my final lot in life. Everything I had done in my professional career was aimed at helping other lawyers and serving the public. The Bar Associations were used as vehicles to accomplish the ultimate goals. I wipe my eyes with the back of my hand as I realize that I've just kicked nearly half of a century of trying to do good deeds right in the ass. I've done such a good job that I've even lost the title of "Attorney."

The only saving grace is that the money I took from my clients will ultimately be paid back to them. The Clients' Security Fund maintained by the BBO is for cases such as this. The interest on lawyers' trust accounts (IOLTA) is forwarded monthly by the banks to the BBO, which uses the funds to support its activities including the Security Fund. I've been contributing the interest earned in my Iolta Account ever since the program was first adopted over 30 years ago.

No more Bar meetings, no more conciliations, and no more seminars. Never again to appear in court waiving the flag in defense of a client. I've brought shame to my comrades, as they will soon realize when the press picks up the story, and there's a resurgence of all those lawyer jokes. They're bad enough even without a reason to tell them. I'm glad that my father and mother are no longer here to share in the shame which I've brought to the family name.

My eyes are no longer just watering. They're filled with tears. My shoulders are heaving. I'm having a full-blown crying jag. It gets worse when I reflect that I've appeared in a courtroom as a prosecutor, criminal defense lawyer, a plaintiff's lawyer and a defendant's lawyer in civil cases, a conciliator, and even as a witness. My next appearance will probably guarantee that I've hit for the cycle. When criminal charges are filed I could very well be a prisoner in the dock with cuffs. If it comes to pass, it will be the ultimate humiliation and degradation that I can imagine, short of being committed to jail which is also a distinct possibility.

How can I no longer be an attorney? How can I no longer serve the lawyers and the courts? How can I no longer serve the public? How can I exist and be prohibited from doing those things that I love?

A commanding voice within me says, "C'mon Sachar! Get with it! Stop wallowing in all of this self-pity garbage! Get your act together and face reality! For cripes sake you're 75 years old and you've never backed down from a fight! You brought it all upon yourself! You should have known better! Stand tall and face the music!"

I stop crying and regain my composure. Amidst the debate going on somewhere within my inner soul a large and almost life-size portrait of Daniel Webster appears. I can visualize it prominently displayed on the wall behind the Judge's bench. It suddenly comes to life. He's standing right in front of me. It's just a dream! No, it can't be an illusion! It's true. I'm losing my mind!

Sachar, this is really the epitome of conceit! It's no longer a painting! I'm now looking directly at Daniel Webster himself who's standing right in front of my desk. He's facing a faceless witness on the stand. His morning coat is open in the front and the thumb of each hand is hidden in a vest pocket. He forcefully and quite loudly begins his questioning. He walks towards the witness but suddenly turns to face the jurors in the box. With his back to the witness stand, he begins.

"What do you mean when you say that he brought it all upon himself?" He doesn't even wait for an answer. He just continues in a sarcastic tone of voice. "You have been qualified by the Judge as an expert witness, haven't you doctor?"

"Yes."

The sarcastic tone continues. "Would you be so kind, doctor, as to refresh the minds of the jurors and tell us once again your exact field of expertise, and just what it is that you do?"

"Absolutely. As I previously indicated I'm a graduate of Harvard Medical School. I also have a Master's Degree and a PhD in the field of pharmacology. In layman's terms, pharmacology deals with the chemical composition of drugs and their uses. My particular function is to study side effects and to follow closely the results and effectiveness of a particular drug. The results of our studies are eventually transmitted to various Federal agencies, as well as to the manufacturer."

"Thank you, doctor. Isn't it a fact that your team of so-called experts approved the marketing of a drug called Mirapex sometime in the 90's?"

"Yes."

"Isn't it also a fact, that your office recommended its use before your study of possible side effects was completed?"

"Yes, but that's quite common."

"Isn't it also a fact, that your research was partially funded by means of a grant from the manufacturer of Mirapex?"

"Yes."

"Isn't it also a fact, that doctors were allowed to prescribe Mirapex for use in RLS cases even though your studies had not been concluded in that area?"

"Yes."

"Isn't it also a fact that the use of Mirapex for treatment in RLS cases was not officially sanctioned by your studies until 2005?"

"Yes."

"Isn't it also a fact, that the empirical data gathered by your office indicated that the use of Mirapex could cause obsessive-compulsive behavioral patterns, as well as pathological gambling?"

"Yes."

" Isn't it also a fact, that the manufacturers of Mirapex offered the drug for sale knowing full-well that its use could lead to pathological gambling?"

"Yes."

"Isn't it also a fact, that even though Mirapex was known to cause pathological gambling, it was released and sold to the general public without any warnings whatsoever as to possible side effects?"

"Yes. That is apparently the case."

"Hypothetically, doctor, could the use of Mirapex over an extended period of time transform an otherwise 'social' card player or gambler into a full-blown slot machine addict?"

"The studies indicate, that it is quite possible and probable."

"We've all watched television doctor. Have you ever seen stories involving junkies, who commit serious crimes in order to support their habit and obtain a fix?"

"Yes."

"Then you must have seen dope addicts on television commit larceny, or even murder, to get a fix?"

"Yes."

"Finally, doctor, assume hypothetically that my client had hitherto been a fine upstanding member of the community, certainly knew the difference between right and wrong, and had been using Mirapex for over twelve years. During those years there was a subtle and undetectable change in his personality and behavioral patterns. He became a compulsive gambler and developed an addiction to slot machines. Do you have an opinion, yes or no, as to whether or not such a person could commit a crime in order to satisfy his addiction?"

"Yes."

"And what is your opinion, doctor?"

"Yes. Given the facts, as you have posed in your question, it is absolutely plausible and quite probable that such a person could commit a crime to satisfy an irresistible impulse to gamble."

"Thank you, doctor. No further questions."

He vanishes as quickly as he appeared. Jesus, Sachar, what the hell have you been drinkin'? Just when and how did the voice in my conscience suddenly become a doctor? I question my sanity once again...Daniel Webster talking about television?...

...*Mirapex, Mirapex, Mirapex, thou art at once my Lord and Master and the very bane of my existence...*

CHAPTER THIRTY-THREE

...I'm doing my best to exist within my limited means. For the first time in my life I'm trying to live within the confines of a budget. It's difficult to change old habits. "You can't teach an old dog new tricks" comes readily to mind, as I attempt to disprove the adage with every waking minute. Income from Social Security and a small VA disability pension mandate a new way of life. Gone forever are the fancy restaurants. For that matter gone also are the days of eating out anywhere.

It's been a major adjustment to learn to live in a modest three-room apartment in a subsidized housing complex. I remember when the building housed the Hoague Sprague Shoe Box Manufacturing Company. As a youngster growing up in Lynn its fleet of trucks were a common sight throughout the city. I gladly and willingly pay 30% of my income for rent and am slowly getting used to doing my own laundry again. It's a reincarnation of dormitory and army life. The bright side is that my cooking skills are slowly returning. I now do my shopping in a distant city so that I can avoid familiar faces and embarrassment.

The every Friday afternoon jaunts to Foxwoods have been replaced by evenings attending a Gamblers anonymous session. GA has managed to keep me clean despite my continued necessary use of Mirapex. The biggest downside to my new life-style involves monetary issues. Budgetary constraints are truly shot to hell every month, and good intentions remain just that. Good intentions. If it's not brakes, it's the air-conditioner, or a toner cartridge for the printer, or the replacement of sneakers which leak, or an obligatory family function requiring a gift. My excuses for not dining out or accepting a date invitation are wearing thin, but all in all I believe that I've adjusted rather well.

On a par with monetary issues is my concern for the future. During the first week in August I receive a message to return a call from Captain Mark O'Toole of the Lynn Police Department. There's no question about it now. The "other shoe" has finally dropped. I return the call.

"Captain O'Toole, this is Bruce Sachar returning your call."

"Thank you very much. I've been assigned the DeFuria Matter and have concluded my investigation. I called to see if you wanted to make a statement or if you had any comments."

There's a long pause before I answer. "I have a lot to say and I'd like to make a statement, but I think that I should first check with my attorney. If you call either Bill O'Shea, Jr. or his brother, James, I will do whatever they say."

"OK. I'll make the call, but either way I intend to file a criminal complaint against you at the Lynn District Court in the next day or so."

"OK Captain. Thanks for the call."

None of the O'Sheas are in the office when I call, but I leave a message. Eventually I learn that I will not be arrested. A summons will be mailed to me advising of my arraignment date. It arrives. I'm due in Court on Friday September 18, 2009 to answer to charges of Fiduciary Embezzlement. It calls for imprisonment in the state prison for ten years, or two years in the House of Correction coupled with a fine of not more than two thousand dollars.

The O'Sheas and I aren't sure if the case will remain in Lynn. The Commonwealth has the option of presenting the matter to the Grand Jury seeking an indictment and removing the case to the Superior Court. Another option would be to file a Motion seeking to remove the case out of Essex County entirely.

My dreams and thoughts are consumed with visions of possible courtroom scenarios. I can practically see and hear the closing arguments. The Judge's "charge to the jury" is also an equally important part of the equation. Just thinking about the many versions of what might be said or asked makes me dizzy. Most troublesome is the fact that I have no real answers even though my future is at stake.

Try this version on for size:

JUDGE: Ladies and gentlemen of the jury, you have now heard all of the evidence in this case and have seen the various exhibits introduced by the parties. Both the Government and the Defense have now rested. You will now hear closing arguments by each party. When they have concluded I will then instruct you on the law. When you retire to deliberate you will apply the facts which you find to the law.

Just one last caveat. The closing arguments you are about to hear are not evidence. If either lawyer comments upon the evidence, exhibits, or anything else, which occurred during the trial, and what you hear is not the same as you remember it, then it's your memory which governs and not the words of the lawyer.

The Judge nods to defense counsel. He rises, walks over to the lectern, shuffles some papers and looks at the jurors.

DEFENSE COUNSEL: Ladies and Gentlemen of the jury, you have now heard all of the evidence in this case. As the Judge told you, if I make reference to anything that happened or was said during the trial, and your recollection differs, then it's your memory which controls.

I would like to suggest to you that this case is somewhat different than the ordinary run of the mill criminal case. In most criminal cases the defendant absolutely denies the allegations of the Commonwealth, and calls upon the prosecution to prove each and every allegation beyond a reasonable doubt. Again, in most criminal trials the defendant denies that he or she committed a crime. There's almost always a different version of the facts presented by the defendant. The object in those cases is to attempt to show that the Commonwealth has misinterpreted certain salient relevant facts, and that the defendant's behavior did not constitute a crime.

The big difference in this case is that we readily admit most of what the commonwealth alleges. We admit that my client took money which didn't belong to him. He stole money from his IOLTA Account and used it for his own purposes. He used the bulk of it for gambling.

I'm the first to acknowledge, that in most criminal cases that kind of an admission would justify the immediate entry of a finding of guilty. The Court could then take the case from the jury and sentence the defendant without any further ado.

Based upon the testimony of the expert witnesses who were called to the stand, and considering the nature of the questions propounded to them, you have obviously concluded that my client's defense is based upon something entirely different than a discrepancy in the facts.

I'll come right to the point. Our defense is based upon the legal doctrine known as an *"irresistible impulse."* I believe that the Judge in his charge to you will fully explain the term and how it comes to play in this case.

With the Court's indulgence and without usurping the role of the Judge, I find it necessary to discuss a little law with you now. If what I have to say is found to be in conflict with what the Judge will tell you later, then of course his instructions will prevail.

I feel no need to single out each witness and recite his or her testimony. Instead, I will refer to the testimony in general and hope that your recollection is the same as mine. You will recall, I'm sure, that my client suffered from an affliction known as, Restless Leg Syndrome. You should also recall the history of the many drugs taken by my client and the effect which each had upon him. I call your attention to the evidence presented which eventually led to a prescription for Mirapex some thirteen years ago. You have heard testimony regarding its effect upon his RLS condition, as well as upon his personality and inner self.

You heard testimony from my client who chose to take the stand in his own defense. A stance which he was not legally obligated to take, but which he chose in order that you would have all the necessary facts before you when you enter the sanctity of the jury room to deliberate his fate.

You've heard from him about the subtle changes in his behavior and especially the obsessive-compulsive nature of the same. I ask you to recall the mandatory positioning of his ashtray and cigarettes, while gambling. Without rehashing the rationale, I'm sure you recall his testimony about the need to take of his shoes and socks on the golf course, and the reasoning behind his actions.

I now ask you to call to mind the evidence presented surrounding the television ad of Mirapex. Remember also the long list of side-effects which appeared on its web site. I call to your attention the testimony indicating that Mirapex marketed its drug without adequately warning the public. Despite the knowledge that continued use of Mirapex could cause an addiction to slot machines and pathological gambling, it said nothing. It deliberately failed to warn consumers about the pitfalls associated with its use.

I further submit to you that the evidence presented indicates that prior to his ingestion of Mirapex, he was only a social or casual gambler. Like most of us sitting here in this courtroom today he purchased an occasional lottery ticket, and earlier in his youth he played cards with other members of his family. He felt no compulsion to gamble. I believe that his exact words to you were, "I could take it or leave it! I couldn't have cared less!"

I ask you now to push the "fast forward" button and recall how this casual buyer of lottery tickets became transformed into a compulsive gambler. Just remember the trips to Foxwoods in snow storms. Just visualize him running up a moving escalator in order to get to a particular machine and begin gambling.

Ladies and gentlemen let's now talk about *"irresistible impulse."* As I previously indicated, I hope that the Judge in his own words will tell you that a person who commits a crime, whatever it might be, may be excused from the same and found to be not guilty; provided however, that he or she was acting under the throes of an *irresistible impulse.*

In short, if a person commits a criminal act, but is unable at the time to control his actions due to the influence of some external force, such as a drug, then he cannot legally be found guilty of the crime. In reality Ladies and gentlemen it's is a form of temporary insanity.

I ask you to think about this logically. Is it reasonable to assume, that a person with my client's credentials and background would deliberately throw it all away, if he was truly able to take a different course of action? Think about it! Here's a past president of both the Greater Lynn and

Essex County Bar Associations, the recipient of the highest award which each organization can bestow upon a person, a former member of the Swampscott Board of Selectmen, a hearing officer for the Board of Bar Overseers, a former Assistant Attorney General of the United States and of the Commonwealth of Massachusetts, an Assistant District Attorney for Essex County, and so many other titles and wonderful achievements. And you certainly must remember the many distinguished Judges who appeared voluntarily on his behalf. I'm sure you recall their testimony as to his character, exemplary conduct and *pro bono* work, which has ultimately benefited us all.

In conclusion, I sincerely hope that you didn't leave your common sense at home this morning. And please don't leave it in the jury box when you retire to deliberate. I merely ask that you use that common sense when you apply the facts of this case to the law. If you do this one simple thing, justice will be served today by finding my client *Not guilty*.

Thank you for your attention throughout this ordeal.

PROSECUTOR: Ladies and gentlemen of the jury, I too am obliged to remind you that whatever I say is not evidence, and that in all cases it is your memory of the evidence which controls and not mine.

I would like to thank you for your interest in this matter and the attention which you have given it. Apparently, defense counsel and I are in agreement on two issues. Firstly, we both hope that your common sense will follow you into the deliberation room at the proper time. Secondly, that as far as criminal cases are concerned, this one is rather simple and somewhat different than most.

Based upon all of the evidence which you have either heard or seen in this case, you must simply determine whether or not the defendant was acting under the influence of some *irresistible impulse*, when he stole money which belonged to his clients.

Now, this is where I ask you to apply your common sense. Just think about it. Here we have a defendant who practiced law for forty-eight years. He served as both a prosecutor and defense counsel. He represented defendants in criminal cases as well as plaintiffs and defendants in civil cases. Not only did he serve as President of two Bar Associations, but he was also a Hearing Officer for the Board of Bar

Overseers. Just think of it. He actually was involved in lawyer disciplinary cases for the Board.

I ask you to recall his answer to my question on cross-examination regarding the type of acts committed by the lawyers appearing before him. Do you remember his answer? Let me refresh your memory in case you have forgotten. He said that most of the cases involved the stealing or misappropriation of clients' funds. He, of all people, was keenly aware of the position of trust which required the preservation and safe-keeping of funds entrusted to him by others. He actually agreed with me when I suggested that clients' funds were considered to be sacrosanct.

The defendant certainly was well aware of the law when he stole. He knew that it was a crime to take the money and use it for personal reasons. I further submit the obvious to you. At the time he stole the money he certainly knew the difference between right and wrong.

Despite this knowledge, which he readily admits, he would now have you believe that he couldn't control himself. He claims that his prolonged use of the drug, Mirapex, caused him to steal to feed his addiction to gambling. Common sense should tell you that it's all a smoke screen. It's just a bunch of hogwash. If you believe his story, then I wanna tell you all about the tooth fairy!

The defendant was a gambler long before he ever ingested a Mirapex pill. As I recall his testimony, he was nine or ten years old sweeping the floor of a chicken store, when he made his first bet. He said that he started playing the numbers with a bookie. He even remembers spending Indian Head pennies and buffalo nickels to finance his youthful gambling.

Did it stop there? No way! He readily admitted to shooting craps during his high school luncheon recesses. He often played cards with his buddies. In high school he often attended Wonderland Dog Track and made some bets. Following his graduation from law school he resumed a weekly card game. Oh, lest I forget, he also purchased lottery tickets on a regular basis.

Common sense should also tell you that one's environment plays a large role in molding one's character. It has often been said that we are victims of our environment. Much depends upon those things to which we are exposed at an early age.

So let's take a look at his background and the environment of his youth. One of his brothers owned greyhounds and raced them at Wonderland Dog Track in Revere. He even had a box at the finish line where the defendant often sat. He readily tells us that his other brother and his father were also regulars at the track. The defendant made bets even though he hadn't reached his twenty-first birthday and shouldn't have been at the track in the first place.

His father was a bread salesman. The defendant often accompanied him after work to the barber shop. In the back room he saw his father gamble at poker, gin, bridge, or cribbage. He often accompanied his father and brothers when they played poker with their friends. He was an observer at first, but if anyone had to go to the restroom, he would sit and play the hand. And mind you, that was at the age of ten! When he got older he became a regular at the poker sessions.

I submit to you ladies and gentlemen of the jury that this defendant was ordained at an early age to become a compulsive gambler. He had a predisposition for gambling long before he ever took a Mirapex pill. How can he now come to Court and tell you to acquit him because he was gambling under the spell of Mirapex?

I suggest to you that he suffered from no such thing as an *irresistible impulse*, when he stole that money. It was not Mirapex which made him a pathological gambler. He was already a gambler. He had free choice not to take the money belonging to clients. He could have and should have exercised that choice.

Based upon all the evidence presented in this case, I ask you to return a verdict of guilty.

JUDGE: Ladies and Gentlemen of the jury, I will now instruct you on the law as it applies to this case. You are the sole finders of fact in this matter. Your obligation will be to apply those facts to the law as I give it to you.

You've had an opportunity to see and observe the witnesses. You are free to believe or disbelieve any of the testimony. In fact, you can believe part of what a witness may have said and disbelieve other parts. It's your decision only.

In your attempt to evaluate or assess the testimony of a particular witness, you are free to remember a witness's mannerisms or perhaps even gestures. There are no rules. You are to exercise your god-given common sense...and...

...In a civil case the burden of proof on a plaintiff is merely to tip the scales slightly in his or her favor. In a criminal case, such as this, the burden is on the Commonwealth to prove each and every allegation beyond a reasonable doubt. The scales are to be tipped more than slightly. They may even appear to be lopsided, when all is finally said and done.

The term *'reasonable doubt'* does not mean beyond *all* doubt. If that were the standard, then there would be very few criminal convictions. You, and you alone, are to determine what is reasonable or not...You are to use your everyday judgment in making that determination. I remind you that not *all* doubt is reasonable.

The defendant in this case is charged with Fiduciary Embezzlement. The Commonwealth must prove every element of the crime beyond a reasonable doubt. Did the defendant take money? If he did, was it someone else's money? Did he have permission or authority from the rightful owner of the funds to take the money? Was the defendant a trustee or other form of fiduciary, who's duty it was to preserve and safeguard the funds?

...The Commonwealth must also prove beyond a reasonable doubt, that the defendant intended to permanently deprive the rightful owner of the money. In your determination of this fact you may consider the testimony regarding the defendant's intent to replace the funds, as he had done before. If you find that that there was no intent to permanently deprive, then you must return a verdict of *not guilty*.

In the usual larceny case, if the defendant took funds belonging to another without permission and with the intent to permanently deprive the owner, he would be guilty of the crime. But, as both lawyers have indicated in their respective closing arguments, this case is a little different. I will now point out those differences so that you may render a true and just verdict.

Your job is made a little easier in this case, since the defendant readily admits that he took someone else's money without permission. But he then claims, that he was unable to control his actions due to the influence of some external force. He claims that the taking of the money was caused by an *irresistible impulse*. In other words he could not control his actions.

Massachusetts recognizes a defense of *irresistible impulse* in criminal cases. Strangely enough, the defense is set forth and is considered to be a part of our law pertaining to claims of insanity. In a typical insanity defense case a defendant must prove beyond a reasonable doubt, that as a result of mental disease or defect, he lacked substantial capacity either to appreciate the criminality of his conduct or to conform his actions to the requirements of the law.

We are here dealing with the claim of the defendant that he was unable to conform his actions to the requirements of the law, even though he knew that what he was doing constituted a crime. The relevant law in this Commonwealth provides, that if a person is unable to conform his actions to the requirements of the law due to an *irresistible impulse*, which existed at the time of the wrongdoing, and which compelled him to commit the crime, then it would be a complete defense by reason of temporary insanity.

If you find this to be a fact, then you must return a verdict of *not guilty*.

The instructions which I previously gave you regarding assessments of the credibility of witnesses, applies equally to the expert witnesses who have testified in this case. You should not assess any greater weight to a person's testimony merely because he or she happened to be wearing a uniform, or had been otherwise qualified as an expert witness. Once again, you are free to believe or disbelieve the opinions of experts. You may even disbelieve such testimony in the total absence of evidence to the contrary. It is your sole province as finder of the facts.

In an effort to reduce your role to its most simplistic form in this case, you must basically decide upon the answer to one single question. "Did the defendant's prolonged use of the drug Mirapex create an *irresistible impulse* within him to take someone else's money?"

The answer to that question will require you to assess the credibility of the defendant himself. You will have to consider his claims of personality changes and the gradual development of obsessive-compulsive behavior. You are free to believe or disbelieve the defendant, as well as his expert witnesses, who claimed that the defendant's addiction to gambling was an illness, and that his wrongful misappropriation of funds in order to placate his addiction, was virtually no different than the acts of a junkie, who steals or kills in order to satisfy an addiction.

You will have an equally compelling task in attempting to evaluate the material contained on the web site of Mirapex, as well as the message contained in its television ad. But must importantly, you must determine the role of Mirapex in attempting to resolve the ultimate issue before you even though Mirapex is not a party to this action.

If you find that Mirapex played no role in the defendant's behavior, and

that he knowingly took the money without authority and with the intent to permanently deprive the rightful owner, then you must return a verdict of *guilty.*

You have heard the closing arguments of both parties to this case. What they have said is not evidence. It is what they would like you to infer from the evidence presented. In all instances, however, it will be your memory of the evidence which governs and not theirs.

Lastly, I suggest that during your deliberations each of you should keep an open mind and listen to the views of others. The exhibits introduced in this case will accompany you to aid in your deliberations.

I am now going to confer at side-bar with both lawyers. I'm sure that each of them thinks that I left something out and will want me to address you again. Just bear with us for a few moments.

The conference produces no further requests for instructions. The jury is then escorted by Court Officers to the deliberation room.

THIS IS EITHER THE END OR THE BEGINNING

YOU BE THE JUDGE